CAMBRIDGE TEXTS AND STUDIES IN
THE HISTORY OF EDUCATION

General Editors

A. C. F. BEALES, A. V. JUDGES, J. P. C. ROACH

PUBLIC EXAMINATIONS IN
ENGLAND, 1850–1900

PUBLIC EXAMINATIONS
IN ENGLAND
1850–1900

JOHN ROACH

Professor of Education in the University of Sheffield
Fellow of Corpus Christi College, Cambridge

CAMBRIDGE

AT THE UNIVERSITY PRESS

1971

Published by the Syndics of the Cambridge University Press
Bentley House, 200 Euston Road, London N.W.1
American Branch: 32 East 57th Street, New York, N.Y.10022

© Cambridge University Press 1971

Library of Congress Catalogue Card Number: 71–123668

ISBN: 0 521 07931 4

Printed in Great Britain by
William Clowes & Sons Limited
London, Colchester and Beccles

CONTENTS

To my parents

PREFACE

Examinations arouse strong emotions among writers on education and even, as in the case of the 'eleven plus', among the ordinary public. They are much more often attacked than defended, though their hold shows no sign of slackening. They have for a century been an essential part of the context of English society. They are unpopular, but we have found no better means of fulfilling the tasks which they set out to perform.

In recent years several books have been published which show a growing interest in them. Among these books may be mentioned the collection of lectures, *Examinations and English Education* (1961), edited by Stephen Wiseman. In 1965 R. J. Montgomery's *Examinations* gave an account of their evolution as administrative devices. *The World Year Book of Education*, 1969, is entirely devoted to them. It discusses their aims and efficiency, their organization and structure, the problems of selection, and their effects, economic, social and educational. This very wide-ranging book will obviously become a standard work of reference.

The purpose of this study is different and more limited. It is an account of the historical origins of the modern examination system, particularly in England though some material is included on Scotland and on the colonies. The works already named and others which might also be mentioned, are chiefly concerned with modern problems and consider historical issues as ancillary to them. The objective of this book is to seek out the source from which the early Victorians drew the ideas of open competition and public examination. The answer given is that the Oxford and Cambridge honours examinations provided the model which could be applied to a whole range of educational and administrative purposes. The process began about 1850. The Northcote–Trevelyan Report of 1853 was an important landmark. The movement was in full swing by 1870 when Gladstone introduced open competition into the home civil service.

The question of historical origins has generally been discussed from the point of view of Civil Service Reform. This study, though it discusses administrative change, concentrates on educational questions, on the universities to some extent and more particularly on the secondary schools. The Victorian secondary schools have been studied far less than either the civil service or the universities, and much attention has been given to the growth and broadening of examining devices and techniques in the middle-class range. Even so there is much more which could be said; for instance, the examinations of the Science and Art Department have been referred to only briefly.

The organization of the book follows the following plan. Part I begins with a study of the competitive principle in general as applied in education and in administration in the middle of the last century. The weakness and inefficiency of 'middle-class education' (to use the contemporary term) are then examined, and an attempt is made to show how the idea of public examination was used to improve the condition of secondary schools. This was done chiefly by the foundation of the Oxford and Cambridge Local Examinations in 1857 and 1858.

Part II is a detailed study of the Locals between their beginnings and the end of the century. During approximately forty years they were the only system of secondary-school examinations with a national constituency, alike in grammar and in private schools. The College of Preceptors had only a limited range, and London Matriculation, though very important, was not really a school examination at all. The records of the Local Examinations give a unique picture of the great range of schools in which middle-class children were educated. These records also throw light on national movements of importance, especially on the higher education of women.

Part III is a more general study of opinion from 1855 to 1900. It deals with the public debate on examinations which went on throughout the age. First of all it looks at the Civil Service examinations, the standards which they demanded and the opportunities which they offered to young men and women. Next it surveys the advantages and disadvantages of school examinations as contemporaries assessed them. Finally it reviews the public debate on the whole principle of open competition.

The book ends about 1900. Many of its arguments are still being contested today, but the end of the nineteenth century does mark a turning point. By 1900 it was clear that public examinations had come to stay. Controversy revolved much more about ways of making them more efficient than about ways of replacing them by other methods of assessment and selection. Examinations also represented a general standard imposed by central agency, and in the new century state control and collective action were to loom much larger than individual initiative. This change was especially important in secondary education with which this book is largely concerned. Between the Report of the Bryce Commission in 1895 and the Education Act of 1902 the situation was radically altered. The state direction of secondary education, which the Victorians had generally resisted, was finally accepted because the problems seemed insoluble without it. The imposition of new solutions in turn generated new problems, and issues different from those discussed in this study were to arise. It is remarkable how the twentieth century, in tackling these issues, has made use of both the principles and the methods bequeathed to it by the Victorians.

Some of the material used in this book has appeared, in a rather different form, in two articles: 'Middle-Class Education and Examinations: some Early Victorian Problems', *British Journal of Educational Studies*, May 1962; and 'Examinations in Nineteenth-century England. State Power versus Private Control', *Paedagogica Europaea*, 1965. The invitation to deliver three lectures on 'Education and society in the nineteenth century' in the University of Newcastle in 1964 gave me the opportunity to develop the argument of Part I of this book.

I have been greatly helped by the kindness of many institutions and of many individuals, and I wish to thank them all. Without the very generous help of the Local Examinations Syndicate at Cambridge and its general secretaries, Mr J. L. Brereton and Mr T. S. Wyatt, and of the Delegacy of Local Examinations at Oxford, the book could never have been written at all, for a large part of it is based on their records. I have been able to see letters and papers of some of the pioneers of the modern examination system – those of Sir Thomas Dyke Acland, through the kindness of Sir Richard Acland; of Prebendary Brereton through that of Mr J. L. Brereton and of the late Canon Philip Brereton; and of the third Earl Fortescue through that of the Trustees of Homerton College, Cambridge.

Many libraries and archives have helped me, among them the University Library and the University Archives at Cambridge, the Bodleian Library and the University Archives at Oxford, the University of London Library, Sheffield University Library, the Department of Education and Science Library, the Public Record Office, the British Museum Newspaper Library, Colindale, and Pusey House, Oxford. The College of Preceptors, the Incorporated Association of Head Masters and the National Society all allowed me to use their records, and the Master and Fellows of Trinity College, Cambridge have permitted me to use the papers of T. B. Macaulay in their library. School records were made available to me by the heads and others connected with the North London Collegiate School for Girls, West Buckland School, St Mary's Hall, Brighton, and Tavistock Grammar School. Mr K. Crooks of the Cambridge Local Examinations, Kingston, Jamaica sent me the minute book (1887–1911) of the Jamaica centre, and Miss Glory Robertson of the West India Reference Library, Kingston, made extracts for me from the Jamaica press.

Among individual scholars who have helped me I wish especially to thank Professor A. V. Judges, one of the editors of this series, and Mr J. P. T. Bury, both of whom read my typescript and greatly improved it with their criticisms. Like many students of Victorian England I owe a great and general debt to the late Professor W. L. Burn and to Dr George Kitson Clark. Information on particular points has been given me by Dr F. E. Balls, Dr J. R. B. Johnston, Miss H. Williams, and the City Librarian of Cambridge.

J.P.C.R.

ABBREVIATIONS

CUA	Cambridge University Archives
CUL	Cambridge University Library
Camb. Univ. Rep.	*Cambridge University Reporter*
CSC	Civil Service Commissioners
Del. Local Exams.	Oxford Delegates of Local Examinations
Local Exams. Synd.	Cambridge Local Examinations Syndicate
OUA	Oxford University Archives
PP	*Parliamentary Papers*
SIC	*Report of Schools Inquiry Commission*
Bryce Comm.	*Report of Royal Commission on Secondary Education*

PART I
THE COMPETITIVE PRINCIPLE ESTABLISHED

1

PATRONAGE AND COMPETITION

Public examinations were one of the great discoveries of nineteenth-century Englishmen. Almost unknown at the beginning of the century, they rapidly became a major tool of social policy. They were used to recruit men for government service. They selected the ablest students in the universities, they controlled the work of the secondary schools, they were used by the state to regulate grants to elementary education under the Revised Code of 1862 and to encourage scientific studies through the Science and Art Department. E. E. Kellett, in an autobiography published in 1936, argued that during his life-time opinion on the subject of examinations had greatly changed. In his youth they had been 'almost the be-all and end-all of school life ... If, in fact, I were asked what, in my opinion, was an essential article of the Victorian faith, I should say it was "I believe in Examinations".'[1] His own headmaster had been a devotee of the system, and his successes had been proportionate to the trouble he took in training his pupils for the course and in ensuring that they paid due respect to the foibles of the examiners. In his eyes lack of success imputed moral failure to those who had not done well. This confidence in the inerrancy of the examination test was, however, not to endure. Men soon came to appreciate that examiners make mistakes and that their individual judgments often differ. A feeling, Kellett thought, had steadily grown which was summed up in Sir Walter Raleigh's epigram: 'The Oxford Final Schools and the Day of Judgment are *two* examinations, not one.'

This move from confidence to doubt represents a whole chapter of English educational and social history. Written examinations had come to stay because no effective substitute for them could be found, but men were not altogether happy with the results of their great discovery. The same doubts remain today though expressed in a different medium, but we are no nearer to solving them than were the Victorians. In a study of the relationship between education and examinations, the point which needs emphasizing is the

[1] E. E. Kellett, *As I Remember* (1936), p. 276.

very sudden and sweeping victory won by the examination idea within some two decades – roughly between 1850 and 1870. Before the middle of the century standards of qualification both in universities and schools and in government service had been rising, but older traditions died hard. In public administration the principle said to have been laid down by King George III that 'any one was fit to occupy any place he could manage to get'[1] was not thought outrageous. At Oxford and Cambridge, as we shall see, the principle of public examination was already well entrenched, but the schools made very little use of such an incentive. The Clarendon Commission in its report (1864) drew an interesting contrast between Shrewsbury, where much stress was placed upon examinations and upon promotion by merit, and Eton, which in many ways represented, among the great schools, the ideas of an earlier and more aristocratic age. In the latter, the commissioners remarked, 'the spur of emulation' was very little used: 'In the system of promotion, the learning of lessons, even the awarding of prizes, there is comparatively little of direct competition, and the distinctions which are given are not conspicuous enough to make them objects of general ambition or respect.'[2]

After 1850 the position had changed very quickly. In 1853 the India Act opened appointments in the Indian Civil Service to competitive examination. In November of the same year the adoption of the same principle for appointments at home was recommended by the Northcote–Trevelyan Report, though in the Home Civil Service changes were slower to come than in India. Limited competition began in 1855 and open competition was introduced by Gladstone in 1870. External examinations at the secondary level for both grammar schools and private schools were begun by the College of Preceptors after 1850 and by the Universities of Oxford and Cambridge in 1857 and 1858. In 1854 a scheme of examination designed for adults studying in Mechanics' Institutes was published by the Society of Arts, and after 1859 the Science and Art Department began to make grants on the basis of examination performances in scientific subjects. Finally, in 1862, the Revised Code imposed examinations in reading, writing and arithmetic upon all elementary schools receiving government grants.

[1] From a speech by Lord Cromer, quoted in P. J. Hartog, *Examinations and their relation to Culture and Efficiency* (1918), p. 38.
[2] P[arliamentary] P[apers] 1864, XX, vol. I, pp. 90, 312.

By that time there were very few parts of public life or of educational effort upon which the examiner had not laid his hand.

The subject is of sufficient importance to have left its mark upon Victorian letters. Often the examiner presents a good target to satire as in W. S. Gilbert's *Iolanthe* (1882). The sentence of the Fairy Queen upon Strephon, the hero, is that he shall go into Parliament and that every Bill shall be passed which gratifies his pleasure:

> Peers shall teem in Christendom,
> And a Duke's exalted station
> Be attainable by Com-
> Petitive Examination!

As Lord Mountararat remarks later in the opera: 'I don't want to say a word against brains – I often wish I had some myself – but with a House of Peers composed exclusively of people of intellect, what's to become of the House of Commons?'[1] Earlier and probably less familiar is Thomas Love Peacock's *Gryll Grange* (1861), where competitive examinations are displayed as a foible of:

> Your steam-nursed, steam-borne, steam-killed,
> And gas-enlightened race.

Young men are no longer thought to be fitted for a profession, Dr Opimian argues, unless they have crammed their minds with incongruous and useless information. Later in the story Lord Curryfin mounts an aristophanic comedy in which seven competitive examiners appear. The spirits of young men who are candidates for the military life come before them, but all are rejected, among them those who are to become famous as Hannibal, Oliver Cromwell and Richard Coeur de Lion. Finally Richard, who is the last candidate, 'flourished his battle-axe over the heads of the examiners, who jumped up in great trepidation, overturned their table, tumbled over one another, and escaped as best they might in haste and terror'.[2]

The best-known accounts in Victorian literature of the abuses in the public offices which competitive examination was intended to stop are those given by Anthony Trollope. In his *Autobiography*

---

[1] W. S. Gilbert, *The Savoy Operas* (World's Classics edn. 1962), vol. 1, pp. 261, 266.

[2] T. L. Peacock, *Gryll Grange* (Penguin edn.), pp. 104, 191, 192.

(published in 1883) he tells the story of his own admission to the Secretary's office of the General Post Office in 1834. He had much earlier told the same story in fictional form in his novel *The Three Clerks*, published in 1858, as Charley Tudor's entry to the Internal Navigation. At the office in St Martin's le Grand Trollope was asked to copy some lines from *The Times* with an old quill pen, and when he made a series of blots and false spellings, he was told that he must make a fair copy at home and bring it the next day. He was then questioned about his proficiency in arithmetic, of which, he says in the *Autobiography*, that he knew nothing, and was told that he would be examined in this the following day if his handwriting was found to be satisfactory. That evening he duly made a transcript of four or five pages of Gibbon, and took it with him to the office. When he arrived, he was seated at a desk and no one asked to look at his penmanship or examined him in anything else. He had become a public official. *The Three Clerks* also makes it quite clear that the 'Internal Navigation' was a particularly bad office and that change was on the way. Indeed, one of the characters in the novel is that redoubtable reformer, Sir Gregory Hardlines, whom Trollope modelled on Sir Charles Trevelyan of the famous report.[1]

Trollope was writing of the period just before the great revolution produced by competitive examination took place. The educational consequences of that revolution in the lives of many poor and aspiring young men can be traced in the works of H. G. Wells who, two generations later, described his own experience in both autobiographical and fictional form. Wells' headmaster at Bromley, Mr Thomas Morley, was a Licentiate of the College of Preceptors, one of the pioneer examining bodies, and he himself left school at the age of thirteen, 'bracketed with a fellow-pupil first in all England for book-keeping' in the examinations of the same college.[2] Later in his youth he first studied and then taught under Horace Byatt, the headmaster of Midhurst Grammar School, who supplemented his own stipend by running evening classes under the Science and Art Department in 'freehand, perspective and geometrical drawing and in electricity and magnetism'. Byatt later put on classes in additional subjects, which were really quite bogus; they were merely a means of enabling Wells to enter for the examina-

---

[1] A. Trollope, *An Autobiography*, ed. Bradford A. Booth (Berkeley, Los Angeles, 1947), pp. 30–31, 94; *The Three Clerks* (World's Classics edn.), ch. 2.
[2] H. G. Wells, *Experiment in Autobiography* (1934), vol. I, pp. 86, 90–1.

tion, for which he worked on his own, and thus to earn grants for his master's benefit.[1]

The novelist did not neglect these early experiences. In *The New Machiavelli* he explains the activity of grant-earning which was quite distinct from any honest form of genuine education since it aimed not to teach people science but merely to teach them how to answer predictable questions.[2] His own sentiments and ambitions as a young teacher are described with marvellous clarity in the following account, in another novel, of Mr Lewisham's room:

Over the head of the bed, for example, where good folks hang texts, these truths asserted themselves, written in a clear, bold, youthful florid hand: 'Knowledge is Power', and 'What man has done man can do' – man in the second instance referring to Mr Lewisham. Never for a moment were these things to be forgotten. Mr Lewisham could see them afresh every morning as his head came through his shirt. And over the yellow-painted box upon which – for lack of shelves – Mr Lewisham's library was arranged, was a 'Schema' ... In this scheme, 1892 was indicated as the year in which Mr Lewisham planned to take his B.A. Degree at the London University with 'hons. in all subjects' and 1895 as the date of his 'gold medal'. Subsequently there were to be 'pamphlets in the Liberal interest', and such like things duly dated. 'Who would control others must first control himself', remarked the wall over the wash-hand stand, and, behind the door against the Sunday trousers was a portrait of Carlyle.

These were no mere threats against the universe; operations had begun. Jostling Shakespeare, Emerson's Essays, and the penny Life of Confucius, there were battered and defaced school books, a number of the excellent manuals of the University Correspondence Association, exercise books, ink (red and black) in penny bottles, and an india-rubber stamp with Mr Lewisham's name. A trophy of bluish green South Kensington certificates for geometrical drawing, astronomy, physiology, physiography, and inorganic chemistry adorned his further wall, and against the Carlyle portrait was a manuscript list of French irregular verbs.[3]

It is easy to poke fun at Mr Lewisham – and Wells tells us that he had himself made such a 'Schema' – and grant-earning is a long way from education. Yet it was by means such as these that educational opportunity was gradually extended more widely as the

[1] *Ibid.* pp. 141, 173.
[2] H. G. Wells, *The New Machiavelli* (2nd edn., 1911), p. 24.
[3] H. G. Wells, *Love and Mr Lewisham* (Nelson's Library edn.), pp. 4–5.

nineteenth century passed into the twentieth. The matriculation and the degrees of the University of London, open to external students after 1858, cleared the way to many who could not otherwise have obtained a higher education. It was Wells' own success in gaining 'South Kensington' (or Science and Art Department) Certificates which gained him a studentship at the School of Science in South Kensington.[1] His studies there gave him the chance to become a successful man of letters instead of a draper's assistant or an usher in a private school.

Gilbert, Peacock, Trollope, and Wells make an interesting quartet of authors whose books handle this theme. Our next task must be to turn from illustration to analysis, and to ask what were the objectives which those who promoted open competition were trying to attain. These objectives were really threefold. The first was to provide a means of maintaining academic standards and an incentive for raising them. This can be seen most clearly in examinations for university degrees. These in England have not normally been linked directly with professional qualifications but have been based on advanced study of a general nature. Their aim has been to grade students according to their individual levels of ability, and at a further remove they have also provided incentives for students to work hard and to do well. A good performance in a university examination has long been regarded as a favourable introduction to later professional success. An example here from the Victorian period is the tremendous interest shown by everyone at Cambridge in the competition for the senior wranglership. Not only were dons and undergraduates involved in this, but college servants laid bets on the favoured candidates![2] A subsidiary aspect of the same objective was the use of external tests to increase the efficiency of schools by bringing them into contact with one another and by making known to all the best standards available. This purpose is seen especially clearly in the work of the various university bodies concerned with school examinations.

The second objective, which is related to the first though independent of it, is that of deciding the fitness of candidates for public office or for an independent profession. Tests of this type have historically often been related to university tests, but they are essentially independent since their purpose is directly vocational.

---

[1] H. G. Wells, *Autobiography*, vol. 1, pp. 174–5.
[2] J. M. Wilson, *An Autobiography 1836–1931* (1932), p. 47.

Their aim is essentially administrative rather than educational. They look to some model of professional efficiency rather than to an ideal of general culture or of intellectual attainment. Examples within this general class are obviously the Civil Service Examinations and professional examinations for solicitors or doctors, which were greatly tightened up during the mid-nineteenth century. In the case of medical men, the Medical Act of 1858 set up a general council to register all those who had obtained the scheduled qualifications.

The third objective, which is more characteristic of the twentieth century than of the nineteenth, though it is also found in the earlier period, is that of social engineering. Open competitive tests may serve to bring forward able boys and girls from a lower social level and to give them opportunities of advancement through higher education. In this sense competition may be used as a means of remedying social inequalities and of broadening the basis of the educated class. Such was the basic philosophy behind the opening of the road from elementary to grammar school through the free place system in the early twentieth century. The Victorians sometimes argued on similar lines; for instance the Taunton Commission argued that the foundation of exhibitions to higher schools was a proper way of using educational endowments.[1] They were however more inclined, as we shall see, to believe that open competition in the award of scholarships and exhibitions would favour those who had enjoyed the best – and therefore the most expensive – preliminary education rather than the poor. In that sense open competition could have, sometimes unintentionally, anti-democratic and anti-egalitarian results.[2]

These three objectives – of classifying students, of testing candidates for the professions, and of providing new opportunities for less privileged members of society – were all present, either singly or collectively, in the minds of those who advocated competitive examinations. The motives of these advocates varied a good deal and the factors which they had to consider covered a very wide range of problems in education and government. Consequently the whole process can be studied today from many

[1] *PP* 1867–8, XXVIII, vol. 1, pp. 208–9.
[2] For discussions of the objects and uses of examination, see also P. J. Hartog, *Examinations and their relation to Culture and Efficiency*, pp. 9–10; N. Morris, 'An Historian's view of Examinations', in *Examinations and English Education*, ed. S. Wiseman (Manchester, 1961), pp. 1, 25–6.

different aspects. Scholars have most commonly discussed the whole subject as an essay in government and in political philosophy. From this point of view the victory of competitive examinations provides an exemplification of the new ways of looking at politics and administration which developed in England between 1840 and 1870. One programme of legal and administrative reforms had been formulated by Jeremy Bentham and his followers. The new attitude, among Utilitarians and non-Utilitarians alike, concentrated on more efficient ways of solving the problems of a complex industrialized society for which the methods of an older and more easy-going world were not effective enough. Government needed servants who possessed, as Nassau Senior wrote to Lord Melbourne, 'diligence, impartiality, decision, discretion, knowledge of human nature ... invention and resource',[1] and many came to believe that competitive examination was the best way to get them. A study from this angle would concentrate on the higher ranks of the Civil Service and on the universities which produced those Civil Servants. This is, of course, the world of Lord Macaulay, of Sir Charles Trevelyan and of Benjamin Jowett.

A second possible approach is methodological rather than ideological. It takes for granted the motives of those who planned the new system and the effects which they thought it would have, and concentrates instead on how the changes took place. Its starting point is to consider examinations as 'the tools of those whose business it is to execute policies'.[2]

A third field of study, which is that adopted in this book, is to consider the development of examinations primarily in relation to educational institutions and to curricula. From this point of view, questions of this type must be asked: what deficiencies in the educational structure was it thought that examinations would help to make good? How far were they successful in meeting these needs, and how far were they able to meet new needs which had not been envisaged when they began? Was their effect on the work of the schools good or bad? Did they help or hinder teachers to work effectively? These questions are a random sample and

---

[1] David Roberts, *Victorian Origins of the British Welfare State* (New Haven, 1960), p. 164: In a memorandum of 1834 on the appointment of assistant poor law commissioners.

[2] R. J. Montgomery, *Examinations: An Account of their Evolution as Administrative Devices in England* (1965), p. xi. This is the purpose of Mr Montgomery's book.

many more could be asked, but they will serve to define the general subject-matter of this study. It is not an essay in government. It does not attempt to chart in detail the workings of our educational machine. It approaches the subject of competitive examinations from the sides of the teacher and the learner. It is focused very much on the class-room, and it tries to see, through the particular vistas opened up by the examination system, how the practical business of educating the young went on in Victorian times.

These limits are themselves very broad for they might include everything from the primary school to the university. Attention will in fact be chiefly concentrated here on secondary education or on 'middle-class education' as the Victorians often called it. The terms will need much more detailed explanation later for they did not always mean the same a century ago as they do today, but broadly they cover the private schools and the grammar schools in which the middle-class educated its children. This sector of Victorian education has been comparatively neglected by modern scholars, for writers on the subject in general have tended to concentrate on two other fields. The first of these is the introduction of general elementary education and its connection with the whole development of political democracy. The second is the development of the universities and the public schools and the creation, through their agency, of a new type of governing class which reached its apogee in the early years of the present century. In comparison with these themes, 'middle-class' education has been very little studied, though it is of crucial importance for the ideas and assumptions of a society in which the middle classes both played a large part and were very vocal about their own role. Since the schools for middle-class children were often extremely bad, great efforts were made to improve them, and the introduction of external and competitive examinations was a method much favoured for bringing such improvements about.

In considering competitive examinations from the point of view of the teacher and the learner, more particularly in the secondary school, it is impossible, of course, to exclude the other considerations of governmental principle and administrative practice which were outlined earlier. Any discussion of one must also bring in the others, particularly in the formative period when competitive examination was an untried theory rather than an accomplished fact. The connection between more effective education and more effective administration was very close. Government appointments provided good careers for men of ability who lacked influence, whether they were the products of Jowett's Balliol or the alumni of commercial schools. Lord Robert Cecil, the future Lord Salisbury and prime minister, had very good reasons for saying in 1856 that the proposal to open the Civil Service to competition 'was neither more nor less, from beginning to end, than a schoolmasters' scheme'.[1] Cecil was not alone in making the point. Henry Latham of Trinity Hall, Cambridge, in a most useful book on the subject published in 1877, pointed out that examinations had a double purpose. They had a strictly educational objective as an aid to study, and they were the means of selecting candidates for appointment, but the methods used in the two cases need not be the same.[2]

This connection was true of all countries which used the system. Both the Prussian *Abitur* and the French *baccalauréat* were essential qualifications for state service as well as school examinations, and mid-Victorian Englishmen were well aware that efficient systems of state education gave their neighbours great advantages both in testing the basis of school work and in laying down the bases for state employment. But in England the academic origins of the examination system are particularly important.

There can be no doubt that the idea of examinations and of the competitive principle in English official life came originally from the prestige of the honours examinations in the two universities, in particular from the Senate House Examination (later the Mathematical Tripos) at Cambridge. Latham, who has already been quoted, says: 'From the success at the universities of examinations as a means of awarding distinctions and emoluments with perfect impartiality, they were brought into use as a means of disposing of all kinds of appointments.'[3] And again: 'moreover this Examination [the Mathematical Tripos] acquired quite early in the present century a high reputation for the integrity and ability with which it was conducted ... In consequence, when a difficulty arose about

---

[1] E. Hughes, 'Civil Service Reform 1853–5', *Public Administration*, vol. XXXII (1954), p. 27.
[2] H. Latham, *On the Action of Examinations considered as a Means of Selection* (1877), pp. 414–16.
[3] *Ibid.* pp. 3–4.

the bestowal of Government patronage, the public caught from [it] the idea of introducing competitive examinations.'[1]

The history of the Senate House Examination is a long and complex one and can only be briefly sketched here. It developed in the first half of the eighteenth century out of the traditional system of disputations. There had always been in addition to the disputations some sort of examination of the candidates in the schools. This examination, which had originally been supplementary to the exercises, gradually became much more important than they; it was a written test in English, as opposed to the Latin of the disputations, and its content was primarily mathematical, though rather in the sense of providing a training in logical reasoning than in advanced mathematical thought. The examination results were printed after 1747, and after 1752 they assumed their permanent division into wranglers, senior optimes and junior optimes. The candidates were, of course, classed in descending order of merit from the senior wrangler at the top, and though, during the eighteenth century, there were occasional accusations of partiality in drawing up the lists, this had ceased by 1800. In the early nineteenth century the Tripos was a genuine though narrow test of intellectual ability. Its standing in the university and the country was very high, and there was no question that the men who came out at the top reached their positions by real ability and hard work and without any question of patronage or favour. 'A belief in the sanctity of examinations thus became an article of every Cambridge man's creed, and a charge of favour or neglect would have been most damaging to an examiner', to quote Latham again.[2] At Oxford one of the first successes of university reform was the enactment of the Examination Statute of 1800 which created the nucleus of the modern examination system. The development of 'Greats', so different in its nature from the Cambridge Tripos, had an equally stimulating effect upon the ablest minds in the University of Oxford.

It was clear very early on that examinations did not suit everyone. Macaulay, who bears as much responsibility as anyone for imposing the examination system on English public life, failed to gain honours in the Tripos of 1822, though he was subsequently elected to a Trinity fellowship. Newman's name in the schools of 1820 appeared 'under the line' – the equivalent of a third or fourth class –

---

[1] *Ibid.* p. 124.   [2] *Ibid.* p. 153.

though he was subsequently elected to a fellowship at Oriel, the foremost Oxford College of the day, which picked its men for their general ability and not because of their examination performance. Yet, if these distinguished anomalies are left aside, it is true that in the first half of the nineteenth century more and more of the high places in public life were being taken by men who had enjoyed successful careers at the university – that is, successful in the great test of public examinations.

Macaulay himself rested his defence on the India Bill, which was designed to open the Indian appointments to competitive examination, on this very point.[1] 'Men who distinguish themselves in their youth above their contemporaries in academic competition', he argued, 'almost always keep to the end of their lives the start they have gained in the earlier part of their career.' The Church, the Parliament and the Bar all provided examples. In Parliament Canning and Peel had been followed by 'Lord Derby and my right hon. friend the Chancellor of the Exchequer' (W. E. Gladstone). In India, Warren Hastings, Charles Metcalfe and Lord Wellesley had all been distinguished students before they became men of affairs. At the Bar the examples were numberless:

Have not the most eminent of our judges distinguished themselves in their academical career? ... Look round the Common Law or the Equity Bar. The present Lord Chief Justice was senior wrangler; Mr Baron Alderson was senior wrangler; Mr Justice Maule was senior wrangler; Mr Baron Parke was eminently distinguished at the university for his mathematical and classical attainments; Mr Baron Platt was a wrangler; and Mr Justice Coleridge was the most eminent man of his time at Oxford.

Macaulay's point was certainly valid. The Bar had always attracted a very high proportion of the national talent, and it is noteworthy how many of the leading lawyers of the early nineteenth century were men of academic distinction and in particular how many of them were men who had won mathematical honours at Cambridge. The qualities of speed and accuracy which brought success in the Senate House were much the same as those who ensured it in the law courts. Among the judges in Macaulay's list

---

[1] For his speech on the second reading of the India Bill, 24 June 1853, see *Hansard*, 3rd ser., vol. CXXVIII, 739–59; *Speeches, Parliamentary and Miscellaneous* (1853), vol. II, pp. 256–76.

Baron Parke had been a fellow of Trinity, fifth wrangler and senior chancellor's medallist. Among Lord Chancellors Lord Lyndhurst had been a fellow of Trinity and second wrangler; among Masters of the Rolls, Lord Langdale, senior wrangler and a fellow of Caius. The same tendency can be noted among the politicians, though it is naturally less marked since in an aristocratic age there were many roads to political success other than academic ability. Peel and Gladstone both took double firsts at Oxford. The fourteenth Earl of Derby, three times prime minister, took no degree at Oxford, but was a university prizeman. Among politicians of the second rank with distinguished academic records, and many of them connected with the administrative reforms of the fifties, were Stafford Northcote, George Cornewall Lewis, Edward Cardwell, Charles Wood and Robert Lowe. Certainly by the middle of the century a good university record provided an excellent entry to public and professional life.

Yet, if this be all accepted, it is remarkable that it should have taken so long for the idea of competition and of assessment by competitive examination to spread from the universities into public life generally. If the prestige of the Cambridge Tripos and the Oxford Schools was high by, say 1825, why should it have taken another quarter of a century for the idea to spill over, so to speak, into the non-academic world? One obvious reason is, of course, that any new idea takes time to become accepted. In any situation other than the purely revolutionary it probably takes a generation for an idea to be communicated by a group of brilliant young men, for those young men to get to the top of their respective professions and then to generalize and make effective the ideas which they had imbibed thirty years before. In the early nineteenth century Trinity was incomparably the most active intellectually of Cambridge colleges. Since the protest of a group of ten fellows in 1786 its fellowships had been awarded as the result of rigorous examination. Macaulay, who was a devoted Trinity man, had been elected to a fellowship in 1824. His nephew and biographer, in discussing this period of his life, refers to:

the reflection that these privileges were the fruit, not of favour or inheritance, but of personal industry and ability, [these] were matters on which he loved to dwell long after the world had loaded him with its most envied prizes. Macaulay's feeling on this point is illustrated by the conscious reverence which he cherished for those junior members of the college who, some ninety years ago, by a spirited remonstrance addressed to the governing body, brought about a reform in the Trinity Fellowship examination that secured to it the character for fair play, and efficiency, which it has ever since enjoyed.[1]

In 1848 the first two volumes of his *History* achieved one of the greatest of literary successes in the annals of nineteenth-century letters. As a national figure he was an active supporter of the India Bill of 1853, and he became chairman of the committee which planned the new arrangements for the Indian appointments. By 1853 the young fellow of Trinity, elected in 1824, had reached the centre of the national stage. His own career partly proves, partly disproves the advantage of early competitive success. He did not, as we have seen, obtain honours in the Tripos, for he had no talent for mathematics in which alone at that time honours could be attained. On the other hand he won a Trinity fellowship, a Craven university scholarship in classics and the chancellor's medal for English verse (on two occasions). By the fifties he had become a leading advocate of the advantages of open competition, though he always appreciated that too much weight could be attached to undergraduate achievement.[2]

The whole question is, however, a good deal more complex than the mere passage of a generation in public life because it is bound up with the whole tempo of English life and society in the second quarter of the century. The idea of competition was in accord with the spirit of the new age. The thirties and forties had been decades of far-reaching changes. Parliament and local government had been reformed. The finances of the Church of England had been reconstructed after the establishment of the Ecclesiastical Commission. In economic affairs free trade had been achieved. A fair field and no favour was what the British business man, in control of the most powerful productive machine ever known by man, was demanding. This was the inspiration behind the movement to repeal the Corn Laws; this was the impetus which carried British manufacturers, British shipping, British commercial contacts all over the world. What was effective in business might also be expected to succeed in government service and in education. The triumph of free competition in all these fields took place between

[1] G. O. Trevelyan, *Life and Letters of Lord Macaulay* (popular edn. 1889), p. 60.
[2] *Ibid.* p. 63.

1850 and 1870. In education and administration it started more slowly than in commerce and manufacture, but once the changes gathered impetus, they bit so deeply into the intellectual and cultural structure that their hold has never been shaken, and, in a social order very different from that of the nineteenth century, they have gone on from strength to strength.

One interesting example of this 'Leitmotiv' of nineteenth-century history lies in the field of organized games. Though sports are very ancient in England, games in this sense are comparatively modern, and it was during the last quarter of the century that they became so important. Many academics and schoolmasters then deplored the hold which athleticism had gained in schools and universities, and thought that, though games provided a new interest for many young men, who would have had no such interest in earlier generations, they also led to philistinism and to the neglect of ideas and hobbies of greater intrinsic value. To discuss this would carry us very far afield, for the history of organized games is a fascinating and unwritten piece of English social history. The point to be emphasized here is that games were not only organized, they were competitive as well. To quote Latham once more: 'The spirit of contest goes all through life. It is found in the professions and in politics and lies at the bottom of all our recreations. English boys learn to love contest from our English games.'[1] The popularity of games – and in higher and secondary education the cult of the athlete was at its height at the beginning of the twentieth century – represented the apotheosis of competition, and of competition endowed with a mystical, almost spiritual value. That this was so is an indication of how deeply the competitive idea runs through the values and ideas of the middle and late Victorian age.

By 1850 all these waves of change were breaking around the universities and the endowed schools, but the fortress had hardly yet been breached by the tide. Of all the major traditional institutions the schools and the universities were the last to be tackled by the reformer. While Parliament and the town corporations, the law and the law courts, and the Church of England had all undergone great changes, they had remained extraordinarily untouched. Many of the grammar schools had tried to reform themselves in the

---

[1] Latham, *On the Action of Examinations*, p. 501.

thirties and forties, and pressures for reform at Oxford and Cambridge, both internal and external, go back to the beginning of the century. Until the fifties very little was achieved. There were still scandals which partook more of the atmosphere of the eighteenth century than of the supposedly purer morals of the nineteenth, though it ought also to be said that academic standards had risen greatly between 1800 and 1850. One dispute which attracted much attention was the conflict between Robert Whiston, the headmaster of the Cathedral Grammar School at Rochester, and the Dean and Chapter of that cathedral, whom Whiston accused of appropriating revenues which ought to have been devoted to the school and its old scholars (1848-52).[1] At much the same time occurred the very strange events of the rectorial election at Lincoln College, Oxford in the autumn of 1851. It was this contest, so vividly described in Mark Pattison's *Memoirs*, which, in the view of a recent historian, 'reinforced the belief in the necessity for university reform and the public concern with the apparently low standards at the senior university'.[2]

Since administrative and educational reform were thought of in such close conjunction by the men of the time, since the whole idea of competitive examination in these spheres was something which stemmed originally from the universities, it was likely that changes in the universities and in administration would come at much the same times. By the early fifties men of Macaulay's background and interests had reached the forefront of public life. If the universities themselves could be reformed, the time was ripe for the new ideas to be taken into the great world by men who had experienced them and had been influenced by them in their student days. It was out of *academe* that the seed would grow. In political life the soil might be receptive, once the young tree had been planted, but there was no primary opportunity for the seed to germinate. The traditions of the political and administrative world – though again the standard had gone up during the first half of the nineteenth century – were those of patronage and influence; new ideas could find a footing but they could come in only from the outside. The academic world was the best available source.

---

[1] See Ralph Arnold, *The Whiston Matter* (1961); W. L. Burn, *The Age of Equipoise* (1964), pp. 234–6.

[2] V. H. H. Green, *Oxford Common Room* (1957), p. 164.

The story of reform which is developed in this book is closely connected with the growth of the universities. In the early part of the nineteenth century Oxford and Cambridge play the leading role because they were the only universities in England until the 1830s. At that time the Scottish universities offered opportunities of higher education to a far wider social group than was influenced by Oxford and Cambridge. By the middle of the century the University of London, non-residential and non-sectarian, was creating similarly wide opportunities in England. The growth of London University is of major importance in the development of higher education. Moreover the provincial colleges of the industrial cities, which were to become the civic universities of the twentieth century, grew up under its wing, and were, by the end of the century, beginning to make their own contribution. The achievement of the new universities in helping to create a larger, more expert and more diverse group of educated people will be considered in a later chapter.[1] In the early decades of Victoria's reign the movement for radical change, both at Oxford and at Cambridge, was coming to a head.

At Cambridge an attempt in the thirties by the liberals to sweep away religious tests for degrees had come to nothing; any such step was too far in advance of university opinion to have any real chance of success at that time. During the same decade both universities were being sharply attacked by the distinguished Edinburgh philosopher Sir William Hamilton, and there was a mounting tide of criticism in the outside world. In the forties practical suggestions for reform were made by two of the leading Cambridge men of the day, George Peacock, Dean of Ely, and William Whewell, who became Master of Trinity in 1841 and who, despite many faults of temper, was the most creative of the Cambridge academics of the time. Whewell was no radical and in his later life he moved away from reform, but in the forties it was very important that one of the leading figures of the academic establishment was in favour of change. In 1847 Whewell suggested the choice as chancellor of Prince Albert, who was elected, though by a narrow majority. The Prince was seriously in favour of reforms and really concerned about education. By this time the waters were moving, and in 1848 the university, as a first step in major change, created two new triposes, one in moral and one in natural sciences.

[1] See pp. 259-61.

At Oxford the whole question of academic reform had been pushed aside by the onset of the Oxford Movement. The story of the Tracts, of Keble, of Newman and of Pusey, of the condemnation of Ward and Newman's secession to Rome is one of the most fascinating in English history and its charm and interest never palls. But it diverted the attention of Oxford to subjects other than those of academic reform. After Newman's secession, the first phase – the distinctively Oxford phase – of the Tractarian movement was over, and men's minds experienced a great reaction against theological and metaphysical conflict. In the outside world negative and critical forces were strengthened. In Oxford there was a pragmatic reaction towards practical issues, a sense that the university must justify its position in a very changed world. There is a very well-known passage in Mark Pattison's *Memoirs* which, though familiar, deserves quotation:

> The truth is that this moment, which swept the leaders of the Tractarians with most of his followers out of the place, was an epoch in the history of the University. It was a deliverance from the nightmare which had oppressed Oxford for fifteen years. For so long we had been given over to discussions unprofitable in themselves, and which had entirely diverted our thoughts from the true business of the place. Probably there was no period in our history during which, I do not say science and learning, but the ordinary study of the classics was so profitless or at so low an ebb as during the period of the Tractarian controversy. By the secessions of 1845 this was extinguished in a moment, and from that moment dates the regeneration of the work we had to do. As soon as we set about doing it in earnest we became aware how incompetent we were for it, and how narrow and inadequate was the character of the instruction with which we had been hitherto satisfied.[1]

There is no need to accept all Pattison's remarks at their face value but there remains a great deal of truth in them. Of the great Tractarians, Pusey alone remained to uphold the old ideas in a new Oxford, and we shall meet him later in this role.[2]

But the leaders of the new age were liberals like A. P. Stanley and Goldwin Smith of University College and Benjamin Jowett of Balliol. Their watchwords were the abolition of ancient privileges, the throwing open of all opportunities in the university and the colleges to the best men, ability being generally defined in terms of

---

[1] Mark Pattison, *Memoirs* (1885), pp. 236–7.
[2] See p. 104.

examination success. A few years later the Northcote–Trevelyan report marshalled in defence of its arguments a formidable array of academic opinion, for the academics were as enthusiastic for the changes recommended as the professional civil servants were doubtful about them.

So for different reasons the reforming party, or perhaps it would be more correct to say reforming influences, since different reformers wanted different things, was getting stronger in both the ancient universities at the end of the forties. Whether they would have been able to put their houses in order without outside help is a theoretical question for in 1850 Lord John Russell, a prime minister who did not believe that they could do this, appointed royal commissions to enquire into the affairs of both universities. This step was bitterly opposed by many people – more violently in fact at Oxford than at Cambridge – and even many of the reformers were doubtful whether it was wise. But it had been proposed on several occasions in preceding years, and it was almost bound to come when the government was prepared to take the responsibility for acting. Once the commissions had enquired and reported, statutory commissions to frame new university and college constitutions followed and the floodgates were opened. The waters of change which had been banked up for so long swept over the land. The university reforms of the fifties left many things undone and the reformers pressed for changes for another generation. But a beginning had been made in sweeping away obsolete regulations, restraints and privileges which had endured for many centuries and which were felt to hamper the efficiency of the universities in the modern age. One very important step was the partial opening of the universities in 1854 and 1856 to men who were not members of the Church of England. In general the commissioners were greatly influenced by the ideas of the university reformers, by the theory of open competition, of awards for merit freely given to the best men available. In a sense the spirit of equal competition which had for half a century inspired the examiners in the Tripos and the schools was being applied to all the concerns of the university. The prizes were to be won by a fair field with no favour. To a conservative like John Keble, thinking of an older Oxford, the changes were repugnant. He complained to a friend of 'a notion that examinations and talents are everything, and another notion, which I deprecate from my heart, that natural preference for home,

2

kindred etc. are not to be allowed in eleemosynary endowments. I think it is an indication of a certain hard priggishness which is getting to be characteristic of this generation.'[1] What Oxford and Cambridge did was bound to have effects outside their own walls. Here Gladstone is an important figure. A distinguished Oxford graduate himself, he was M.P. for that university. As chancellor of the exchequer 1852–5 he commissioned the Northcote–Trevelyan enquiry. His concern for both academic and administrative reform is very clearly expressed in a letter of 1854 to Sir James Graham:

In the case of Haileybury we struck an undisguised and deadly blow at patronage; in the case of Oxford we are likely to propose measures which I think are strong but I hope will be salutary for the purpose of setting up competition as against restriction or private favour: I am convinced that we have it in our power to render an immense service to the country by a circumspect but energetic endeavour to apply a like principle to the Civil Service and the great administrative departments.[2]

By 1850 the belief in 'competition as against restriction or private favour' was in the air, for it fitted the ethos of the age. Public examinations were a useful tool for achieving the reformers' objectives. In 1850 the *English Journal of Education* commented that there was no other way of discovering proficiency in any department of knowledge, although 'almost half a century ago examinations were nearly unknown in England'.[3] Great efforts had been made during the previous twenty years to improve popular education, and after 1833 the state steadily increased its expenditure in this field. The key to the success of the new schools was the training of a sufficient number of qualified teachers, a task which was undertaken by the state after 1846. Grants were made to pupil-teachers, who were apprenticed to schoolmasters and mistresses, and further grants were made to students at training colleges. The whole process was managed and the grants allocated through annual examinations conducted by Her Majesty's Inspectors of Schools, which were the first large-scale examinations held

---

[1] Georgina Battiscombe, *John Keble: A Study in Limitations* (1963), p. 313.

[2] Emmeline W. Cohen, *The Growth of the British Civil Service 1780–1939* (1941), p. 85. Haileybury was the college in which the East India Company had trained its civil administrators under the old system. Its closure was decided in November 1854.

[3] Vol. IV (n.s., 1850), p. 288.

at a number of different centres in this country. More will be said about them later;[1] the point to be noted here is that, when the Civil Service reformers were asked whether large-scale examining was a practical proposition, their existence was used to prove that this difficulty had already been overcome.

The changes which were affecting the universities were also being felt in the public service. In the period of reform after 1830 the public administration did not escape criticism, and after 1848 enquiries were made into a number of departments. An important part in these investigations was played by C. E. Trevelyan who, after service in India, had been assistant secretary to the Treasury since 1840, and who was made a K.C.B. in 1848 for his work in administering relief during the great Irish famine.[2] Trevelyan was not himself a university man. He had been trained at the East India Company's college at Haileybury, and he brought to English problems his experience of administration in India which was, throughout the century, a laboratory where the English tried out ideas which were too revolutionary to be initiated at home. During his Indian service, Trevelyan had married Hannah Macaulay, the sister of the historian who was then (1834) a member of the Supreme Council of India. He developed very close personal links with Macaulay and with other university men, such as Jowett, who have already been mentioned, links which, as we shall see, played a very important part in helping to launch administrative reforms.

The Northcote–Trevelyan report itself was the culmination of many years of thought and work, mainly on Trevelyan's part.[3] In 1848 he criticized the organization of the Treasury in evidence before a select committee on miscellaneous expenditure and argued, as in the report of 1853, in favour of separating routine from work of a more complex nature.[4] He was supported on this occasion by J. G. Shaw-Lefevre, assistant secretary at the Board of Trade, like Macaulay a Trinity man, who will appear again in these pages – not least as one of the original Civil Service Commissioners of 1855. Trevelyan's letter-books show that the following establishments

---

[1] See p. 50.
[2] For his work on the Irish famine, see Cecil Woodham-Smith, *The Great Hunger* (1962).
[3] The following paragraph is based on Jenifer Hart's article, 'Sir Charles Trevelyan at the Treasury', *English Historical Review*, vol. LXXV (1960), which makes use of Trevelyan's letter-books.
[4] Cohen, *Growth of the British Civil Service*, pp. 88–9.

were investigated after 1848: the Home Office in 1848, the Irish Public Record Office and the law courts in 1849, the Foreign Office in 1850, the War Office in 1852, and the Board of Control in 1854, while there was possibly an investigation of the Admiralty and the dockyards in 1848–9. Already departments were introducing their own examinations,[1] and the services were moving tentatively in the same direction. Thus in 1849 an examination in English, history, geography, arithmetic, algebra, fortification and a language was introduced before the purchase of a commission in the army, though this was not a severe test.[2]

The Act of 1853 introduced competitive examination for the Indian appointments, as we have seen, and Macaulay in his speech on the second reading of the India Bill reminded the House of Commons that this was no new idea. Competition had been suggested by Lord Grenville as long ago as 1813, and he had himself advocated a similar scheme in the House in 1833. The Charter Act of that year had provided that there should be four nominations for each appointment and that the nominees should compete among themselves. This, in fact, proved a dead letter because the directors of the company did not put it into practice. In 1837 the system was suspended and new arrangements were made for entrance to Haileybury College which effectively restored the nomination system. In reminding the House of this past history, Macaulay said: 'It is now proposed to introduce this principle of competition again, and I do most earnestly entreat this House to give it a fair trial.'[3]

The India Act of 1853 in fact marked the first decisive step towards the adoption of the new system of competition in the public service. After the Act had become law, a committee of which Macaulay was chairman was set up to report upon the means of carrying into effect the new system. The report of the committee, which Macaulay wrote himself, was published in November 1854, almost a year after the report of Northcote and Trevelyan, and it is interesting to compare the basic assumptions of the two documents.[4]

[1] Hughes, 'Civil Service Reform 1853–5', *Public Administration*, vol. XXXII, p. 20.
[2] W. J. Reader, *Professional Men: The Rise of the Professional Classes in Nineteenth Century England* (1966), pp. 79–80.
[3] *Hansard*, 3rd ser., vol. CXXVIII, 750; Naresh Chandra Roy, *The Civil Service in India* (Calcutta, 1958), pp. 63–5, 69.
[4] They are most conveniently available in *Report of the Committee on the Civil Service, 1966–68* (Cmnd 3638, chairman Lord Fulton), vol. I, appendix B.

There are in the nature of the case certain differences; for instance Northcote and Trevelyan made recommendations about methods of examining candidates for the very large numbers of lower appointments, a problem which did not arise in Macaulay's report where only the higher administrative group had to be considered. Macaulay's report, not surprisingly, is much more strikingly written and more interesting to read. But both share a common structure of ideas.

First and foremost both aim to attract the most promising young men available (to quote Northcote and Trevelyan) 'by a competing examination on a level with the highest description of education in this country'.[1] The suggested age limits which were much the same in either case – nineteen to twenty-five for the higher home appointments, nineteen to twenty-three for India, followed by one or two years' probation at home – were likely to attract young men with a good university background, and both reports emphasize that the proposed plans would have a great effect upon the universities. Macaulay put his point in a very arresting way:

The educated youth of the United Kingdom are henceforth to be invited to engage in a competition in which about 40 prizes will, on an average, be gained every year. Every one of these prizes is nothing less than an honourable social position, and a comfortable independence for life. It is difficult to estimate the effect which the prospect of prizes so numerous and so valuable will produce. We are, however, familiar with some facts which may assist our conjectures. At Trinity College, the largest and wealthiest of the Colleges of Cambridge, about four fellowships are given annually by competition. These fellowships can be held only on condition of celibacy, and the income derived from them is a very moderate one for a single man. It is notorious that the examinations for Trinity fellowships have, directly and indirectly, done much to give a directive to the studies of Cambridge and of all the numerous schools which are the feeders of Cambridge. What, then, is likely to be the effect of a competition for prizes which will be ten times as numerous as the Trinity fellowships, and of which each will be more valuable than a Trinity Fellowship?[2]

Both reports considered that candidates should be selected on the basis of general ability rather than on the possession of any technical or special attainment. Macaulay believed that an excellent general education was the best foundation for a Civil Service career and

[1] *Ibid.* p. 112.   [2] *Ibid.* p. 120.

argued in addition that, since many competitors were likely to be unsuccessful, they should not be required to devote time to specialized studies which would be of no subsequent use to them. In the case of the successful Indian candidates, the period of probation was to be given up to the technical studies of law, economics and Indian history and languages. This ideal of general ability was likely to favour the university man, whose previous studies had been directed on very similar lines, but, in their view about the subjects in which candidates were to be examined, the reports diverge widely from the concentration on a small number of subjects which already dominated honours degree courses at Oxford and Cambridge. This was probably done deliberately in order to give an opportunity to students of other universities, particularly to the Scots with their much more widely ranging courses. The Macaulay report for instance pointed out that the new examination should not be framed so as to favour any particular type of university, and mentioned that the Scottish universities did not carry advanced classical studies as far as the English.

The wide range of subjects examined was to be a continuing feature of the later Civil Service Examinations. Northcote and Trevelyan argued that if men took a wide range of subjects, the greatest and most varied amount of talent would be secured – 'the superiority of the best would become evident'. They mentioned, in addition to classics and mathematics, 'history, jurisprudence, political economy, modern languages, political and physical geography, and other matters'.[1] The Macaulay report gives a suggested mark scale which covers English history, language and literature, Greek, Latin, French, German and Italian, mathematics, natural and moral sciences, Sanscrit and Arabic. No candidate was likely to obtain as many as half of the total maximum of marks, and no candidate should obtain any credit for a subject of which he had a mere smattering of knowledge. With a confidence which was not substantiated by later experience the same report affirmed that if the examiners were well chosen, 'cramming' could never be successful!

Though the two reports were so similar in their basic ideas the subsequent course of events in England and in India was very different. The first competitive examinations for the Indian Service

---

[1] *Report of the Committee on the Civil Service, 1966-68* (Cmnd 3638, chairman Lord Fulton), vol. i, p.114.

were held in July 1855, but in England full competition was delayed for fifteen years. In the same year the Civil Service Commission, consisting of Sir Edward Ryan, J. G. Shaw-Lefevre and Edward Romilly, was indeed set up to test the qualifications of Civil Service candidates. It is possible that its creation was assisted by the storm over administrative inefficiency caused by the disasters of the Crimean War, but its powers were very limited. Heads of departments were still permitted to decide whether vacancies should be filled by simple nomination or by limited competition among nominees. In its early years the commission merely administered qualifying examinations of a low standard. The change to full competition challenged too many traditions to come very easily. Macaulay had pointed out the difficulties in a letter written a year earlier: 'I am afraid that Trevelyan's plans about the Civil Service will be frustrated by the opposition which strong interests and strong prejudices are raising up in all quarters. The pear, as I always told him, is not yet ripe.'[1]

The opinions expressed about the proposed changes can be studied in the famous blue book of 1855 which published the opinions of both educationalists and Civil Servants.[2] Many of the latter resisted change and argued in favour of the traditional system but the educationalists were enthusiastically on Trevelyan's side. Among them were representatives of the universities like Francis Jeune, Master of Pembroke College, Oxford, W. H. Thompson of Trinity College, Cambridge, and R. W. Jelf, Principal of King's College, London, headmasters like H. G. Liddell of Westminster, Charles Vaughan of Harrow and E. H. Gifford of King Edward's, Birmingham, Her Majesty's Inspectors of Schools like Henry Moseley and Frederick Temple, whom we shall meet again as one of the founders of the Oxford Local Examinations. Benjamin Jowett of Balliol, who was becoming one of the most influential of the academic reformers, had expressed his views in a letter to Trevelyan dated January 1854, which was printed as an appendix to the Northcote–Trevelyan Report. Speaking of the proposed change, Jowett wrote, 'I cannot help feeling, as a college tutor, its great importance to the University, supplying as it does, to

[1] To T. F. Ellis, 4 March 1854 (Macaulay Papers, Trinity College, Cambridge). The passage appears in a somewhat altered form in Trevelyan, *Life and Letters of Macaulay* (pop. edn.), p. 612.
[2] Papers relating to the Reorganization of the Civil Service, *PP* 1854–5, XX.

well-educated young men a new opening for honourable distinction. The effect of it in giving a stimulus to the education of the lower classes can hardly be over-estimated.'[1] The same points are repeated over and over again in Trevelyan's correspondence of this time, published by Professor Edward Hughes.[2]

Little more need be said here about the connection between the universities and the higher government appointments, because this has already been examined, though one quite different example is of interest. Clearly in the new era universities must meet the needs which competition imposed upon them. Although the Macaulay report had specifically mentioned the importance of giving Scottish students a fair opportunity in the Indian Examinations, they did very badly in them. This failure was quickly noted in Scotland and it may be linked with the reforms of 1858 which imposed stricter rules about examination and graduation upon the Scottish universities.[3]

An equal stress was laid by the reformers of the mid-fifties on the beneficial effects for secondary and primary education which would follow from the opening of the lower posts to open competition. This area of education will be explored more fully in the next chapter. Briefly it was argued that, if people in the humbler positions of life knew that their children would have a chance of competing for minor government posts, they would be encouraged to keep them longer at school and to ensure that they obtained a better education. This would greatly assist the efforts which were being made to stimulate popular education. It would provide alternative opportunities for pupil-teachers and certificated teachers who finally decided that they did not wish to teach. It would encourage middle-class schools to attain far higher standards in their work.

Two good examples of propagandists who argued on these lines were Jowett himself and Dean Dawes of Hereford, one of the most active of parson educators whose village school at King's Somborne in Hampshire had been one of the most advanced of the time. It is interesting that Jowett devoted almost the whole of his published letter to Trevelyan to proving that the proposed new arrange-

[1] Papers relating to the Reorganization of the Civil Service, *PP* 1854-5, XX, p. 477.

[2] E. Hughes, 'Sir Charles Trevelyan and Civil Service Reform 1853-5', parts I and II, *English Historical Review*, vol. LXIV (1949).

[3] G. E. Davie, *The Democratic Intellect: Scotland and her Universities in the Nineteenth Century* (Edinburgh, 1961), pp. 42-4, 70-1.

ments could be carried out in practical terms and that they were not merely a theorist's dream. In the case of the higher appointments this was not particularly difficult; in the case of the lower the case was harder to make both because of the great numbers and of the very wide variety of occupations involved. Jowett made his case by using the example of the examinations for pupil-teachers and schoolteachers which have already been mentioned. 'The experience of the Education Department of the Privy Council Office', he wrote, 'in which as many as 1,800 certificates of merit have been given, after examination, to schoolmasters and pupil-teachers in a single year, shows that no numbers occasion any real difficulty.'[1] It was no more absurd to submit excise-men and tide-waiters to a literary test than to examine village schoolmasters, and to institute such tests would have four beneficial results: they would have a beneficial effect upon popular education; a good basic education would give even the humblest official the chance of doing his job well and of rising to a higher rank; the examinations would relate to common things in a common-sense way; and finally there was no other means of getting rid of the evils of patronage.

Jowett had visited Richard Dawes at King's Somborne just before he left in 1850 for the deanery of Hereford, and quite naturally, since Dawes was a well-known pioneer in the field of popular education, tried to draw him into the propaganda of the reforming circle. In February 1854 he wrote to ask the dean to write 'a few pages showing the bearing of the measure on the education of the lower classes',[2] and a pamphlet by Dawes duly appeared the same year.[3] His arguments follow lines which are now familiar. The proposed scheme is practicable and it would encourage ordinary people to educate their children better. A new demand would be created, just as examinations for schoolmasters have by their very success, created a need for highly qualified men in areas where this would never have been felt in earlier times. No reform would 'do more to attach the lower and middle classes of society to the institutions of their country'.[4] Dawes also put considerable stress on the moral argument at both the individual and the national level. For the individual, examinations are a test of common-sense

---

[1] *PP* 1854–5, XX, p. 475.
[2] *English Historical Review*, vol. LXIV (1949), p. 87.
[3] *Remarks on the Reorganization of the Civil Service and its bearing on Educational Progress: In a letter addressed to the Rt. Hon. The Earl of Aberdeen* (1854).
[4] *Ibid.* p. 4.

and of character as well as of book-learning. To do well in them demands perseverance and self-denial which strengthen the character. For the nation, a competitive system would be based on high moral principle and would help to reduce corruption and place-seeking.

The moral argument was, in fact, two-edged. The reformers claimed that the man who worked hard and passed a good examination was likely to have the strength of character which would make him a good public servant. In this sense the examination criterion provided a test of suitability for state employment. Many people doubted the force of this argument because they thought that this work, particularly in the more confidential departments, demanded qualities of loyalty and dependability which could not be measured by an examination. Among this school of thought were included both Disraeli and Queen Victoria. Much later, in 1874, when he was prime minister, Disraeli wrote in a letter to the Queen that Gladstone had been mistaken in introducing open competition for Treasury posts, because these and Foreign Office appointments 'require so much trust in their holders that some social experience is requisite of those who hold them. There should be a moral security for their honour and trustworthiness.'[1] The permanent secretary to the Foreign Office expressed the same fears when he gave evidence to the Ridley Commission of 1886. Were the office to be opened to free competition, there would, he thought, be a danger that 'foreign governments, or perhaps people engaged in large financial operations, might train up men or send up young men for examination, and keep them in their pay'.[2]

The conflict of opinion is clearly expressed in an exchange of letters between the Queen and Gladstone, who was then chancellor of the exchequer, during the original discussions of 1854.[3] The Queen wrote expressing her doubts about the 'proposed plan', and pointing out that 'a check … would be necessary upon the admission of candidates to compete for employment, securing that they should be otherwise eligible, besides the display of knowledge which they may exhibit under examination. Without this a young

[1] Robert Blake, *Disraeli* (1966), p. 683.
[2] Evidence of Sir Philip Currie, permanent secretary to the Foreign Office: Royal Commission appointed to Inquire into the Civil Establishments, 4th report, *PP* 1890, XXVII, p. 50, para. 26189
[3] *The Letters of Queen Victoria* 1837–61, ed. A. C. Benson and Viscount Esher (1907), vol. III, pp. 13–14. Both letters are dated 17 February 1854.

man might be very ineligible, and still after having been proclaimed to the world as first in ability, it would require very strong evidence of misconduct to justify his exclusion by the government.'

Gladstone in his reply preached the pure reforming gospel of the moral strength of good examinees when combined with careful enquiries about character:

Experience at the universities and public schools of this country has shown that in a large majority of cases the test of open examination is also an effectual test of character; as, except in very remarkable cases, the previous industry and self-denial, which proficiency evinces, are rarely separated from general habits of virtue.

But he humbly assures Your Majesty that the utmost pains will be taken to provide not only for the majority but for all cases, by the strictest enquiries of which the case will admit; and he has the most confident belief that the securities for character under the system, although they cannot be unerring, will be stronger and more trustworthy than any of which the present method of appointment is susceptible.

Precisely the same argument was used by Macaulay in his Indian report and by Jowett in the letter of January 1854 to Trevelyan.[1] Indeed not only were the arguments the same but the very words and expressions used were very similar. The three men represented a wide range of interests – Gladstone high politics, Macaulay the borderlands of politics and literature, Jowett the universities. Yet all spoke with a single voice. There is much more evidence than this to suggest that the cause of competitive examination was being promoted at this time by what would now be called a very well-organized pressure group.

The progress of university reform in the first half of the century has already been briefly surveyed. One of the major objectives of the reformers was to replace the ancient constitutions of Oxford and Cambridge by a new order based on merit and on freedom of opportunity. In extending these opportunities and recognizing this merit the honours examinations, which had gained such prestige in the century between 1750 and 1850 were the natural instruments to use. When, after 1850, major changes in the universities began, the reformers were eager to spread their gospel into the outside world of politics and government. Partly they believed that

---

[1] For Macaulay, see *Report on the Civil Service 1966–8*, vol. I, p. 127; for Jowett see *PP* 1854–5, XX, p. 470.

a system based on competition was morally preferable to one based on patronage; partly they had a direct interest in finding employment for the educated men whom the universities and schools might be expected to produce in ever increasing numbers. Civil Service Reform would have come in any case at some time, but it need not have taken the very academic and intellectualized shape which it did. The way the process developed was due to the university men and in particular to the way in which Trevelyan organized his campaign. Not a university man himself he had very close connections with the university-trained intelligentsia who were becoming interested in administrative change. The family link between him and Macaulay is important, but there were many other personal ties between those who preached the new doctrines.

Trevelyan's position at the Treasury gave him access to Gladstone who, as chancellor of the exchequer, commissioned the Northcote–Trevelyan enquiry in March 1853. Gladstone was the most prominent politician committed to the new course, and Macaulay's involvement is obvious. Among other politicians of similar views, Stafford Northcote himself was a Balliol man, and Robert Lowe, who was secretary of the India Board while the Indian discussions were taking place, was a distinguished graduate of Oxford who was in close touch with Jowett.[1] The tutor of Balliol was, as we have seen, an active university reformer who gave evidence before the Royal Commission on the university of Oxford. It was probably because of this, and through Northcote and Lingen, another Balliol man, who was secretary of the Education Department, that he came into touch with the administrative reformers.

Trevelyan made good use of his academic allies. He collected the opinions of the many educationalists who supported his report so enthusiastically.[2] Both Jowett and Shaw-Lefevre, who had supported his views before the select committee of 1848,[3] were members of Macaulay's Committee on the India appointments. Trevelyan regarded the former as representing Oxford and the latter as representing Cambridge and London, and he advised Wood, president of the Board of Control, against making further

[1] Cohen, *Growth of British Civil Service*, p. 85.
[2] See p. 27; *Public Administration*, vol. XXXII, pp. 27–8.
[3] See p. 23.

additions to the committee, though in fact Wood added two more members to it.

The influence of the educationalists on Indian reform has been emphasized in a recent article which suggests that, when the India Act of 1853 was passed, there had been no intention of abolishing Haileybury College. The decision to do so was promoted first by Jowett and by Charles Vaughan, headmaster of Harrow, who convinced first Trevelyan and then the politicians of the advisability of this step. The decision to abolish Haileybury removed a serious obstacle to the claims of university graduates to the Indian appointments.[1]

About the same time as he became a member of this very important committee, Shaw-Lefevre was advising Trevelyan that his 'connection with Cambridge and with the University of London' made him confident that there would be no difficulty in examining 400 or more candidates simultaneously or in obtaining competent examiners.[2] A year later Lefevre became one of the first Civil Service Commissioners along with Sir Edward Ryan, who was a friend of Macaulay's and had been Chief Justice of Bengal where both Macaulay and Trevelyan had served. Like Lefevre and Macaulay himself, Ryan had been at Trinity College, Cambridge. There can be little doubt that at this crucial time public opinion was being influenced by a small group of men who knew one another well and who were quite clear what they wanted. Like all such groups, their unity made them formidable.

Oxford, Cambridge, India – these were the roots of the new system which Lord Robert Cecil described with great force as a 'schoolmasters' scheme'.[3] The establishment of the Civil Service Commission in 1855 is an appropriate event with which to conclude this preliminary survey. Administrative reform was for many years after 1855 a subject of controversy and of eager debate, and something will be said of this later. Our next task will be to review the parallel events of the forties and early fifties in primary and secondary education where very similar influences had been at work. It was clear by the mid-fifties that education was going to play a far larger role in social and political life than it had done

[1] R. J. Moore, 'The Abolition of Patronage in the Indian Civil Service and the Closure of Haileybury College', *Historical Journal*, vol. VII (1964), pp. 255–7.

[2] *English Historical Review*, vol. LXIV (1949), pp. 79–80.

[3] See p. 12.

hitherto, because the way to promotion would lie through intellectual training and hard work. The point may be summed up by two
contemporaries. Trevelyan himself told the Playfair Commission
twenty years later that the competitive system had been welcomed
by professional men of moderate means who gave their children a
good education and who lacked political influence.[1] A grammar
school headmaster, writing in 1856 in praise of the new arrangements
saw them as providing a new role for his profession: 'Henceforth,
the able and successful teacher takes the place of the parliamentary
whipper-in, as the guide to government employment, and the only
question now remaining to be solved is, how the great educational
work before us is to be effectually accomplished.'[2]

[1] Civil Service Inquiry Commissioners, second report, *PP* 1875, XXIII,
App. F, pp. 556–67.
[2] *England's Educational Crisis: A letter addressed to the Rt. Hon. Viscount
Palmerston, Prime Minister of Great Britain* [By the Headmaster of an English
Grammar School, E. R. Humphreys] (1856), p. 8.

2

MIDDLE-CLASS EDUCATION

Though the universities were the birthplace of the changes which have just been outlined, the effect of them was bound to be felt through all the educational institutions of the country. Indeed the reformers were anxious that this should happen, for they were very conscious, as we have seen, of the interrelationships between education at all levels. Yet these terms must not be misunderstood. The reformers believed that one part of the whole would not flourish unless the other parts were in a healthy state, yet neither they nor other Victorians understood this interrelationship to mean genuine interdependence. The parts of the educational structure cohered together but they did not depend on one another in the sense in which the mid-twentieth century sees education as a single national concern which oversteps local or class boundaries. To the Victorians each of the great class groupings – upper, middle and lower – required its own separate institutions because each class had its own separate needs. This statement needs explaining by a fuller examination, which will follow later, of Victorian ideas about the class structure but for the moment a simile may help to make the point. Schools created for the needs of different classes were like a grove of trees which owes much of its beauty to the fact that all the trees are seen as a whole. Yet each tree is a separate living creature, drawing its own nourishment from the soil, and independent of the other trees around it

Though reform was badly needed at Oxford and Cambridge in 1850, it was even more imperative in the secondary schools. An observer looking at the scholastic landscape, would have noticed some remarkable discrepancies in the speed at which changes were taking place. Improvements had been greatest at opposite ends of the educational scale. The public schools, patronized by the upper classes and very closely united with the universities, had been steadily improving for a generation and were well on the way to the stability and security of the late Victorian age. Elementary schools, founded by the great religious societies and partly supported by public funds, had sprung up all over the country, and though to us their horizons seem limited and their achievements small, they were already mining away at the great crag of popular ignorance and beginning to create a literate population. The great weakness lay in the centre of the social spectrum, in the schools of the middle classes. The theme of this chapter is the poverty and weakness of these schools and the attempts which were made to improve the situation. As we shall see, all of these attempts ran into very serious difficulties. Finally the establishment of public examinations under university control appeared to be the easiest and the most effective way of raising standards, which were universally acknowledged to be far too low.

The distinctive institution which catered for middle-class children was the private school, like Mr Morley's school at Bromley which H. G. Wells attended,[1] though many of them used the ancient grammar schools as well. How much they used the grammar schools depended a good deal on local circumstances and may have changed from time to time, for instance according to the personality and abilities of a particular headmaster. Both schoolmasters and parents were anxious to preserve their charges from mixing with the classes below them. Much of this came from a rigid view of class relationships which has already been suggested; something came from the fact that in habits, cleanliness and dress there were far greater differences between the child of a labourer and the child of a business-man than those which exist today. Yet, although men operated within a rigid pattern of social relationships, many individuals were on the move. Indeed society as a whole was proud of the fact that great fortunes were made by men who had begun their lives in very humble circumstances. 'Self-Help' was a popular conception; there were many like the future Sir Daniel Gooch, chairman of the Great Western Railway and one of the creators both of the *Great Eastern* steamship and of the Atlantic cable, who had been told by their mothers when they left home: 'always to keep my thoughts fixed on obtaining for myself a good position in life, never to be satisfied to stand still; and although I was going to the Vulcan Foundry [near Warrington] as a boy and a pupil, to strive one day to become the manager.'[2]

Careers like Daniel Gooch's illustrate the fact that a richer and more complex society demanded a larger managerial class. Yet, during the first half of the century, the educational institutions available to this class hardly developed, either in quality or in

[1] See p. 6.   [2] Sir Daniel Gooch, *Diaries* (1892), pp. 25–6.

quantity, at a rate commensurate with the pace of social and economic change. Indeed it seems very likely that the opportunities available to the middling ranks of society for educating their children may, comparatively speaking, have been getting worse rather than better. Traditionally the work of secondary education and the path of access to the universities had been in the hands of the grammar schools. By the end of the eighteenth century many of them had ceased to perform their ancient functions. On the one side, the aristocracy and the higher professional classes, like the lawyers and many of the clergy, had drawn away to the public schools. This process was to gain far greater momentum after the increased ease of communication provided by the railways and the foundation of many new public schools in the fifties and sixties.[1] After the mid-century many business-men who would in an earlier generation have kept their boys at home or sent them to private schools were beginning to use the public schools for their sons. Dr Kitson Clark has pointed out that 'even so stern an opponent of the aristocracy and the governing class as Joseph Chamberlain sent his sons to Rugby, and the one, Austen, who was designed for a political career, to Trinity College, Cambridge, where he took his degree in 1885'.[2]

At the poorer end of the 'middle-class' range the farmers or the shopkeepers were rapidly losing the advantages which they had earlier possessed over the labourer as the result of the rapid growth of popular education through the work, first of the religious societies and then of the state. The grammar schools had in most cases ceased to be the centre of the secondary education of their area and many of them had declined into giving elementary education less efficient than that provided by the national schools. Where the grammar schools did reach a higher standard, their classical curriculum was not necessarily what the middle classes wanted as a training for a career in commerce or industry. The private schools which were the only alternative were often pretentious and ineffective, though some of the criticisms which were made of them may have been exaggerated. The national and British schools provided little help for middle-class parents because they were not willing to have their children educated alongside the children of the

---

[1] For a general discussion see T. W. Bamford, *The Rise of the Public Schools* (1967).

[2] G. Kitson Clark, *The Making of Victorian England* (1962), p. 273.

working classes. As Frederick Temple pointed out in 1856, it was impossible to persuade the middle classes to mix with the lower when the upper classes did not mix with them. 'The Education of the upper classes has distinctly separated itself from that of the rest of the nation. The middle classes will insist upon a similar relative position. This may be an evil. But, unless members of Parliament would consent to send their own sons to these [primary] schools, the evil is incurable.'[1]

Sometimes in country districts attempts were made to educate the children of farmers and of labourers in the same school. The best known and most successful of these was the school at King's Somborne in Hampshire, conducted by the rector, Richard Dawes (1793–1867), one of the most interesting of the parson-educators whom we have already met in connection with Civil Service reform.[2] In some country areas, where farms were not large, class differences could be less sharp than they were in the towns. But the King's Somborne plan was rarely effective and there are many contemporary references to the poor education of the farmers and their reluctance, as a consequence of this, to provide better opportunities for their labourers. Kay-Shuttleworth, himself one of the greatest of the English educational pioneers, had written:

The Gentry and clergy have little encouragement or assistance from the farmers in the erection or improvement of schools. The common argument employed by the farmer is that he had little or no instruction himself, and that he does not see why his labourers' children should be as well instructed as his own. No general sympathy in the improvement of the education of agricultural labourers can be expected until proprietary schools for the education of the children of farmers have been established and we hope that every intelligent landowner, and especially our aristocracy, will recognise the importance of their providing such an education for farmers' children as shall enable the next generations to keep exact accounts of the income and outlay of their farms – to comprehend the mechanical improvements recently introduced into husbandry.[3]

---

[1] F. Temple, 'National Education', Oxford Essays 1856, p. 253.

[2] R. Dawes, Hints on an Improved and Self-Paying System of National Education, suggested from the working of a Village School in Hampshire (1847), and Suggestive Hints on Improved Secular Instruction (3rd edn., 1849). See also J. W. Adamson, 'A Hampshire Village School', in 'The Illiterate Anglo-Saxon' and Other Essays in Education, Medieval and Modern (Cambridge, 1946).

[3] J. P. Kay [-Shuttleworth], Recent Measures for the Promotion of Education in England (10th edn., 1839), p. 86.

It is noteworthy that in the discussions on the difficulties of middle-class education in the middle of the century the farmers are very often cited as an example. Economically, until the onset of agricultural depression in the late seventies, they were an important group. Since much of the writing on educational problems was the work either of members of the landed gentry or of the higher professional groups like the lawyers and the clergy who were in close touch with the gentry, the farmers were the middle-class group who lay much more open to inspection than the inhabitants of the large towns. But the farmers' problems, though accentuated by greater distances and rural remoteness, were very similar to those of other middle-class groups, and may help to emphasize the point that, as educational provision was extended both for the classes above and below, the great social group in the middle found itself comparatively worse off than in earlier times.

The problems of middle-class education were exhaustively discussed by contemporaries, and many solutions were proposed. Many of them foundered for one reason or another, but one of the more successful was the creation of external examinations for secondary schools which will be discussed in detail later. The best known of the critics of the day was Matthew Arnold, but what he was saying, in vigorous and memorable English and in a sometimes exaggerated tone, was very much a commonplace of educational thought and discussion in the fifties and sixties. Arnold complained that the English middle class was the worst educated class of its type in the world. Since there was a complete lack of central administrative devices which existed in France, Germany and Switzerland, educational opportunities were not provided throughout the country on an adequate scale.

A few great public schools were excellent, but below that level nothing could challenge the state secondary schools of France and Germany. As a result the English middle class lacked 'personal dignity', a characteristic weakness which most clearly marked it off from the aristocracy. 'We have to meet the calls of a modern epoch', Arnold wrote in 1874,[1] 'in which the action of the working and middle class assumes a preponderating importance, and science tells in human affairs more and more, with a working class not educated at all, a middle class educated on the second plane, and the

---

[1] M. Arnold, *Higher Schools and Universities in Germany* (1874), pp. 217–18.

idea of science absent from the whole course and design of our education.'

Familiar as Matthew Arnold's arguments still are, it is perhaps less well known that his father, the great headmaster of Rugby, was saying something very similar in the year of the passing of the Great Reform Bill. Thomas Arnold commented in a letter to the *Sheffield Courant*, that the middle class was growing and that its education was a 'question of the greatest national importance'. This education was largely in the hands of private schoolmasters with no external standard to guide them, no external reward to expect, and very much at the mercy of opinion in their own locality. The situation could be put right, Thomas Arnold argued, only by the creation of a national system through the interference of government, a system which would 'provide for the middling classes something analogous to the advantages offered to the rich classes by our great public schools and universities'.[1]

Both Thomas and Matthew Arnold pinned their hopes for middle-class education on a nationally organized system promoted by the state. This emerged as a serious possibility after the report of the Taunton Commission on the endowed schools (1868) and will later be discussed in that connection.[2] It did not become accomplished fact until the twentieth century because there was very serious opposition to the whole concept of public provision. Already by 1850 it was becoming clear that the education of the people was too vast an undertaking for individuals and private groups and that the government must take a hand. One outstanding example of this had been the creation and financing of a state-sponsored system of teacher-training. Yet the means which were appropriate for one social group were thought quite unfitting for another. The middle classes cherished their personal independence. They expected to pay for the education of their own children. They felt that they neither needed nor wanted the state aid which was recognized as inevitable for their social inferiors. 'The more civilized the homes', wrote the Rev. J. P. Norris, HMI, 'the less need the government interfere with the education of the children. As we ascend through the several gradations of schools, the control

---

[1] T. Arnold, *Miscellaneous Works* (1845), pp. 227, 230.
[2] See pp. 230–1.

of the state should become less and less.'[1] Middle-class parents
and schoolmasters believed that they had the money, the knowledge
and the experience to look after themselves: 'we want no state assistance or interference', wrote a prominent private schoolmaster to one
of the progenitors of the Oxford Local Examinations of 1857.[2]
This fear of state intervention was allied to a hierarchical view of
social structure. State control, it was feared, might interfere with
the schoolmasters' private property. It might involve secularization
of institutions with a strongly religious character. It might result
in the levelling of social distinctions. The men of the time
believed that for practical purposes classes should remain distinct
and their educational institutions separate. The point is made very
clearly in the reports both of the Newcastle Commission on popular
education (1861) and of the Taunton Commission on the endowed
schools (1868). The Newcastle Commission commented on the
tendency of competitive examinations for minor government
appointments to teach people to 'value education as a means of
rising to a higher station in life'. This, they accepted, was in many
cases a reasonable ambition: 'but the main object of promoters of
education must be to teach the people to value it as a source of
morality, enjoyment, and comfort, in the station in which the great
masses of them are necessarily destined to remain.'[3] The Taunton
Commissioners were anxious to use endowments to enable poor
boys to carry on their education, but they pointed out the strong
objection to a preparatory education common to all classes, in that
parents of a higher class disliked their children associating with
others of a lower class and being taught by men, whom they
regarded as their social inferiors. Private schools and the newer and
more ambitious proprietary schools all depended to some extent on
the social distinctions which the schools were powerless to ignore
and to which indeed they often owed their very existence. Many
inferior private schools survived, the commissioners argued,
because of 'the unwillingness of many of the tradesmen and others
just above the manual labourers to send their sons to the National
or British School. Rather than let their children mix with the class

[1] J. P. Norris, *The Education of the People, our Weak Points and our Strength:
Occasional Essays* (Edinburgh, 1869), p. 16.
[2] T. D. Acland, *Some Account of the Origin and Objects of the New Oxford
Examinations* (2nd edn., 1858), p. 90.
[3] *Report of the Commissioners appointed to Inquire into the State of Popular
Education in England*, vol. I, *PP* 1861, XXI Pt. I, p. 224.

beneath them in a large well-fitted room where they would be taught by a thoroughly competent master, they will send them to an inferior teacher in a miserable room, and pay twice or four times as much.'[1] At some of the more exclusive proprietary schools 'the governing body retain in their hands the power of rejecting any boy whom they do not consider qualified socially for the school; and as a fact would not admit the son of any resident tradesman'.[2] At these opposite extremes, where middle-class education touched the national schools at one end and the public schools at the other, the same sense of social separation was deeply felt.

These two observations of the Taunton Commissioners about the upper and the lower ranges of their field of enquiry also bring out the important point that people of very different social and economic standing might be described as 'middle-class'. Since this was so, it is necessary to define more precisely what the Victorians meant by that term. It was a platitude of contemporary discussion that the middle class shaded off at one end into the gentry, and at the other into the poor, and the range was naturally enormous from the industrialist or the merchant prince at one end of the spectrum to the clerk or book-keeper at the other. It is a commonplace to say that England has never had a merchant patriciate and that wealth made in industry and trade has always been quickly assimilated into the landed and aristocratic class. After 1870 industrial wealth was to mix more completely with wealth made from the land and from the older professions like the law. Indeed the unifying forces provided by public school and university education were not the least important factors in bringing this change about.

Even if the wealthiest sector of the middle class was tending more and more to coalesce with the old aristocracy, a very large section of the total population remained in the middle-class ranks. For a clearer definition we may use the ideas of two men who devoted their lives to the provision of middle-class education. The first of these, Nathaniel Woodard, is still a well known name because the Woodard Schools still flourish. The second, Joseph Lloyd Brereton, of whom more will be said later, is now almost forgotten. Brereton thought that the term 'middle-class' could be applied to some 20,000,000 people ranging from 'men who earn their liveli-

[1] *SIC, PP* 1867-8, XXVIII, vol. I, pp. 90, 297.
[2] *Ibid.* p. 317.

hood by the least esteemed manual labour' to 'men who follow the most honoured professions'.[1] This definition may appear so sweeping as to be almost useless, though its very breadth reminds us of the host of ambitious people like Daniel Gooch of the Great Western Railway, who were moving from one class into another. Brereton was particularly interested in the education of farmers' sons; the farmer occupying between 200 and 300 acres was, he thought, 'the midmost man in England', and he pointed out that the farmers as a group exceeded in number any other above the rank of labourer.[2]

Woodard excluded the really well-off who were provided for by the existing public schools and divided the remainder into two main groups. The first were the 'gentlemen of small incomes, solicitors and surgeons with limited practice, unbeneficed clergymen, naval and military officers'. The second was 'the trades-class ... persons of very different grades, from the small huckster who obtains his livelihood by his dealing with the poor, up step by step, through third and second rate retail shops, publicans, gin-palace-keepers etc., to the influential and highly respectable tradesmen, whose chief dealings are with the higher ranks of society'.[3] On another occasion he named as representative groups 'the tradespeople, the farmers, the merchants and the superior class of mechanics'.[4] It was people such as these he thought, who had been neglected by the Church and had in consequence become estranged from it; the small tradesmen were a particularly important group 'and with a little diligence and management might be *picked up by thousands*'.[5]

When Woodard's plans took concrete shape, the schools which he founded were planned to meet the needs of these different groups. Of the three original schools in Sussex, Lancing, the first founded, provided a public school type of education for the sons of gentlemen and professional men of moderate means. Hurstpierpoint was designed for the sons of those who wanted a less extensive education which would not normally lead to the university, while Ardingly

---

[1] J. L. Brereton, *County Education: A Contribution of Experiments, Estimates and Suggestions* (1874), pp. 1–2.
[2] *Ibid.* pp. 8–10.
[3] N. Woodard, *A Plea for the Middle Classes* (1848), pp. 4–5. For a recent treatment of Woodard, see B. Heeney, *Mission to the Middle Classes: The Woodard Schools, 1848–1891* (1969).
[4] N. Woodard, *Public Schools for the Middle Classes* (1851), p. 7.
[5] N. Woodard, *Plea*, p. 13.

was to serve the sons of men of very modest means who wanted merely what we might call a junior secondary course. In the seventies the annual payment at Lancing was £60 to £100 a year, at Hurstpierpoint £30 to £35, at Ardingly 15 guineas.[1] Later on more schools were founded and taken over in other parts of the country, and all were joined in a federative structure in the Society of St Mary and St Nicholas. The same idea of classification was taken over by the Taunton Commissioners who wanted to organize the endowed schools into three grades. The first with a classical curriculum would prepare boys for the universities. The second would train boys up to the age of sixteen or seventeen with a view to professional and managerial careers, while the third would carry them up to fifteen or sixteen years only.

The fact that the Taunton Commission took over in this way an idea which had been put forward by Woodard twenty years previously shows that state activity in secondary education followed belatedly behind the efforts of private individuals to achieve reforms. For the purpose of this study three such efforts may be isolated. The first is the attempt in the forties of the National Society to create middle-class schools in conjunction with colleges for training teachers. The second is the endeavour of numerous individuals to found schools to give a good education at a modest rate. There were many such individuals of whom Woodard was the most important, but here J. L. Brereton will be taken as an example, partly because his work is very little known and partly because his plans give a definite place to public examinations as a means to effecting improvements as Woodard's do not. The third, which is linked both with Brereton and with the National Society, is the idea of public examination as a means of achieving higher standards in secondary education. This idea was embodied both in organizations like the College of Preceptors and the Society of Arts and in the writing of many individuals who will be studied later.

The idea of public examinations for secondary schools did not, however, come onto the horizon until the late forties. By that time the first major effort to improve middle-class education on an extensive scale had been made and was already proving unsuccessful. The Church of England, enlivened to new activity, saw middle-class education as an important extension of the work which the National

[1] N. Woodard, *The Society and Schools of St Mary and St Nicolas College* (1878), p. 6.

Society was doing among the poor. The impetus was provided in 1838–9 by fear of state interference, which led a group of active churchmen to conclude that the Church must be first in the field. Among these were Lord Ashley (later Earl of Shaftesbury and one of the greatest of Victorian philanthropists), W. E. Gladstone, Lord Sandon (later Earl of Harrowby), T. D. Acland, who was later to be one of the fathers of the Oxford Local Examinations, and G. F. Mathison of the Mint, a man now forgotten but who appears to have been the instigator of the whole scheme.[1]

The root of his ideas was that the Church should establish both training colleges for schoolmasters and 'middle schools' to provide for the middle classes a higher level of education than that available in the primary schools. Mathison explained his ideas in a pamphlet published in 1844.[2] He makes the same point as Woodard was to make a few years later that the Church must extend its influence among 'farmers, tradesmen, and mechanics', for 'to train the Peer and the Pauper in one direction, and leave the Ten Pound house-holder to grope his way in another, without guide or juvenile bias of any kind is surely at variance with the ordinary laws of moral and social progression'. Like Woodard and William Sewell of St Columba's, Rathfarnham and Radley, Mathison wanted his new foundations to be corporate in character. Collegiate bodies should be established, engaged in teacher-training and associated with 'national boarding schools admitting day scholars'. These schools would provide practical experience for the students and would, in turn, send candidates to the training department. 'The same foundation', Mathison concluded, 'would support and direct the junior and senior departments; one Principal being over all, and one form of discipline common to both. Periodical examinations of a formal character, corresponding with university examinations and degrees, might take place at St Mark's College as a common centre, or at Oxford, Cambridge, St David's, Lampeter, and Durham, by means of special endowments.'

[1] See A. H. D. Acland (ed.), *Memoir and Letters of the Rt. Hon. Sir Thomas Dyke Acland* (privately printed, 1902), pp. 86–9.

[2] *How Can the Church Educate the People? The question considered with reference to the Incorporation and Endowment of Colleges for the Middle and Lower Classes of Society: In a letter addressed to the Lord Archbishop of Canterbury,* by a member of the National Society. See also the rather similar argument of R. Hussey, *A Letter to Thomas Dyke Acland Esq., M.P., on the System of Education to be Established in the Diocesan Schools for the Middle Classes* (1839).

The ideas of the Mathison–Acland group were taken up at once by the National Society. A Committee of Inquiry and Correspondence, of which the group were members, was formed in 1838. Among its tasks was to encourage the formation of diocesan boards of education and the establishment of training colleges. 'Middle Schools' in towns were to be taken into union with the society and a similar type of education was to be provided in the country districts. The committee went actively to work. It obtained counsel's opinion that there was nothing in the National Society's charter to prevent it from erecting and supporting schools for the sons of tradesmen and farmers. It projected a central institution in London to be connected with King's College in the Strand and diocesan normal schools, connected with the Cathedral Chapters, containing both a training department and a middle or commercial department.

The curricula which they planned for middle schools to be founded by or taken into union with the society included general subjects and such special subjects as mathematics, languages, drawing, surveying, and 'the sciences of agriculture and commerce'. They planned that each school should contain several class-rooms, a library, museum and, where necessary, a laboratory. Their endeavours would, they hoped, produce better trained teachers, improved methods of school management, and a useful general education, based on the religious principles of the Church for the middle classes.[1] A great appeal for funds, particularly for the central training institution, was launched at Willis's rooms in London on 28 May 1839; one of the resolutions presented at the meeting mentioned with satisfaction the establishment of diocesan and local boards of education 'as well as the establishment and encouragement of schools for the education of the middle classes, upon principles akin to those which are embodied in the Society's charter'.[2]

The work of the committee had important results. St Mark's Chelsea was founded in 1841 as the central training institution with Derwent Coleridge as the first principal, and a number of diocesan colleges were quickly set up. Gladstone, in addressing the society's annual meeting in 1847, claimed with justice that the society had started to grapple with the problem of teacher-training before the

---

[1] See the Minutes of the Committee of Inquiry and Correspondence in the National Society Archives.

[2] *National Society Twenty-Eighth Report* (1839), p. 84.

state had taken any hand in it and that, during the previous two years, a class of trained schoolmasters, though still small in number, had been created which did not exist before.[1] The training colleges, though they suffered many vicissitudes, had come to stay and were to make a very important contribution to English education. The fate of the middle schools was less happy. A number were set up, but they did not flourish. The curriculum of the Lincoln school, which is probably fairly typical, covered religious knowledge, English, writing, arithmetic, and elements of mathematics, psalmody, geography, French, history, elements of natural history and philosophy, with Latin and linear drawing if required.[2] In general the schools aimed at a good non-classical or commercial education. In London, a commercial school was founded in 1839 in Rose Street, Soho Square, which is said to have been the first of its kind.[3] Several of these schools were run in connection with training colleges as Mathison had planned. Among these, the 'Yeoman School' at York had 137 boys, 86 of them non-boarders, in 1847.[4]

These schools, however, did not prove successful and interest in them gradually died away. The history of the York School was outlined by one of the witnesses before the Taunton Commission in December 1865. Mr H. S. Thompson explained that the principal of the training college had also been headmaster of the school, with another master in charge of the teaching and a certain amount of help from the students in training. These were, he argued, two main reasons for the failure of the school. Every effort had been made to keep it cheap in order to attract the smaller farmers. With fees at only £22 per annum, the managers got into debt. Secondly the link with the college had been a disadvantage because many parents had been frightened by what was regarded as 'very high church teaching'. Eventually the Yeoman School had been united with the old Holgate Grammar School foundation, and, though this

---

[1] *National Society Thirty-Sixth Report* (1847), pp. 68ff.

[2] *National Society Twenty-Ninth Report* (1840), p. 85.

[3] *National Society Thirty-First Report* (1842), p. 23. George Chandler, *An Address delivered at the Opening of the Church of England Metropolitan Commercial School, Rose Street, Soho Square, January 28, 1839* (1839).

[4] *PP* 1847–8, L, p. 583. The College at Chester was also meant to include a 'commercial and agricultural school' for boys from 8 to 15 years. In 1845 there were 30 pupils. See H. Barnard, *Normal Schools and other Institutions, Agencies and Means designed for the Professional Education of Teachers* (Hartford, Conn., 1851), pp. 396, 402, 407.

was running successfully as both a day and a boarding school, it had never succeeded in attracting many farmers' sons.[1] Probably the history of other such schools was very similar. Acland, who had been very active in the early days of the movement, wrote in 1858 of 'the signal failure of terms of union for middle schools about 1839'.[2]

Certainly fear of Church influence was one reason for failure. Among the lower middle classes Dissent was particularly strong, and many parents and schoolmasters distrusted a body such as the National Society which made specific requirements about Anglican religious teaching. H. S. Thompson, later on in the same submission of evidence, stated that there was not likely to be 'any religious difficulty if the committee of management contained men of different opinions, and was not confined to any particular religious body'.[3] The National Society, by its constitution and its ethos, could not stand on such a footing and was bound to appear proselytizing in contrast.

There were practical and financial difficulties, too, as some of Her Majesty's Inspectors showed in their reports. The Reverend Henry Moseley, in his report for 1850, pointed out that the middle schools had not made a profit to help in the maintenance of the colleges, that running two basically different institutions was very distracting for the principal, while the teachers produced were more likely to be 'ushers for commercial schools' than primary school teachers.[4] After the introduction in 1846 of the system of government grants for teacher-training there was the further difficulty that the middle school was not eligible for a grant and it was very difficult to manage the finances of the two institutions separately. There are a number of indications of the difficulties caused by the grant situation; for instance the Worcester Diocesan Board when planning their college at Saltley in the fifties, had originally intended to add a middle school to it. This plan was later abandoned. The Reverend Frederick Temple in his report for 1857, pointed out that the government grant could not be used for the purpose of erecting or supporting a middle school, and that the subscribers had thought it best 'to finish first that part of their design for which they could

[1] *SIC*, vol. v, pp. 268–71: 11660–80.
[2] Acland, *New Oxford Examinations*, p. xxix.
[3] *SIC*, vol. v, p. 273: 11698.
[4] *PP* 1851, XLIV, pp. 297–8.

obtain aid from the public revenue, leaving the rest to be completed at a more convenient time'.[1]

The further history of the training colleges is outside the scope of this study, but they influenced the development of secondary education in two important ways. First of all they strengthened the middle-class dislike of state interference and its anxiety to keep itself separate from the classes below. As the colleges grew, they became more and more dependent on state aid which created, under the Minutes of 1846, a new social group of trained teachers. The middle classes strongly disliked what they considered to be the intellectual and social pretensions of these people. The elementary teachers were very unpopular figures in early Victorian England. Their critics said that they were subsidized by the state to cross the natural lines of class division. Their education took them out of the world of the poor from which by social origin they generally derived and they were despised by the higher classes to which they aspired to belong. Mr Collins in his book *Dickens and Education*[2] has pointed out the very unfavourable pictures of the teachers Bradley Headstone and Charley Hexam in *Our Mutual Friend*. The report of the Newcastle Commission shows the influence of these criticisms. It noted the existence of a feeling among teachers that they did not enjoy sufficient social consideration and that they had no chance of promotion to the inspectorate. Its own fears that the teachers might claim too high a status is seen in the explicit statement that they should not be regarded as public servants and that their terms of employment should be made with the school managers and not with the state.[3]

These discussions of the status of the trained teacher are indirectly important to the history of secondary education because the teachers' unpopularity discredited the state initiative which had brought them into existence, and in that sense made reforms, which were bound to depend in some degree on state intervention, more difficult to achieve. There was, however, one feature of government aid to the training colleges, which was uncontroversial and easily adapted in other purposes. This was the system of regular examinations before the award of grants to students and to pupil-teachers. At first Her Majesty's Inspectors of Schools paid an

[1] *PP* 1857–8, XLV, p. 720.
[2] P. Collins, *Dickens and Education* (1963).
[3] *PP* 1861, XXI, Pt. I, p. 161.

annual visit to each college and gave it a separate examination. Subsequently, under the system of 1846, common examinations were set simultaneously to all colleges. The examinations and the grants awarded on the results were, wrote Moseley in his annual report for 1852, a principal motive to exertion among the students and, since special weight was laid on subjects necessary for an elementary schoolmaster, means were provided of directing the attention of candidates particularly to these subjects.[1] The example of the training college examinations was used, as we have seen, by the Civil Service reformers to prove that the simultaneous examinations of large numbers of candidates was possible.[2] Indeed this was really the only precedent they could have used, for the training college examinations were the first common test in England set on a general syllabus and taken in a number of separate places. It should be remembered that such 'periodical examinations of a formal character' had already been suggested in Mathison's pamphlet of 1844.[3] The model they provided might prove to be useful for other educational purposes, and was not necessarily connected with the state interference which was so much disliked.

This dislike of state interference was shared by many of the Victorian founders of schools and by none more strongly than by Joseph Lloyd Brereton (1822–1901). His active career as an educationalist stretched from the fifties to the nineties, and a brief examination of his career, though it will carry us far beyond the early Victorian period which has so far been discussed, will bring up many issues which will be developed more fully as this study proceeds. Indeed Brereton himself will reappear at a number of points in it. His father was rector of Little Massingham in Norfolk and was actively concerned with social and economic questions as they affected the labourer and the land, an interest which he himself inherited. He had been a pupil of Arnold's at Rugby and had been deeply affected by his headmaster's views, particularly by Arnold's belief that Church and State alike were divine institutions and that neither could be considered subordinate to the other. Later on Brereton's anxiety to get men of different religious opinions to co-operate may not have helped him as an educationalist because it deprived him of the support of any definite church party. Here,

---

[1] *PP* 1852–3, LXXIX, p. 404.
[2] See p. 23.
[3] See p. 45.

of course, his attitude was very different from Woodard's who propounded definite High Church views in his schools. As a curate in London Brereton became concerned with the problem of filling the gap in educational provision between the new public schools such as Marlborough, founded in 1843, and the parish elementary schools. His London experience together with Arnold's influence and his father's concern about the problems of rural life, led him naturally towards education as one of the most important means of social improvement.[1]

He had no opportunity to put his ideas into practice until he was presented to the living of West Buckland in North Devon in 1852. There he persuaded the farmers to agree to a voluntary rate to pay for a village schoolmaster. He was also an enthusiast for agricultural improvement. He organized agricultural shows and was active in a newly constituted farmers' society. The neighbourhood was a poor and remote one, and, like so many of the reforming agriculturalists of the time, Brereton appreciated that better farming was possible only if the farmers were better educated. He was fortunate in gaining valuable support for his schemes from the Fortescues, the great local family who lived at Castle Hill near West Buckland. The second Earl, who had been Lord Lieutenant of Ireland, was Lord Lieutenant of the County. His son, Viscount Ebrington, later to become the third Earl, was a Whig politician who was deeply interested in social reform and agricultural improvement. The support of the Fortescues, father and son, was of the greatest importance to Brereton.

His educational plans developed fast after his arrival at West Buckland, and in 1856 he published a comprehensive plan of school organization.[2] The scheme bears certain resemblances to Woodard's three-tier structure which was developing at about the same time and to the later recommendations of the Taunton Commissioners. Brereton considered that in each hundred or similar county division there might be a school for boys and girls between the ages of twelve and fifteen which should be partly maintained by the labour of the pupils on a small farm to be attached to it, the remainder of their time being spent in studying the usual school

[1] This is based on an MS account by Brereton himself and on an unpublished biographical note by his son, Canon Philip Brereton.

[2] J. L. Brereton, 'County Education': A Letter addressed to the Rt. Hon. Earl Fortescue (1856), reprinted as Appendix I in Earl Fortescue, Public Schools for the Middle Classes (1864).

subjects. Above these schools there might in each county be a college to educate boys from fifteen to seventeen years old, again in connection with a larger farm and financed partly by fees and partly by the labours of the students. The keystone of the whole system would be an annual county examination, to be held under the patronage of the county magnates, at which youths between sixteen and twenty-four whose parents were in 'respectable and independent circumstances' might sit for a 'County Degree' and compete for 'County Honours', with which, through the liberality of individuals, various prizes and scholarships might be connected. The system should be self-supporting and should rest fundamentally on the efforts of the farmers themselves as the group who would principally benefit from it.

This 'County Education' plan of 1856 was one of the roots from which grew the Oxford Local Examinations of 1857, and it will be considered later in that connection, though the Locals eventually developed on lines rather different from Brereton's original ideas. His first practical achievement as a founder of schools was the 'Farm and County School' opened at West Buckland in 1858. The fees, he explained in an explanatory pamphlet, were to be graded from £45 to £10 according to the amount of farm work done, and he hoped for a school of fifty boarders with 100 acres of land, though he would be willing to begin with considerably fewer than that.[1] The school had its ups and downs, but it was a modest success, and it will appear later in this book.

Brereton continued to write and speak actively on educational subjects for the next thirty years. His ideas are worked out most fully in a book published in 1874.[2] In this book he further developed the graded structure of schools which he had suggested in the pamphlet of 1856 on the lines set out in the Taunton Commission report. The Devon County School at West Buckland had, he explained, been started as a second-grade school. The desirable size for such a school was 200 boys and about £32 per annum was a reasonable annual charge in such a school to cover board, tuition and the interest on capital. A first-grade school, he thought, might be provided at an annual expense of £52 though this was much less than was usually thought a viable figure. A third-grade school for

---

[1] J. L. Brereton, *Principles and Plan of a Farm and County School* (Exeter, 1858).
[2] *County Education: A Contribution of Experiments, Estimates and Suggestions* (1874).

boys who were going to be small farmers and bailiffs should, if it were to meet the needs of the parents who required such an education, not cost more than £15 to £20. Such a farm school should be small – about fifty boarders only – and it would be possible to make it so cheap only by the boys doing agricultural work. These fees are about the same as Woodard was charging at the same time for second- and third-grade schools, but Lancing was much more expensive than Brereton's figure for a first-grade school.[1]

The general organization, as in the 1856 pamphlet, was to be centred on the civil divisions. Second- and third-grade schools would be based on the county and the poor law union respectively, while each division of several counties should support a first-grade school. At the summit there should be a national structure of four educational provinces each based on a university, Oxford, Cambridge, London and a centre in the north, and each with an educational Council, which should conduct examinations, certificate masters and supervise endowed and other schools. Each province would be independent and would be free to develop its examinations in its own way. At each area university there should be a training college for secondary teachers. The finance for all this was to be found by a mixture of the charitable and the commercial principles. Endowment capital should be invested in educational development through the purchase of shares in a district school fund in which private investors might also invest if they wished and on which dividends would be paid.

These plans were very similar to some of Matthew Arnold's ideas and to the proposals of the Endowed Schools Bill Part II of 1869, to which we shall return later.[2] Most of Brereton's own schemes remained pure speculation, though he did create one very interesting institution of higher education, which survived for twenty years, the County College (later known as Cavendish College) at Cambridge. The County College was meant to form the apex of the pyramid of County Schools. The original plan was that the College was to be connected with middle-class schools, and residence in those schools should form a part of the total course, at the end of which the university was to be asked to recognize those who had passed the Oxford and the Cambridge Senior Local Examinations as 'County Graduates' or some such title. The students would

---

[1] See p. 44.
[2] See p. 231.

spend a year of the total course in residence at the university, and great stress was laid in the scheme on the need to provide better preparation for teachers. No sanction was ever given by Cambridge University to the proposed title, but the college itself opened successfully in 1873. It accepted students for the B.A. course at considerably less than the usual age in order to reduce the total cost of a university education. A large building was erected, and a total of 300 students aimed at.[1] Brereton also planned and partly carried out a similar educational structure for girls. The Graduated County Schools Association was registered in 1884 and several schools opened. There were to be schools of a higher and of a lower grade and a ladies' hostel at Norwich House, Cambridge, on similar lines to Cavendish College.

Unlike Woodard, whose schools were successful, most of Brereton's schemes have not endured. The Graduated County Schools Association was wound up in 1887. Cavendish closed in 1892. Another county school in his native county of Norfolk had closed in 1891, though West Buckland survived. It looks as though Brereton was an over-ambitious financier and the joint-stock principle of finance, in which he believed, was unpopular with many people, and could not easily be fitted into the era of greater state aid which began in the nineties. He was a devotee of private enterprise and self-help, and such views were falling out of fashion. At the social and economic level on which he was trying to operate, it was becoming increasingly clear as the century drew to a close that secondary education could not be provided without some kind of government assistance. Brereton was strongly opposed to anything of the sort, and was anxious through the county machinery to maintain 'local life and energy ... against the absorbing tendency of wealth and education to one centre'.[2]

Both Woodard and Brereton, though they differed in many ways, had two principles in common. They were very anxious to avoid state interference, and they understood that one of the major needs of secondary education was better organization. If this was not to be provided by the state, it must be created by the educational pioneers themselves. Existing schools were isolated, lacking

---

[1] The building still exists. It was bought by the authorities of Homerton College when Cavendish closed, and is today a college of education.

[2] J. L. Brereton, *'County Education': A Letter addressed to the Rt. Hon. the Earl of Devon* (1861), p. 15.

common standards and the means to apply the best available methods. The federation which Woodard achieved in his Society of St Mary and St Nicholas and which Brereton projected was designed to overcome these weaknesses. Brereton had, as we have seen, made considerable use in his plans of the 'County Examinations' as a centralizing and unifying force. At the time when he began work at West Buckland in 1852, the idea of using external examinations in this way was in the air, and the next chapter will be devoted to early plans of this kind. Founding new schools was expensive and difficult as the National Society had discovered. Therefore some means had to be found for making those which already existed as effective as possible. The introduction of external examinations for secondary schools might turn out to be the best method of doing this. If controlled by an impartial arbiter, such examinations would offer a target to ambition and a means of raising the general standard. Efficient teachers would achieve success in them, the inefficient would have the chance to learn from their failures, and parents would be able to assess the value of the education which their children were receiving. Just as the administrative reformers saw public examination as a remedy for political corruption and a test of personal competence, so the educational reformers saw it as a remedy against local pressures on the teacher and as a means of raising professional standards.

3

EXAMINATIONS AND
SCHOOLS - TO 1857

Examinations can by their nature be nothing more than tools, the means of attaining certain objectives external to themselves. The real interest of the story, both in administrative reform and in education, is in the problem why at a particular moment of time these tools should have appeared to so many people to be a useful way of achieving certain desirable goals. The story can be comprehended only if it be related to the general background of social and administrative change in the forties and fifties, and, in the case of the schools, more particularly to the complex problems of middle-class education which were reviewed in the last chapter. The examining method was making converts very rapidly in the late forties. It appears as a subject for discussion in the school world at much the same time as the creation of new honours schools at Oxford and Cambridge, the beginning of departmental entrance examinations in the Civil Service, and the establishment of state certification for teachers in training.

The idea in its relations to the schools was carefully examined in 1847 in an interesting pamphlet by James Booth, who was at that time vice-principal of the Liverpool Collegiate Institution and an active writer on educational and mathematical subjects with a strong interest in the further education of adults.[1]

Booth began his pamphlet with a lament of the usual type about the backwardness of middle-class education and of the danger that the poorer classes might become much better taught than their social superiors. It was, he thought, the duty of the state to promote education if necessary and this should be done by the enactment of the rule that, after a certain date, no one should be eligible for office under the Crown or for any public appointment who had not either taken a degree or been through one of the military colleges or 'obtained a *certificate from the Government Board of Examiners*'.[2] Such a certificate should not itself entitle a man to such a post but

[1] J. Booth, *Examination the Province of the State: or the Outlines of a Practical System for the extension of National Education* (1847).
[2] *Ibid.* p. 12.

should place him in the cadre from which all holders of such posts were to be drawn. The country would be divided into educational districts each with its board of examiners holding annual examinations and awarding certificates of three different grades. These examiners would not be authorized officially to inspect any school, their duty being to examine those candidates who voluntarily presented themselves and to abstain from interfering with the details of local education.

Booth believed that almost all middle-class youths who were not going into the army or to the universities would take the examination because it would be an excellent testimony to their general ability. He estimated the number of middle-class boys annually reaching the age of fifteen at about 30,000.[1] One great advantage of the proposed scheme would be that it would provide a standard of education at which middle-class schools might aim and which at the moment was conspicuously lacking. The public schools looked to the universities and were ranked according to the performance of their pupils there. If something similar could be provided for middle-class schools, the sound teacher could be more easily distinguished from the charlatan. The influence of the university examinations in Booth's mind is very clear: 'The truth is,' he said, 'such a Board of Examiners would influence education, much in the same way that the Colleges at Oxford and Cambridge indirectly sway the teaching and course of instruction given in the great public schools, and as they themselves are ruled by the permanent characteristics or varying tendencies of the Degree Examinations.'[2]

This scheme of general examinations could be applied throughout the whole kingdom. It would create a uniform system of education for the middle classes and provide a common goal of achievement for young people. It would enable new schemes to be tried out, new subjects like chemistry to be introduced. It would encourage young people to stay at school longer, an important point when most of them left too early to learn very much. All this might be achieved, through the examinations, without the dislocation caused by the introduction of a brand new system, for use might be made of institutions which were already in existence. Voluntary effort could be stimulated and local benefactors encouraged to endow prizes and exhibitions. The middle classes did not require charity and to tell them to look to the reform of the endowed

[1] *Ibid.* p. 67.   [2] *Ibid.* p. 47.

schools for better education merely deadened their present exertions. The efficiency of examinations for professional education had already been proved. They encouraged effective methods of teaching and ensured that the adult had in youth acquired sound habits of application and industry. They provided a goal of achievement for the less talented boy. To argue, Booth concluded, that education ought to be left to the law of supply and demand was nonsense. 'How is it less consistent with a wise and benevolent public policy to send forth Commissioners of Education than Commissioners of Bankruptcy? Is it not as rational to have inspectors to detect falsehood and dishonesty in education, as in weights and measures of commerce?'[1]

Booth's pamphlet is of exceptional interest because it draws together almost all the lines of contemporary thought which have been suggested in the last two chapters. The influence of the universities is obvious. Like Jowett and the educational reformers he looked at the business of government through educational spectacles and believed that an educational qualification could serve both as evidence of proficiency in knowledge and of aptitude for government service. He argues, like them, that success in examinations ensures the formation of habits of diligence and self-control. As Macaulay put it: 'Early superiority in science and literature generally indicates the existence of some qualities which are securities against vice.'[2] Booth appreciated, like Thomas and Matthew Arnold, that one great problem of the middle-class schools was their lack of any common standard of excellence. Such a standard might, he argued, be provided through examinations without the dislocation involved in introducing a brand new educational system. Perhaps he had in his mind here the difficulties experienced by the National Society in their plans for middle-class schools. Booth was far more ready for the state to intervene in this field than were most of his contemporaries, but, like them, he put strong emphasis on voluntary effort. There was widespread agreement that the middle classes did not require charity but needed to depend on their own exertions. So far as state activity is concerned, Booth's position was midway between that of Brereton and of Matthew Arnold.

---

[1] J. Booth, *Examination the Province of the State: or the Outlines of a Practical System for the extension of National Education* (1847), p. 66.
[2] Trevelyan, *Life and Letters of Lord Macaulay*, p. 611.

Echoes of ideas very similar to Booth's were to be heard in many other places in the ensuing years. A correspondent in the *English Journal of Education* for 1851, who complained in the usual terms about the education of the middle classes, suggested that it would be of the greatest use to them if 'a board of nine or ten responsible men of acknowledged qualification could be appointed, and kept constantly sitting', to examine boys whom their parents might wish to present to them for trial.[1] The suggestion of a government board or a council of examination of some type reappeared regularly during the following thirty years, particularly in the report of the Taunton Commission.[2] In the blue book on the reorganization of the Civil Service which followed the Northcote–Trevelyan Report the idea of a general qualifying examination for government employment was urged by the Scottish scientist, Lyon Playfair, who thought that the Education Department might hold a general 'maturity' examination, and by Henry Cole, joint secretary of the Science and Art Department, who was against a central examination but who thought that the work might be done by accredited local bodies of various kinds.[3] Canon Richson, an active Manchester educationalist, linked a similar scheme with a reforming programme which also covered another of Booth's interests, the education of adults. In a pamphlet published in 1856 Richson advocated 'periodical public examinations' for schools of different types, together with the foundation of bursaries to encourage parents to help their children at school, of examination for adults studying in their spare time, and of Polytechnic Institutions for higher educa-tion.[4] The scheme was far too ambitious to be practicable but it does illustrate the opinion held by many during the fifties that far-reaching educational changes were necessary.

Booth, Richson and the others whose opinions have been quoted were speaking purely as individuals, and the idea of public examination which they advocated was not likely to spread, unless it was taken up by institutions whose influence and prestige would have a far wider effect upon opinion than any single person could hope to achieve. In fact, such corporate activity began very early

[1] Vol. IV. (n.s.), p. 461.
[2] See p. 230.
[3] *Papers relating to the Reorganization of the Civil Service, PP* 1854–5, XX, pp. 250–1, 379–81.
[4] C. Richson, *The Agencies and Organization required in a National System of Education* (1856).

in the fifties, the pioneers being the College of Preceptors among the private schools and the Society of Arts in adult education.[1] The private schoolmasters were very early in the field here, surprisingly so when their generally low reputation is remembered. History has not treated them kindly as a group. Their memory is overshadowed by the monstrous shade of Dotheboys Hall and by the more elegant satire of Matthew Arnold's 'educational homes'. The parents were in a position to dictate to them, and ill-educated people often got the showy and ineffective teaching for their children which they demanded. Yet not all private schoolmasters were bullies and charlatans. There were among them innovators and men of ideas like the Hill family with their schools at Hazelwood and Bruce Castle[2] and if they were exceptional, there were many more commonplace men who were anxious to raise the standards of their calling.

Many of them saw that, if this was to be done, the key was to raise the standard of the teaching, for in most cases teachers in private schools were without qualifications, poorly paid, and with very poor prospects. In February 1846 a group of schoolmasters at Brighton formed a provisional committee under the chairmanship of H. S. Turrell, which was the parent of the College of Preceptors, formed in London later in the same year. Its purpose, as defined in the preamble to its royal charter of 1849, was that:

of promoting sound learning and of advancing the interests of education, more especially among the middle classes, by affording faculties to the teacher for the acquiring of a sound knowledge of his profession, and by providing for the periodical session of a competent body of examiners to ascertain and grant certificates of the acquirements and fitness for their office of persons engaged or desiring to be engaged in the education of youth, particularly in the private schools of England and Wales.[3]

The College of Preceptors began, in fact, with the very ambitious objective of providing a professional standard of qualification for teachers to be administered by teachers themselves. It has retained, throughout its history, an active interest in improving teachers' qualifications, but in the early days this side of its work was not a

[1] The Society of Arts was given the prefix 'Royal' in 1908.
[2] W. A. C. Stewart and W. P. McCann, *The Educational Innovators, 1750–1880* (1967), pp. 98–123.
[3] J. Payne, 'On the Past, Present and Future of the College of Preceptors', *Works*, vol. I, *Lectures on the Science and Art of Education* (1883), p. 320.

success. The college did not attain a very high standing, and probably the private schoolmasters were too weak and too disunited to be able to create a successful system of certification. Very few men came forward to be examined and the college diplomas were granted on too easy terms to teachers who had done little to deserve them. The dilemma of the teacher who neither wished to be examined nor was ready to flaunt a meaningless title is expressed clearly in a letter of 1851 in the college's archives:

I do not intend to go up for examination, nor are there many men who teaching as I have done for 25 years will be willing to do so. This being the case, it is undesirable to accept a Fellowship as a compliment or a recognition of past labours and services, while any doubt is cast on the propriety of it.[1]

Though the linked ideas of examinations for teachers or of professional qualifications did not prosper, it was very quickly seen that the examination technique might be extended to the boys under their care. Many of the members of the college council, including Turrell the chairman of the original Brighton committee, resisted this innovation, but they were unsuccessful. The first school examination by the college – that of certain pupils of a school in Nottingham – took place at Christmas 1850, and the plan of school examination was in full operation by 1854.[2] These were the first external examinations of 'middle-class' schools to be held in this country. In 1870 there were 1,571 candidates for the pupils' certificates of the college, while the candidates for teachers' certificates numbered only 53.[3] Though these school examinations performed a useful function, the college itself lacked the prestige or the authority to take any very important part in the overall direction of secondary education. Yet a courageous attempt had been made under difficult circumstances, and those who tried in this way to improve the condition of the private schools deserve to be remembered for what they did. There were private schoolmasters, too, among the pioneers of the University Local Examinations and some of them were active in running local examinations centres. Nor should it be forgotten that Miss Buss, one of the

---

[1] From W. H. Hopkins, Summer Hill, Birmingham, 26 January 1851—a letter in the rough Minute Book of the College of Preceptors (1854–72).

[2] Payne, *Works*, pp. 320–1.

[3] *Fifty Years of Progress in Education: A Review of the Work of the College of Preceptors from its Foundation in 1846 to its Jubilee in 1896* (1897), p. 37.

greatest pioneers of women's education, was a private school teacher and that the North London Collegiate School for Ladies developed out of a private school belonging to the Buss family. The private school was a product of its age. It gave the middle class what it wanted, and its whole existence was linked very closely, as has frequently been emphasized, with the class presuppositions of the time. Often the work it did was poor and shoddy, but there are things to be remembered on the other side, and not least of them the pioneering efforts of the College of Preceptors.

Many of those, like Booth and Richson and Dawes of King's Somborne, who were interested in improving primary and secondary education, were also animated by the idea of providing better educational opportunities for adults. It is not therefore surprising that the idea of external examination was applied in adult education by the Society of Arts at much the same time as it was applied to secondary education by the College of Preceptors. In 1851 the Society had achieved an outstanding success in organizing the Great Exhibition. At the same period it was much concerned to help the Mechanics' Institutes which had spread widely throughout the country since the 1820s. The institutes had always aimed, among other things, at increasing the scientific knowledge and skills of working adults, though this objective was very difficult to achieve because of the very rudimentary nature of their basic education. In 1851 Harry Chester suggested to the Society's Council that the Society should try to help the institutes, and in July 1852 the council set up a union of institutes with the aim of strengthening their educational activities through better organization. One way of doing this lay in the creation of a system of examinations. This was definitely proposed by Chester in December 1853, and a scheme of examinations was published the following year. This original plan was found to be too elaborate and was remodelled, chiefly by James Booth. In 1856, sixty-two candidates were examined at the Society's house in London in a wide range of subjects, book-keeping, mathematics, the natural sciences, geography, English history and literature, French, German and drawing. The first examination in a provincial town was held at Huddersfield in 1857, the Society's examiners going down to the West Riding for the purpose.[1] Two years previously the indefatigable Richard Dawes had told the

---

[1] H. T. Wood, *A History of the Royal Society of Arts* (1913), pp. 369–70 and ch. 19.

Huddersfield members at their annual soirée that what they needed were qualified, paid teachers and 'systematic examination, in connection with some educational board'.[1]

Dawes had been a pioneer of the popular education of King's Somborne. He had been an active propagandist for competitive examinations in the Civil Service,[2] and he was preaching the same gospel to the workmen and clerks of Huddersfield. The range of his activities, like those of James Booth, shows how vigorous the educationalists were during the late forties and early fifties, and how large a part the concept of public examination played in their thinking. This concept was shared by both private individuals and the state. The Science and Art Department, founded in 1853, began a system of examinations by which grants were awarded at different levels of proficiency in 1859. Before that date, the Devonshire Commission of 1872 argued, the working classes could hardly acquire scientific instruction at all.[3] Subsequently the department's grants played a very large part in the development of scientific education in secondary schools generally and especially in the growth of the higher-grade schools founded by the School Boards. The opportunities which the department's examinations offered to the young H. G. Wells have already been mentioned in the first chapter.[4]

In elementary education examinations came to be used extensively. On occasion they could serve as a means of encouragement; for instance in 1852 the Iron and Coal Masters of south Staffordshire established a system of examinations and prizes in order to persuade children to stay longer at school, an example followed by several other schemes in the same part of the country.[5] By that time there was growing concern over the cost of education to the state and over what was thought to be the neglect of the rudiments of learning by the teachers. This led to the appointment of the Newcastle Commission on Popular Education which in its report (1861) recommended that these problems should be dealt with by the award of grants on attendance and on the performance of

[1] R. Dawes, *Mechanics' Institutes and Popular Education: An Address delivered at the Annual Soirée of the Huddersfield Institute, December 13th 1855* (1856), p. 17.

[2] See p. 29.

[3] *Royal Commission on Scientific Instruction and the Advancement of Science, Second Report*, PP 1872, XXV, p. 19.

[4] See p. 8.

[5] *PP* 1852–3, LXXIX, p. 345; *PP* 1854, LI, p. 391; *PP* 1854–5, XLII, p. 738.

children according to their ages, in tests of reading, writing and arithmetic. The grant proposal in a recast form was embodied in Robert Lowe's Revised Code of 1862; and the principle it embodied was to dominate the elementary schools for thirty years. Controversy still continues about the system of 'payment by results'. For our purpose it is important to note the close kinship between the Revised Code and the examinations of the Science and Art Department; while the examinations of the Society of Arts, of the College of Preceptors, and of the Civil Service Commissioners were perhaps not unaffected by the same influences. A very wide range of territory had certainly beeen captured by the examiners since the early days of the Cambridge Tripos and the Oxford Schools.

Yet, by the mid-fifties, no effective means had been found of applying the new idea of external examination to the 'middle-class' or secondary schools, which, it was generally agreed, were one of the weakest parts of the whole educational system and therefore particularly in need of stimulus and help. Such school examinations could be created either by the state or by a private institution. State intervention, for reasons which have already been explained, was not at that time a serious possibility. The College of Preceptors and the Society of Arts were doing useful work, but neither possessed the prestige necessary for a real initiative. Another possibility was that the universities might act. In the period of reform which began with the Royal Commissions of 1850 Oxford and Cambridge were much more likely to accept wider responsibilities towards national education as a whole, for there was a widespread feeling that the universities had to justify their position in a very changed world if they were to preserve their existing wealth and influence.

The first fruits of this wider interest were the creation by the two universities of the Local Examinations in 1857–8. The story of their institution is a curiously circuitous one, which began in Devonshire, a long way from the banks of the Isis and the Cam. The immediate problem which started off the whole development was the old question of improving the education of farmers' sons. The people primarily concerned with the Devonshire part of the story were four – two landowners and two clergymen. The ideas of two of them, Viscount Ebrington (later the third Earl Fortescue) and the Reverend J. L. Brereton, have already been discussed in the last chapter.[1] The second of the landowners, T. D. Acland, of the

[1] See p. 51.

family long established at Killerton near Exeter, had been, as we have seen, one of the pioneers of the National Society movement of 1838-9. He had maintained his interest in education during the intervening years and he was also an active agriculturalist who had drawn up a scheme by which the Bath and West of England Society should hold exhibitions in different towns of the west and south.[1] The fourth of the quartet, Frederick Temple, is the greatest name of them all, a man who was to be a great headmaster, an archbishop, father of a greater son. He had been brought up in Devonshire and educated at Blundell's School. After a brilliant Oxford career he became a fellow of Balliol, and then entered the Education Department, first as an examiner and then as principal of Kneller Hall, a training college for workhouse schoolmasters. When Kneller Hall was closed in 1855 he became inspector of men's training colleges until in November 1857 he was appointed headmaster of Rugby. A member of the most distinguished Oxford college of the day, Temple was closely connected with the Oxford reformers like Jowett, and was himself a keen supporter of university reform. With his university background and his knowledge of the training colleges and of the Education Department, he spanned the whole of English education in a unique way, and was in a position to bring an unusually wide experience to bear on any problem which he took up. He was in addition a man of great energy and force of character.

The Devonshire part of the story began with Brereton and Lord Ebrington. Brereton's plans for county schools and for a county examination and degree were published, as we saw in the last chapter, in a pamphlet of 1856.[2] The basic ideas had been suggested by Brereton to Ebrington and his father, the second Earl Fortescue, and had been discussed between the three men in the winter of 1853.[3] The following year Ebrington put forward the bare outlines of Brereton's scheme in a published letter to Harry Chester of the Society of Arts, which was at that time working on its own system of examinations. Since this was so, Ebrington urged that it would be best to try and adapt the machinery of the society to rural conditions. He was, however, anxious to maintain the idea of a county degree as representing the standard of attainment which

---

[1] Acland (ed.), *Memoir and Letters of the Rt. Hon. Sir Thomas Dyke Acland*, pp. 142-3. There is an interesting sketch of Acland in W. Tuckwell, *Reminiscences of Oxford* (1900), pp. 88-93.
[2] See p. 51.
[3] Earl Fortescue, *Public Schools for the Middle Classes* (1864), pp. 3, 52.

might be expected of the middle class and of the elite of the class below it.[1]

In the following year (1855) Ebrington offered a prize of £20 for the best examination passed by a young man between eighteen and twenty-three years old, the son or relative of a Devonshire farmer. The examination was to take place in Easter week 1856 at Exeter, the subjects required being English language, the history and geography of the British Empire, and practical mathematics. He explained in a published memorandum the great importance of setting a standard to the schools and the growing habit of establishing 'special examinations to test qualifications with a view to the selection of the right men for the right places'. The Society of Arts, he thought, had an insufficiently strong hold on public opinion to conduct such examinations; the universities were too busy with their own internal reforms; if the government were to act, the result would be to create an army of place-seekers. He again mentioned the scheme for county examinations and degrees, but clearly considered that this was too major a step to be taken at once. The prize-scheme was blessed by the Bath and West Society in October 1855, and some of its members agreed to form a committee to help in carrying out the plan.[2]

The examination was duly held at Exeter in Easter week 1856, though very few candidates came forward. In the same year Ebrington had a very serious illness, losing the sight of one eye and having to go abroad to recuperate.[3] The idea which Brereton and he had fathered was quickly taken up by Acland who, as Ebrington wrote later, 'with characteristic impetuosity, rushed into the field, and first superseded my tentative effort by his scheme for "Prizes for Practical Schools in the West of England"; and then superseded that scheme of his in its turn by another larger one'.[4] Acland had led a retired life after the death of his first wife in 1851. In 1856 he remarried and returned with new energy to public work, the problem of middle-class education being the first subject to which he applied himself.

In January 1857 a committee of which Acland was secretary met

[1] Viscount Ebrington, *Letter to H. Chester Esq. Middle Class Education and Society of Arts Public Local Examinations*, in Fortescue, *Public Schools for the Middle Classes*, App. II.
[2] *Memorandum on Middle Class Education* (1855); *ibid.*, App. III and IV.
[3] *Ibid.* pp. 7–8.
[4] *Ibid.* p. 6.

at Exeter to establish a 'system of Examinations and Prizes for Boys educated with a view to employment in agriculture, arts, manufacture and commerce'.[1] Its prospectus proposed that boys should be examined in two divisions, those below fifteen years and those below eighteen years of age. The object in view was to test a good general education, and prizes would be offered for religious knowledge; languages and literature, including English, Latin, modern languages, geography and history; mathematics, including arithmetic, algebra, trigonometry and 'general principles of natural philosophy'; and for practical science and art, including mechanics, chemistry, physiology, engineering, and surveying, book-keeping, architecture, drawing and music. All candidates would be required either to take the paper in religious knowledge or to produce a certificate from a minister of religion in its place.

The committee's prospectus mentioned Ebrington's scheme of 1855 and Brereton's pamphlet on *County Education*, and elsewhere Acland paid tribute to Ebrington's work in concentrating attention on the improvement of existing means of education and on the utility of examinations as the best way of doing this.[2] He did not specifically mention Brereton's contribution, though it is fair to say that Ebrington had been applying Brereton's ideas and that the whole movement should, in a sense, be traced back to him. Where Acland differed from both of them was in that he did not believe in the practicality of the proposed County Boards of Examination.[3] The attractiveness of the examination plan to him as a means of improving middle-class education was that it avoided most of the snags which had beset the plans of the National Society in the forties. Its advantages were that it would set a standard of general education and keep that separate from apprenticeship; it would teach the parent to distinguish the sound from the showy; it would help the honest teacher to surpass the charlatan. It would achieve this without infringing the middle-class love of independence, without presenting problems about religious instruction or about outside interference in the running of a school. It would make the best use of what was available without the expense and difficulty of starting new schools and of reforming old endowments.

---

[1] Acland, *New Oxford Examinations*, p. 105.
[2] Acland, *New Oxford Examinations*, p. 13; *The Education of the Farmer viewed in connection with that of the Middle Classes in general* (1857), p. 49.
[3] Acland, *New Oxford Examinations*, p. 13.

Very early in its career the Exeter Committee appealed to the Committee of Council on Education to ask for the help of some Inspectors of Schools in carrying out their plans, which were to be modelled on 'the Examinations for Training Schools under inspection'. Their request was granted, and they were given the aid of Joseph Bowstead and of Frederick Temple, who, as we have seen, was familiar both with Devon and its problems. If anything permanent was to come of the Exeter plan, some continuing machinery would have to be found. Such machinery was unlikely to be provided by the government. The Society of Arts, to which Ebrington had originally applied, lacked the necessary prestige, and, although it was already in the field, its schemes had been planned far more with the needs of adult workers in mind than with those of schoolboys. Acland himself may have thought of bringing in the universities, for he was a distinguished Oxford man, a double first and a fellow of All Souls, but it looks as though the primary credit for linking the plan of school examinations with university control should go to Temple. He was himself a keen supporter of university reform and keenly alive to the need to make the universities better known and more useful to the country at large. From both school and university points of view the link seemed an ideal solution to the problem.

Acland was sent by Ralph Lingen, secretary of the Education Department, to see Temple probably about the beginning of February 1857. Temple seems to have taken to the idea at once, as is clear from an important letter which he wrote to Robert Scott, Master of Balliol on 25 February.[1] After explaining that the examination idea was very much in the air, Temple continued:

Will there be any chance of inducing the universities to step in? My plan is this: That the University should appoint a competent Board of Examiners; that these examiners should be prepared to examine all boys between certain ages presented to them under certain regulations; that the examination should be divided into schools to cover the subjects at present most needed by boys in the middle class school; that every boy who passes should have a Testamur from the examiners and the title Alumnus or Scholaris in Artibus of the University, and should be considered as in some sense matriculated; and that the expenses

---

[1] *Memoirs of Archbishop Temple*, by Seven Friends, ed. E. G. Sandford (1906), vol. II, p. 541.

of the examination should be covered by a small fee from every candidate.

The University, you see, would give nothing but the title, and would have the responsibility for choosing the examiners. The expenses could easily be met by the fees. The examinations might be held once a year at Oxford; but also in the country wherever the local gentry chose to make arrangements for that purpose.

If Oxford began, Cambridge would soon follow. In this way the universities would give guidance to those schools which is sadly needed. And surely there is no function which Oxford might more appropriately offer to assume than that of guiding education all over the country.

I am quite sure that the right to put 'S.A. of the University of Oxford' after one's name would be eagerly coveted.

This letter makes it quite clear, that if the germ of the school-examination idea was Brereton's and Ebrington's, if the Exeter plans of 1857 were Acland's, it was Temple's mind which generalized the whole notion into an elaborated plan directed by the universities of Oxford and Cambridge.

The rest of the events of 1857 fall into two parts – the actual examination at Exeter itself and the campaign to get the idea taken up by the University of Oxford, with the confident hope that Cambridge would soon follow. The course of events in the west can be sketched quite briefly. The scheme, like Ebrington's plan of 1855, was blessed by the Bath and West Society who offered an honorary life membership as a prize.[1] The examination began at Exeter on 16 June. The subjects were those defined in the original prospectus. First of all a preliminary examination in writing and arithmetic had to be passed. Though the candidates were arranged into two divisions according to their ages, they were all to take the same papers, which were to contain questions of varying degrees of difficulty. In each department there was to be both an elementary and a higher examination.[2] All the details had to be worked out *ab initio*, there being so few precedents which could be followed. Enquiries were made from masters of schools in Devonshire and adjacent counties about the course of instruction and the books used in their schools, while 'intelligent parents in the middle ranks' were questioned about the kind of knowledge required in business. One hundred and six candidates were actually examined from schools of many kinds, 'two little fellows from a National School'

---

[1] Acland, *New Oxford Examinations*, p. 104.
[2] For the syllabuses and examination papers, see *ibid.* pp. 122–8, 139–79.

having walked twenty miles to attend.[1] Arrangements were made with three innkeepers to provide lodgings where necessary, and two large rooms hired at the Clarence Hotel. The friends of the candidates and other interested persons were allowed access to these rooms 'with a view to remove all air of mystery, and to satisfy public interest', though on another occasion it was thought they would be better excluded from the rooms, where written work was being done.[2] The entire expense of the examinations amounted to £42. 3s. 6d. of which £18 was for printing and posting the prize list.[3]

Temple's report on the examination showed that of the 106 candidates, 34 were seniors (up to 18 years old) and 72 juniors (up to 15). The standard had properly been kept low, but he considered that only 16 of the seniors and 22 of the juniors had passed, many of the remainder having failed in the preliminary examination. Temple commented that many candidates had not been properly grounded in the elements of knowledge. Of the work in literature and language, the Latin was far the best. French appeared not to be taught in many schools and few taught it well. Mathematics was the best taught subject of all, though the boys generally had more idea how to work calculations than how to apply their knowledge to solving problems. The papers in practical science and art had been put in rather because of public demand than because they really fitted into school programmes, and Temple did not find much to say about them. In general he thought the results had shown that the pupils had worked hard, and that the masters were willing to improve their methods by all the means in their power.[4] The Exeter Examination had been, in the modern jargon, a pilot scheme. If it had shown up many weak places, it had found some strong ones, and Temple's report suggested that more could be built on the existing foundations, which were reasonably sound.

While the Exeter Examination was being planned and executed, Temple and his supporters had been at work both in Oxford and in the country at large. In Oxford Temple's intermediary with the Hebdomadal Council was Francis Jeune, Master of Pembroke, a reforming head of a house, member of the University Commission of 1850, and a former headmaster of King Edward's, Birmingham. Jeune's advocacy had much to do with the final passing of the necessary University Statute. Temple's views were set out in two

---

[1] Acland, New Oxford Examinations, p. 135.
[2] Ibid. p. 133.   [3] Ibid. p. 134.   [4] Ibid. pp. 180–92.

letters to him of April 1857. The first of these suggested a scheme of examination similar to that followed at Exeter, except that English and languages were divided into two separate schools. Each candidate was to be required to pass in the preliminary examination and in one school or group of subjects, and if they did so success-fully they should be awarded some title such as 'Associate in Arts'. In the second letter Temple established the practicality of the scheme, citing the example of the Society of Arts, of Acland's scheme in Devonshire, and at a lower level, of the prize schemes in Stafford-shire and other counties.[1]

Though he was anxious up to the last moment about the fate of the proposed Statute at Oxford, his cause was strengthened by the evidence of widespread support flowing into Oxford for the scheme.[2] Some of this activity had been stimulated by Temple's own efforts. On 14 April, for instance, a letter which he had written to the Reverend H. W. Bellairs, HMI on lines similar to the first letter to Jeune was brought by Bellairs before the committee of the Birmingham Educational Association. The committee then for-mally decided to bring the subject before the University of Oxford and pledged itself to secure candidates and to provide accommoda-tion if Temple's scheme were accepted and an examiner sent to Birmingham. Bellairs himself went to Oxford with the resolution and subsequently, with Temple and with two members of the Birmingham Committee, presented it to a committee of the Senate of Cambridge.[3] Encouragement came from other great towns. The headmaster of Leeds Grammar School in a letter to Acland mentioned a petition which had been drawn up in Leeds. At the moment, he said, his school was sending only about three boys a year to the universities; for the rest 'we have no means of showing whether they are well taught or not'.[4] Interest was stirring at Cambridge. 'We want something which shall endear us to the middle classes', wrote Harvey Goodwin, later Bishop of Carlisle, 'we want a wider field of action, in order to make even the work that we are doing at the moment more effective and influential.'[5]

---

[1] *Ibid.* pp. 75–81.
[2] See *Report of the Committee on Middle-Class Examinations* (Bodleian Library, G. A. Oxon, b. 29), with the memorials which were presented.
[3] *Minutes of the Committee of Council on Education, 1857–8, PP* 1857–8, XLV, pp. 280–1. The letter is on pp. 285–6 (Appendix B).
[4] Acland, *New Oxford Examinations*, p. 88.
[5] *Ibid.* p. 87.

It seemed, wrote the *English Journal of Education*, as if Temple 'had struck the key to the thoughts of a thousand hearts'.[1] The Statute establishing a Delegacy to conduct examinations of non-members of the University in religious knowledge, English, history, languages, mathematics, physical science and other subjects forming part of the liberal education of youth was passed by the University of Oxford on 18 June 1857 while Temple was at Exeter conducting the examination there. That same evening there was a great meeting in Exeter at which Temple spoke and where he was able to announce that the Oxford Statute had been passed. The universities, he said, educated the upper class and the learned professions, and it was of the greatest importance that this class should be closely connected with other classes. 'The universities should be made to feel that they have an interest in the education of all England, and all England should be made to feel that they have an interest in the prosperity and excellency of the universities.'[2] Acland and Temple had been in active communication with Cambridge as well as with Oxford. A Grace similar to the Oxford Statute passed the Cambridge Senate in February 1858.

'I have little doubt', wrote Temple to Scott from Exeter in June 1857, 'that we have planted the seed of no mean tree.'[3] Indeed the whole development of secondary education in England during the past century has been deeply influenced by the decisions made during these few days at Oxford. The idea of examination was in the air and was almost bound to be applied to secondary education. It was the only scheme of improvement which avoided the bogies of state interference, of religious controversy, of local dissensions between parents and teachers, of the crushing expense of new schools. Of all the ideas for reform in secondary education which had been discussed it alone appeared to make the best use of the resources which were available and, according to the philosophy of the time, to provide people with the means to help themselves. Yet to create a satisfactory system was not at all easy, as the efforts of the College of Preceptors and of the Society of Arts made clear. The Brereton–Ebrington idea of county examinations, too, had fatal weaknesses; they would have had no common centre, no assurance of a sponsoring body with real authority. The real stroke

---

[1] Vol. XI (n.s., 1857), p. 226.
[2] Acland, *New Oxford Examinations*, p. 201.
[3] *Memoirs of Archbishop Temple*, ed. E. G. Sandford, vol. II, p. 549.

of genius was Temple's association between school examinations and the universities.

The idea of public examination had originally grown up at Oxford and Cambridge and in the period of academic reform which began after 1850 it had, as we have seen, been quickly and widely carried into the outside world. For a generation the education problem in its many aspects had been a main topic of concern among those who were interested in social questions. Now it appeared that education was advancing on a broad front with the examiners as the shock troops of the army. J. G. Fitch told the Social Science Association in 1858:

No phenomena in the educational horizon at all approach in importance the rapid extension of a system of examination hitherto almost exclusively confined to the students in the Universities – first to candidates for appointments in the military, naval, and civil service of the Crown; then, to the alumni of mechanics' institutions, by the Society of Arts; then, to the boys of middle class schools, by the College of Preceptors, and by the Universities; and lastly, to the children of National, British and other elementary schools, in the form of prize and certificate schemes.[1]

The connections between university reform and changes in the public service have already been traced. Temple had very close connections with the Oxford reformers, and it was natural that as soon as he was confronted with the problems of middle-class schools, he should have looked to the universities to provide a solution for them, just as Jowett had looked to the same quarter for the means of regenerating the Civil Service. Balliol, like Macaulay's Trinity, had grown great through open competition for its fellowships, and two Balliol men might be expected to think that the principles which had made their college a leading force in Oxford could be transferred with advantage to the public offices and to the schools.

The association between the new examinations and the universities offered to the schools an invaluable connection with the higher education of the country. It preserved their independence. That was its great merit. Moreover it gave them the organization which they desperately needed. From the university side this new sphere

---

[1] 'Examination Schemes and their incidental effects on public education', *Transactions and Sessional Proceedings of the National Association for the Promotion of Social Science, 1858*, p. 220.

of work was something very much outside their traditional limits. They were prepared to undertake it because, as Temple had said during the Exeter Examinations, 'the universities should be made to feel that they have an interest in the education of all England'. This is a new note in university thinking. Acute minds at Oxford and Cambridge had been aware for a quarter of a century that the universities were falling more and more out of touch with a changing society. Their methods and ideals seemed to be linked to an older, aristocratic England, when a new England of democracy and manufacture was rising all around them.[1] The reformers were keenly aware of the need to extend the scope of their work and to get into touch with classes and interests hitherto quite alien to them. The movement of 1857 served the needs of both parties. The universities could give the guarantee of scholarship and impartiality which the parent and teacher needed. The school examinations provided the universities with a priceless means of extending their work, enlarging their constituency and winning new and valuable friends.

[1] See J. Roach, 'Victorian Universities and the National Intelligentsia', *Victorian Studies*, vol. II (Dec. 1959), pp. 131–50.

PART II

THE OXFORD AND CAMBRIDGE LOCALS AND NATIONAL EDUCATION, 1857–1900

4

BEGINNINGS, 1857–1860

There were many signs in the middle fifties of a growing public interest in education, apart from the events at Exeter and at Oxford which have already been recounted. The Manchester and Salford Education Bill, proposing to raise a rate in aid of denominational schools in those towns, was finally defeated in 1854, though in the ensuing years a series of bills was introduced into the House of Commons, and a Royal Commission was appointed to enquire into the state of popular education in 1858.[1] In June 1857 an Educational Conference was held under the auspices of Prince Albert, which concerned itself mainly with primary education and with problems of early leaving, but which also considered prize and certificate schemes and the educational aspects of the Civil Service Examinations. Among the papers read was one by W. L. Sargant on 'The proposed middle-class examinations as a means of stimulating the education of the lower classes'.[2]

It is very interesting to note how much attention was given to educational matters in the 1857 issues of two such important provincial newspapers as the *Manchester Guardian* and the *Leeds Mercury*. The latter was owned by the Congregationalist Edward Baines who was one of the chief opponents of state intervention in primary education, and the newspaper columns naturally reflect his interests in that they oppose state taxation for educational purposes. A great deal of space is given to Mechanics' Institutes and their work and to the examinations of the Society of Arts, which were first held in a provincial town at Huddersfield in 1857. In this connection Dr James Booth makes several appearances;[3] he spoke at the distribution of the Society of Arts prizes at Huddersfield and reminded his hearers that 'the principle of examinations introduced by the Society of Arts had been adopted by the

[1] Frank Smith, *History of English Elementary Education, 1760–1902* (1931), pp. 217–19, 224–5.

[2] *Manchester Guardian*, 24 and 25 June 1857; C[ambridge] U[niversity] A[rchives], University Papers 1856–7, nos. 590, 611.

[3] See pp. 56–8.

Universities of Oxford and Cambridge'.[1] Although the trustees and masters of Leeds Grammar School and the clergy of Leeds and neighbourhood, as well as the School of Practical Art and the Mechanics' Institution, petitioned the University of Oxford to establish the middle-class examinations,[2] the *Leeds Mercury* gives curiously little attention to this subject, perhaps because two prominent churchmen, Alfred Barry, the headmaster of the grammar school, and W. F. Hook, the vicar, were active in promoting one of the memorials. However in December the paper reported a public meeting which had decided to co-operate with the University of Oxford and to ask that Leeds be made a centre for examination, and a few days later welcomed the Oxford scheme in an approving editorial.[3]

The *Manchester Guardian* also gave much attention to the Mechanics' Institutes and their work, but seems to have been far more conscious than its Yorkshire neighbour of the general problem of middle-class education. An editorial in February pointed out the need for better management of educational endowments and for better support for Owens' College (opened in 1851); 'it is high time', wrote the author, 'that something should be done either to make a better use of existing institutions, or to found others fitted to give a high-class education to our young men.'[4] In June much prominence was given to Temple's plan, which an editorial of 10 June interprets as an attempt by the universities to put themselves really in touch with the national life and to admit into connection with them 'classes which are neither orthodox nor wealthy'.[5] A year later, in presenting the prizes and certificates after the first Oxford Examinations held in Liverpool, Gladstone remarked that he never came into south Lancashire without feeling how little connection there was between it and Oxford or Cambridge. The institution of the new examinations would mark the resumption of the proper relationship between the universities and all classes of the community.[6]

[1] *Leeds Mercury*, 30 July 1857.
[2] *Report of the Committee on Middle Class Examinations* (Bodleian Library, G. A. Oxon, b. 29); W. R. W. Stephens, *Life and Letters of W. F. Hook* (6th edn.) (1881), p. 474.
[3] *Leeds Mercury*, 10 and 19 December 1857.
[4] *Manchester Guardian*, 9 February 1857.
[5] *Ibid.* 10 June 1857; see also 5 and 9 June.
[6] *Ibid.* 18 October 1858.

It was, then, against a background of widespread public interest in educational problems that the Local Examinations began their work. Temple's plan and the Exeter Examination of June 1857 have already been treated in the last chapter.[1] At Oxford the scheme was referred by the Hebdomadal Council on 11 May to a strong committee including Williams, Warden of New College, the vice-chancellor, Jeune, Robert Scott of Balliol, Pusey and H. L. Mansel, which reported on 25 May.[2] The widespread support which the scheme elicited is shown by the large number of memorials supporting it. Individuals and societies in great cities like Leeds, Birmingham, Liverpool, Sheffield and even Edinburgh are represented; there are smaller towns like Cheltenham, Gloucester and Durham, headmasters of country grammar schools like Bromsgrove and Berkhamsted, rural bodies like the Hants and Wilts Adult Education Society and the clergy of the deanery of Stonehouse in Gloucestershire.

The report itself argues that the university should endeavour to extend its influence to the middle classes which have no bond with them and for whom nothing is done nor perhaps can be done by the state. It is desirable that the efforts of good teachers should be rewarded and that promising boys should be brought forward in a way which is impossible within the confines of a small school. This may be achieved by 'a well digested and well administered system of voluntary periodical examinations' which the universities are peculiarly well-qualified to undertake, and it is suggested that there should be two such examinations, one for boys under fifteen to test elementary training, one for boys under eighteen to examine more advanced work. This might be very advantageously arranged in Oxford itself but it might also be desirable that the same papers be taken in 'other considerable places' at the same time. Part of the examination should consist of a test in 'the rudiments of religion, suited to the character of the university and the age of the candidates' but this should be excused if parents objected to it. Apart from the award of certificates, success in the senior examination should be marked by some title showing the connection of the possessor with the University of Oxford and, although all such titles are open to some objection, that of Associate in Arts is probably as good as any.

---

[1] See pp. 68–70.
[2] O[xford] U[niversity] A[rchives], Minutes of Hebdomadal Council 1854–66, fols. 179, 181, 185, (4, 11, 25 May 1857).

The rest of the report outlines the system of administration, which should be supervised by a Delegacy, and suggests that, if a similar scheme is adopted at Cambridge, the two universities should act harmoniously but independently of one another. One clause alone disappeared between the first consideration of the report by the Hebdomadal Council and its final publication. This had discussed a suggestion made in Leeds that the universities should examine people of more advanced years, a suggestion which the committee thought might deprive many people of the benefits of university residence. Perhaps it was felt that this clause did not relate very directly to the question of school examinations, and it was therefore dropped.[1]

Discussion in the university ranged chiefly round the question of the title and to a lesser extent round the examinations in religious knowledge, a subject which, as we shall see, was to be a fruitful source of trouble later.[2] When the statute was promulgated in Convocation on 5 June, the title of A.A. was opposed by Provost Hawkins of Oriel who urged that it should be considered by many as equivalent to a degree and that people would ask what was the use of university residence if the equivalent of a degree could be obtained without it. Similar views were expressed by J. W. Burgon who thought that A.A. sounded too much like part of a series of degrees leading through B.A. to M.A. He suggested the use of the simple letters 'O' for Oxford candidates and 'C' for Cambridge candidates as a suffix to their names; similar suggestions made by other speakers included 'A.O' and 'A.C' for Associate of Oxford and of Cambridge and even 'companion' or 'cadet' of Oxford. Burgon was also strongly opposed to the voluntary nature of the religious examination. As J. E. Thorold Rogers the political economist said, although the B.A. degree might now be taken without religious subscription, there was no need for the university to do more than Parliament required. The line taken by the supporters of the measure who spoke in the debate, Robert Scott, Jeune, Acland, was very much that which had already been outlined.

---

[1] OUA, w.p. γ. 28 (1), Hebdomadal Council Reports, 1855–64, fol. 37; *Report of the Committee on Middle-Class Examinations*, G.A. Oxon. b. 29; there is another copy of the report as originally prepared for the Hebdomadal Council in Pusey House Pamphlets, no. 71092; the report as finally published is printed in *Jackson's Oxford Journal*, 6 June 1857. The memorials are appended to the report of the committee.

[2] See pp. 104–5.

Scott and Acland both urged that the title was necessary as an honourable distinction which would encourage young men of good prospects and good abilities to be candidates for it. There was however no danger that the title would be confused with a degree or would rob the university of members. Jeune not only emphasized this but also devoted much attention to the religious question; compulsion would he thought gain no adherents and the arrangements proposed would at least bring many more candidates within the range of Church influence. He spoke here with the authority of a former headmaster of King Edward's, Birmingham. The rector of Exeter (J. P. Lightfoot) reinforced the same view from his experience as a parish clergyman which had convinced him that 'the more liberality was extended to the middle classes of society the more success would attend efforts to win them'.[1]

Although the religious question is important later, the real point at issue in the summer of 1857 was the title, since there was very little objection to the plan as a whole. Temple and Hawkins both went into print to establish their case. In a public letter to Jeune, dated 8 June, Temple urged the title of A.A. because it alone would make a really wide appeal to the middle classes and would encourage them to take a pride in their education with the university. The proposed name would not damage the prestige of the Oxford degree because it was quite different from it; on the other hand the words 'in Arts' should be kept because they provided a real link with existing studies at Oxford and because the idea which they enshrined would protect the schoolmaster against the pressure to provide exclusively 'useful knowledge'.[2] A week later Hawkins counter-attacked in a letter to the vice-chancellor (17 June) in which he repeated that he wished well to the scheme but would have preferred to wait before bestowing any permanent title since its future was so uncertain. The proposed title would give a kind of degree to young men of whom the university knew nothing and to whom, since they were not matriculated, the university had but a doubtful right to give any title at all.[3] The main provisions of the new Statute passed both Congregation and Convocation with very large majorities, but the clause conferring the Associate in

[1] *Jackson's Oxford Journal*, 13 June 1857.
[2] *Letter to the Master of Pembroke on the proposed title Associate in Arts*, G.A. Oxon. b. 29.
[3] *Letter to the vice-chancellor on the proposed conferring of any title such as Associate in Arts*, G.A. Oxon. b. 29.

Arts title passed Congregation by only 62 votes to 38 and Convocation by the even narrower majority of 52 votes to 36.[1]

The detailed story of the passage of the Statute at Oxford is of interest in itself; it is also interesting to compare with events at Cambridge where much the same issues were raised and where the decision as to the title went the other way. The council of the Senate reported on 1 June that they had received a deputation from Birmingham and memorials from Cheltenham, Leeds and from J. S. Howson of the Collegiate Institution at Liverpool and they recommended that a Syndicate be set up to consider the matter. The arguments used by the memorialists were much the same as those which have already been reviewed.[2] The Syndicate, appointed by a Grace of 4 June, reported on 19 November. It recommended a system of examinations for students under the ages of fifteen and of eighteen years in 'the English Language and literature, history, geography, the French, Latin and German languages, arithmetic, mathematics, natural philosophy, and such other branches of learning as the Syndics, to be appointed as hereafter mentioned, may determine'. All candidates were to be examined in religious knowledge unless their parents or guardians objected. The title of Associate of Arts for the Senior Students was recommended, although the Syndicate admitted that it had been very divided on the subject. The title had already been adopted by Oxford and there were great advantages in the two universities acting harmoniously.[3]

The report of the Syndicate was discussed on 24 November at considerable length. Again the main controversy centred round the title. Most speakers were opposed to it like the classical scholar and coach J. W. Donaldson who urged that there was no reason to follow Oxford, that it was quite inappropriate to give a title to people who had no real connection with the university and – most serious point of all – that the proposed title would actually harm

---

[1] *Jackson's Oxford Journal*, 13 and 20 June 1857. The main provisions passed Congregation by 81 votes to 16 and Convocation by 73 votes to 17. Convocation register 1854–71 (fol. 146) gives the votes in Convocation as 81–16 and 62–38, i.e. the figures given in the *Journal* for Congregation. I think that the *Jackson Journal* figures are to be preferred because its figures for the Congregation vote were printed before Convocation voted on 18 June and it is most unlikely that the votes would have been the same on both occasions. Did the writer of the Convocation register get the two sets of figures mixed?

[2] C[ambridge] U[niversity] A[rchives], Guard Book 57.1 (Local Examinations and Local Lectures), no. 1.

[3] CUA Guard Book 57.1, no. 2.

Cambridge because parents would ask 'What is the difference between A.A. and B.A. that they should pay £1,000 for the latter? A great majority [he believed] would be satisfied with the A.A. and would send their sons to the bar, or into the army, or into other professions with no other degree.' Another opponent Professor William Selwyn said that the title was an invention of Temple personally and even those who spoke in favour of the title did so in general because Oxford had adopted it and it was difficult to follow a different line. As at Oxford there was some debate about the religious question and the vice-provost of King's (George Williams) commented with regret on what had been done at Oxford 'where competence in certain rules of arithmetic was made a *sine qua non*, whilst religion was made a matter of choice'. Other speakers supported the Syndicate's religious plans; religious questions however never played a very important part in the history of the Cambridge examinations.

In summarizing the discussion the *Cambridge Chronicle* remarked that the rejection of the proposed title could be safely predicted, even though it had been adopted at Oxford.[1] And so it was; the Syndicate was reappointed on 3 December and reported again on 12 December, leaving out on this occasion the clause granting the title 'Associate in Arts'. The Grace finally passed the Senate on 11 February 1858.[2] So both universities had established an examination in much the same form. The main differences between them concerned the examination in religion, which will be discussed later, and the title. There is no doubt at all that this was distinctively Temple's idea. It raised much opposition in both places, and it seems at least probable that it was adopted in Oxford and not at Cambridge because Temple's personal influence was naturally far greater in his own university.

Important as Temple's contribution was to the establishment of the examinations, his biographers make in one respect a claim for him which is unjustified – that he was the first to suggest that the university should undertake the inspection as well as the examination of schools.[3] The idea of some general system of inspection of secondary schools on lines parallel to that which already existed for

[1] *Cambridge Chronicle*, 28 November 1857. This also includes the report of the discussion which has been summarized above.
[2] CUA Guard Book, 57.1, nos. 3, 4.
[3] *Memoirs of Archbishop Temple*, ed. E. G. Sandford, vol. II, p. 552.

elementary schools was a fairly general one at the time. Matthew Arnold suggested in *A French Eton* (1864) that what English secondary education needed was competent supervision and that the universities might provide this by establishing a body of inspectors to report on and exercise control over both endowed and private schools.[1] A speaker at the first meeting of the National Association for the Promotion of Social Science in October 1857 had suggested that this might be done by the creation of a Government Board of Examiners which would raise the general standard of instruction and make improvements in method generally known.[2]

The idea does not appear at all in the Oxford discussions, but several of those who were interested in the new plans at Cambridge did put it forward. Among them was an HMI, J. P. Norris, a former fellow of Trinity, who proposed in a letter to the Public Orator (W. G. Clark) that the university should appoint two or more inspectors who should visit such schools as wished for inspection and make an annual report to the Senate. They would be armed with no powers and have no public money to spend and would therefore need to gain the confidence of schoolmasters and to report with discretion on what they saw in individual cases, though they would be able to comment much more frankly on general problems.[3] Norris' intention like Arnold's later was that this work should be done by the universities and not by the government. As he told the Taunton Commission when he gave evidence before them, he had always preferred a system of inspection to a system of examination and had tried to raise the question at Cambridge in 1857, though he and his supporters had come to the conclusion that it would be best at first to co-operate with Oxford.[4]

One of those supporters, W. G. Clark, urged the same point of view in an important speech in the discussion at Cambridge on the Syndicate's report. He claimed that it would be better to associate

[1] W. F. Connell *The Educational Thought and Influence of Matthew Arnold* (1950), pp. 260–1.
[2] E. R. Humphreys, 'Examination of Endowed Schools', *Transactions of the National Association for the Promotion of Social Science, 1857: Inaugural Addresses and Select Papers* (1858), pp. 136–7.
[3] For Norris' letter see *English Journal of Education*, vol. XII (n.s., Jan. 1858), pp. 30–2; *Transactions of Social Science Association 1863*, p. 283; Norris, *The Education of the People, our Weak Points and our Strength*, pp. 148–9n.
[4] *SIC*, vol. IV, pp. 46, 396.

schools rather than individuals with the university and cited the example of France:

> A stereotyped form of examination he objected to, as reacting upon and in some measure governing the course of study, uniformity of examination leading to uniformity of study. In France mischievous results had been produced by centralization in this matter. The writer had this on the authority of M. de Tocqueville, with whom he had talked over the whole scheme last July. M. de Tocqueville said there were three evils to be carefully guarded against in carrying out any such scheme as the *Brevet de Bachelier* system of the University of Paris – (1) uniformity of examination; (2) a tendency, almost inevitable in schemes of examination, to push up the standard; and (3) excessive importance coming to be attached to such diplomas, so that the want of them would come to be a *barrière* to entrance into trade, etc.[1]

This comment is interesting because it brings in the great name of Tocqueville – the only allusion, in fact, which I have met in the founding days either at Oxford or at Cambridge to an overseas influence. The problems voiced by Tocqueville here were to be the regular criticisms voiced against Local Examinations themselves once they had got under way. The idea of school inspection as a more flexible alternative to examination without many of the disadvantages of cramming and over-pressure produced by the latter was to reappear on many later occasions. The great difficulties which prevented any general system of inspection being achieved were the lack of any central educational machinery, the great expense involved and the fear of over-centralization and of interference with school management. The universities did later achieve a certain success in inspecting schools, but only on a comparatively limited scale. The idea was certainly too ambitious for the conditions of 1857, though it should be noted here as the one original suggestion made by Cambridge men in the general debate. Otherwise Cambridge worked on the lines already laid down at Oxford.

By the spring of 1858 the 'middle-class examinations', as they were often called, were launched in both universities, and Delegacy and Syndicate alike were laying their plans for the future. T. D. Acland, the co-founder of the scheme, wrote a good deal about it in the ensuing years, and his remarks form a useful commentary on the purposes which the pioneers had in mind. The idea of inspection rather than examination was still in the air at Cambridge.

[1] *Cambridge Chronicle*, 28 November 1857.

4

It was suggested by one author that it would prevent too much attention being concentrated on clever boys and by another that the Syndicate might undertake to examine whole schools and to publish reports of its findings.[1] In Acland's view the perils of such schemes had been shown by the failure of the National Society's plans for middle-class education in 1839.[2] To deal with schools as a whole would mean a perilous involvement in the details of school management. At the moment the vital step was to establish public confidence in the value of the intellectual training provided by the universities in place of the suspicion with which they were often regarded. Until this had been done the wisest course was to leave moral training to parents and to attempt no more than to test the mental cultivation of the individual. 'If these lads turn out well,' Acland wrote, 'their friends will be more disposed than heretofore to trust University men as teachers, and to value the Institution which made the men.'[3] Clearly he feared that, if too much were attempted, nothing would be achieved, and with the failure of the National Society's plans for union with middle schools in 1839–40, he had much justification for such a view. Of course the approach to education through examinations contained its own dangers, as Temple himself was quick to point out. He wrote to Acland, that education is not merely a substitute for apprenticeship and that, although all education must be ultimately practical in the sense of teaching men to do as well as to think, its primary purpose must be 'to make *men*, not to make *engineers*, or *artists*, or any other specialty.'[4] Nor was a system to be created for the middle classes according to a blueprint in the mind of some thinker. Improvements would follow when the need for them was felt and people cared for them enough to take trouble to achieve them.[5]

Acland himself had been affected in his thinking by his experience of the training colleges and he clearly regarded the new examinations

---

[1] [Cambridge University] *Occasional Papers on University Matters and Middle-Class Education: together with full information on the Local Examinations and Recent University Changes*, no. 1 (Dec. 1858), pp. 14–15, 29. Paper IV, 'On the Examinations of Schools by the University' is signed T. M. (probably Thomas Markby, later secretary to the Syndicate). Paper VI, 'University Extension' is signed W. M. C. (probably W. M. Campion of Queens').

[2] See pp. 45–7.

[3] Acland, *New Oxford Examinations*, pp. xxx–xxxi; *The Education of the Farmer, viewed in connection with that of the Middle Classes in General* (1857), pp. 45–9.

[4] Acland, *New Oxford Examinations*, p. 50.

[5] *Ibid.*

as a general extension to the middle classes as a whole of the methods which had already proved their effectiveness in educating teachers. Here, however, the bogey of social prestige and class feeling very soon raised its head. The social standing of the elementary teachers and of their training colleges was low; the term 'middle-class' which was rapidly applied to the new examinations was not much better. In a paper given to the Social Science Association in 1859 Acland denied the appropriateness of the term, saying that the examinations belonged to no class and that many 'distinguished scholars at the head of grammar schools' had furnished candidates. He admitted however that many headmasters of grammar schools had held back on the plea that the scheme was not for them.[1]

It was commonly believed from the beginning that schools with a definite university connection either did not take the examinations or used them only to a limited extent. As a result the examinations lacked prestige. J. P. Norris told the Taunton Commissioners that when he had asked schools why they did not send pupils in, 'the answer I received was "Does Dr Temple send any boys from Rugby?"'[2] Charles Evans, headmaster of King Edward's, Birmingham put the point from the headmaster's point of view to the same Commission. Once the novelty had worn off very few boys had entered. The examinations were found to interfere with the course of study for the universities and parents did not see the practical utility of the certificate or of the A.A. 'They find that a recommendation from the headmaster of King Edward's school is a more valuable passport into a merchant's office than the distinction of A.A.'[3] These arguments naturally applied most strongly in the case of a well-established school with high standards and good local connections. Birmingham was such a school, and the same note appears elsewhere.

The Christmas 1859 school list of Exeter School, only a few miles from Acland's house at Killerton, describes the new examinations and says that boys will from time to time be sent in for them; however, the school has its own examination conducted by examiners from the universities and covering every boy as opposed to a few

[1] T. D. Acland, 'On the Education of the Middle Classes', *Transactions of Social Science Association, 1859*, pp. 303–4.

[2] *SIC*, vol. IV, p. 50: 431.

[3] *SIC*, vol. IV, p. 559: 5873.

selected pupils. The implication is clearly that the second test is much more important than the former, since 'the efficiency of the higher class of Foundation Grammar Schools, which enjoy Exhibitions and Scholarships to the Universities, and are subjected to Public Examination annually, is generally best seen and testified by the success of their pupils in gaining open Prizes at the Universities, and in the several Honor Lists that from time to time appear'.[1] One writer commenting in a published letter to Acland on the results of the first Oxford Examinations criticized the tendency of the higher-class schools like St Paul's, Merchant Taylors and City of London to hold aloof, and pointed out that they and other schools like them had argued that the examinations were designed for boys of a lower social class than theirs. Since they claimed to prepare boys for the universities, 'they could not give up their higher classical studies to prepare boys for examinations in English grammar, geography, and history'.[2]

The English subjects were given a prominent role in the layout of the Locals since they, with arithmetic, formed the Preliminary Examination which all candidates had to pass. Here the example of the Civil Service Commissioners was freely utilized. The Oxford Delegacy in its first report explained that it had obtained the services of 'Mr Sandford of the Council Office, and Mr Walrond of the Civil Service Commission office' to carry out the Preliminary Examination. The first of these gentlemen had wide experience of the examination of pupil teachers, who could be considered as providing a standard of achievement for boys of the prescribed age. The latter, the Report goes on to say, 'has a principal share in conducting the examination of candidates for admission to the Civil Service'.[3] The tie was much deeper than merely employing the same examiners. Acland himself does not discuss this point, but it was much in the mind of his contemporaries. A. H. Wratislaw, a headmaster and a former Cambridge don, writing shortly afterwards, emphasized the importance of the Locals in providing a liberal education for professional men who were not going to the

---

[1] Acland MSS, Killerton – in a bundle of papers *c.* 1860, relating to exhibitions at Exeter School.

[2] James Ridgway, *Oxford Examination of those who are not Members of the University* (Oxford and London, 1858), p. 4.

[3] *Delegates of Local Examinations, First Annual Report* (1858), p. 9. These Reports with the Delegacy's Minute Books are preserved at the Delegacy of Local Examinations, Oxford.

university and looked forward to the day when they might serve as Preliminary Examinations either to professional studies or to the army and civil service.[1]

Despite the difficulties caused by lack of prestige, the barometer was set fair, and the supporters of the new examinations may well have felt that they formed part of a movement which was affecting the whole educational and social pattern of the country. Similar arrangements to those made at Oxford and Cambridge were made by the University of Durham in 1858.[2] Suggestions were made for the extension of the scheme both to Ireland and to Scotland.[3] The extent of the local support which could be mobilized is shown by a petition that Manchester should be made a centre for the Oxford Examinations in June 1858. This was signed, among many prominent local figures, by the Mayor of Manchester and the Members of Parliament for the borough, the Dean of Manchester, the Mayor of Salford, W. J. Fox, M.P. and prominent Unitarian leader, the educational reformer James Heywood, the scientist J. P. Joule, W. B. Hodgson the political economist and the principal and four professors of Owens' College.[4]

Another sign of the interest aroused in Manchester is a memorial sent by the Manchester Society of Middle-Class Teachers and others to the Senate of the University of London asking that Manchester be made a local centre of examination for London Matriculation. This request was backed by arguments which are now familiar and was supported by a letter from Principal Greenwood of Owens' College, explaining that the Oxford Examinations of June 1858 had shown that this would be quite practicable and arguing that it would be very unfortunate if Oxford and Cambridge 'offered to Provincial *Schools* unconnected with them, facilities greater than those which the University of London afforded to

---

[1] A. H. Wratislaw, *Middle Class and Non-Gremial Examinations* (Cambridge and London, 1860). He was headmaster of King Edward VI's Grammar School, Bury St Edmunds, and a former fellow of Christ's College, Cambridge.

[2] *English Journal of Education*, January 1858, pp. 33–4 gives the Durham scheme of 1858.

[3] The author of *Middle Class Education* (1858), a pamphlet in the possession of the library of the Department of Education, signed G. F. S., suggests the application of the idea to Ireland. For Scotland see W. Scott Dalgleish, *University Certificate Examinations with suggestions for a scheme in Scotland similar to the English 'Middle Class Examinations'* (2nd edn. Edinburgh, 1860).

[4] OUA, w.p. γ. 22 (2).

Colleges which were incorporated with her.'[1] The utility of the Local Examinations was already making itself felt, and the London Committee of Senate quickly decided that there was no need at all for their university to confine itself to a central examination. It also pointed out that the Civil Service Commissioners already decentralized their work and recommended that the same course be taken for the Matriculation and the Pass B.A. but not for honours.[2]

One of the most interesting tributes to the potential importance of the Locals is the outcry raised against them in the *Educational Times*, the journal of the College of Preceptors, which had itself established school examinations some years earlier.[3] From the beginning the *Educational Times* attacked the Oxford scheme as trespassing on ground which the Preceptors had already occupied and Oxford examiners as not at all well suited to examine the studies of middle-class schools which tended to concentrate on modern subjects. Moreover it asked were these bodies, which had been unable to reform themselves, at all fitted to control secondary education ? A yet more insidious danger lay behind. Were not the examinations an insidious clericalist scheme to get control of the education of the middle classes ? Were there not at Oxford influences hostile to 'the grand principles of civil and religious liberty, to gain which the precious blood of thousands has drenched British ground through the priestly advocacy of prerogative government, which means tyranny, both temporal and spiritual, under its most dangerous, most insidious form' ?[4] The suspicion, significantly enough, was directed against Oxford in particular. Most of this is merely silly, and represents the actions of men in a weak position shouting to keep their courage up, but it does illustrate the difficulties which made Acland fear a more ambitious scheme like the inspection of schools,[5] and it serves as a reminder of the force of the sectarian feeling which lay only just below the surface.

Gradually the *Educational Times* shifted its ground. E. R. Humphreys, headmaster of Cheltenham Grammar School, who as chairman of the Council of the College of Preceptors had publicly

---

[1] *University of London. Minutes of Committees 1853–1866*, p. 54 (2 December 1858, University of London Library).
[2] *Minutes of Committees 1853–1866*, pp. 60–3.
[3] See p. 61.
[4] *Educational Times*, vol. x, pp. 261–2 (December, 1857).
[5] See p. 86.

opposed the Oxford scheme later helped to set up a local centre at
Cheltenham.[1] The line taken by the *Educational Times* subsequently was to accept that the universities should conduct the
examination for boys of eighteen years old but to argue that the
examinations for younger boys ought to be left to the College.[2] It
was also urged with a good deal of justice that experienced practical
teachers had no say at all in the running of the examinations,[3]
a criticism which was often to be repeated in later years, though
even here Joseph Payne, the later historian of the college, pointed
out that there were advantages in completely independent examiners
and that the universities had consulted schoolmasters' interests very
carefully.[4] The college professed itself anxious to collaborate with
the universities but there were limits to the extent to which co-
operation could go. Thus in July 1858 the *Educational Times*
attacked the idea that the council of the college should form a
permanent London committee for the Oxford and Cambridge
Examinations, because such a project would endanger the very
existence of the College of Preceptors.[5]

Many of these fears felt by private schoolmasters about the
ancient universities, though exaggerated and hyper-sensitive, were
in themselves reasonable enough. The universities had an illiberal
past, their members were not very closely in touch with the schools
with which they proposed to deal, there was a possibility that the
point of view of the teachers might be neglected. However both the
Delegacy and the Syndicate set to work to overcome their suspi-
cions. At Oxford a committee was appointed on 3 July 1857 to get
the examination started.[6] This had a conference on 15 September
with a group of schoolmasters and considered letters from others.
Among those consulted were Edward Thring of Uppingham,
Howson of the Liverpool Collegiate Institution who had been a
prominent supporter of the new plans on Merseyside, the heads of
two great civic grammar schools, Barry of Leeds and Gifford of
Birmingham, and William Johnson, one of the most prominent
Eton masters of the time. Most of the detailed points which naturally

---

[1] *Ibid.* vol. x, pp. 122–3 (June 1857); vol. xi, pp. 145–8 (July 1858).
[2] *Ibid.* vol. xi, pp. 21–2 (February 1858).
[3] *Ibid.* vol. xi, p. 147 (July 1858).
[4] *Educational Times*, vol. xii, pp. 38–9 (February 1859).
[5] *Ibid.* vol. xi, pp. 151–2 (July 1858).
[6] The following section is based on the first Minute Book (1857–77) of the
Delegacy of Local Examinations.

arose in organizing the scheme were considered by the committee. One suggestion, for instance, which raised much opposition and was therefore abandoned was a plan to hold the examination in September, it being considered that 'some period nearer the end of the spring half-year' would be a much better time. Another point mentioned in the first annual report was the abandonment by the Oxford Delegacy of their original plan not to examine the juniors in Greek since some schoolmasters said that this would interfere with their work. A scheme of examination based on the information obtained from the schoolmasters was then drawn up by Temple and was ordered to be printed on 12 November, a copy having been meanwhile sent to Cambridge and a committee set up to sound the opinion of leading people there.

The first regulations for the examination of 1858 provided that both senior and junior candidates must satisfy the examiners in a Preliminary Examination, which was basically the same in its general outlines for both.[1] It covered English – analysis and parsing and a short composition – arithmetic, geography, and the outlines of English history, with, in addition for the juniors, reading aloud and a passage of dictation. The rudiments of faith and religion paper, if taken up, demanded for juniors the books of Genesis and Exodus, the Gospel of St Matthew and the Acts of the Apostles with the catechism, the morning and evening services and the litany. Seniors were to be examined in the historical books of the Old Testament to the death of Solomon, in the Gospels of St Matthew and St John and the Acts of the Apostles with questions on the Greek Testament for those offering Greek, and in the catechism, morning and evening prayer, the litany and the outlines of the history of the Book of Common Prayer.

After this followed details of the optional subjects of which junior candidates must offer at least one but not more than four. The work set was as follows: in Latin, a passage for translation from Caesar's *Gallic War*, Books I–III, with questions on the parsing and the historical and geographical allusions, an easy passage for translation from some other book, and a passage of English for translation into Latin with Latin words supplied; in Greek two translation passages, one from Xenophon's *Anabasis*, Books I and II without any English passage for translation into Greek; in French a

[1] Examination Papers, and Division Lists, etc. for the examination held in June 1858 (*Del. Local Exams., Reports*).

passage for translation from Voltaire's *Histoire de Charles XII*, with another passage for translation from a French newspaper and English sentences for translation into French; in German the arrangements were similar with Schiller's *Revolt of the Netherlands* as the book for translation. Mathematics would require a knowledge of Euclid Books I and II, of arithmetic and of algebra to simple equations; in addition questions would also be set in 'Euclid Books III, IV, VI, on quadratic equations, progressions and proportion, plane trigonometry, not beyond the solution of triangles, the use of logarithms, mensuration and practical geometry'. The scientific subjects were mechanics and mechanism, covering 'the Parallelogram of Forces, the centre of Gravity and the Mechanical Powers' with the mechanism of the steam engine; chemistry, including the testing of solutions containing 'each not more than one acid and one base'; and botany and zoology, that is 'the Classification of Plants and Animals, their uses, and geographical distribution'. In addition candidates might be examined in drawing and in music.

The senior examination consisted of four sections together with drawing and music, and in order to satisfy the examiners a candidate was required to pass in two of the initial four sections or in one of them plus either drawing or music. The primary sections were English, languages, mathematics, and physics. The English section comprised four sub-divisions: English history from Bosworth Field to the Restoration and the outlines of the history of English literature during the same period; Shakespeare's *Lear* and Bacon's *Essays*; the outlines of political economy and English law (the syllabus being defined by the first book of *The Wealth of Nations* and the first volume of Blackstone's *Commentaries*); and physical, political and commercial geography. In order to pass, it was necessary for a candidate to show a fair knowledge of one of these divisions.

The languages section embraced Latin, Greek, French and German, of which a knowledge of one was sufficient. Mathematics covered both the pure and applied parts of the subject; to pass, it was sufficient to show a knowledge of algebra to quadratic equations and of the first four books of Euclid. The physics section was again made up of several sub-divisions and it was necessary to satisfy the examiners in one of these – natural philosophy, chemistry, vegetable and animal physiology, it being required that 'in all cases a practical acquaintance with the subject-matter will be indispensable'. Drawing embraced not only what the word suggests, but design in pen and ink and in colour and the history and principles of design, music both 'the grammar of music' and the history and principles of composition.

After the regulations had been issued the Delegacy busied itself with the selection of local centres, the choice of examiners and the planning of a time-table on the principle 'that no two subjects should be presented to Candidates for choice at the same hour'.[1] A special committee was appointed on 6 May 1858 under the chairmanship of Robert Scott to confer with the examiners so as to produce consistent standards in the papers and the marking and to arrange for Delegates and other Masters of Arts to visit local centres and open the examination. The payments to examiners were agreed in the autumn; these ranged from £25 each to Sandford and Walrond who conducted the Preliminary Examination and £20 each to the two examiners in Latin down to £5 paid to the examiners in some of the smaller subjects, while the Secretary of the Delegacy received £150.[2]

The examination of 1858 was held at eleven centres – Oxford, Bath, Bedford, Birmingham, London, Cheltenham, Exeter, Leeds, Liverpool, Manchester, Southampton. Of the 750 junior candidates 280 obtained certificates, of the 401 senior 150 were successful.[3] The balance of subjects taken is interesting because it gives a useful guide to the studies of the schools examined.[4] Among the seniors, as might have been expected, a large number took history (357) and geography (228). The most popular languages were French (299) and Latin (255), with Greek (118) and German (65) considerably behind. Mathematics (308) was about as popular as French, and the scientific subjects attracted only a few candidates (natural philosophy 77, chemistry 76, physiology 12). The junior candidates concentrated on mathematics (575), Latin (498) and French (524), with Greek (127) a little more popular than mechanics and mechanism (103) and chemistry (98). A considerable number both of seniors and of juniors took drawing (116 and 185) but comparatively few attempted music (24 and 43).

The most obvious facts about these results are the large numbers of candidates and the high proportion of failures, both of which

[1] Minutes, 29 April 1858.
[2] Minutes, 20 October 1858.
[3] *Del. Local Exams., First Annual Report* (1858), pp. 11, 86.
[4] *Ibid.* 87.

points receive considerable attention in the first annual report of the Delegacy which was drafted by Temple.[1] The report admits that the Delegacy did not expect so many candidates as actually came forward from a very wide variety of schools. The large number of failures among them should not however be regarded as a valid index either of the candidates' attainments or of the efficiency of the schools. As the working of the examinations for elementary teachers had shown, the standard rose once the examinations had become a routine and everyone knew what to expect. On this occasion too the time-table had been very crowded, the candidates may have been excited by the novelty and have had little sense of how to make the best use of their time. So far as this argument is concerned Temple may have been somewhat generous in his assumptions. A far more definite cause of failure, which led to the great bulk of casualties, came from inability to pass the Preliminary Examination. Here, the report says, the Delegacy had been unanimous in requiring a certain amount of elementary knowledge and stipulating that failure should disqualify a candidate. The results had shown the need for much more care in elementary instruction. The report in the Senior Preliminary, for instance, pointed out that in English grammar candidates 'were able to cite correct definitions of abstract grammatical terms, and to trace English words to their foreign roots', but 'they could neither parse with intelligence, nor analyse satisfactorily an ordinary sentence'.[2] The geography answers were careless and inattentive and the English history the most unsatisfactory subject of all. As might have been expected, the standard of reference used by the Delegates for the preliminary subjects was firstly, that attained by thirteen- and fourteen-year-olds in the elementary schools, and secondly, the knowledge required to satisfy the Civil Service Commissioners for appointments such as a clerkship in the Customs or Inland Revenue.

Of the higher subjects the best was the pure mathematics. The languages were mixed, with some good work and much that was indifferent. Of the scientific subjects the only one which was really much studied was chemistry and here the knowledge was drawn almost entirely from books, though the Delegacy had been conscious of the great need, if the scientific subjects were to be more

[1] Minutes, 11 December 1858.
[2] *Del. Local Exams., First Annual Report* (1858), pp. 27.

extensively taught, of a proper emphasis on practical work. The summary of the argument is worth quoting:

a good many of the candidates showed proof of having been extremely well taught. The papers of the rest gave the impression of hard work, considerable intelligence, not much cultivation, and a singular want of purpose. There was often a tolerably wide range of information, but sometimes no small amount of original thought: but candidates who showed both these, frequently showed little power of putting their information together, and still less power of expressing it in clear language. There seemed to be in many instances all the materials of a good education, but not the form. There is reason to hope, that the attempt to prepare for definite examinations will gradually lead to improvement in this respect.[1]

The first Cambridge Examination followed in December 1858. There is no need to examine the regulations in detail since their pattern broadly reproduced that of the Oxford Delegacy with two exceptions. The first of these was that the age limit for Junior candidates was sixteen not fifteen.[2] The second and far more important difference was that the section on Religious Knowledge was differently planned. This change had a very important effect on the subsequent history of the two examinations and must be considered in detail later.[3] The number of candidates at the first Cambridge Examination was far fewer than at Oxford – 297 juniors and 73 seniors, though of these very nearly two-thirds satisfied the examiners, a very different picture from that which we have just surveyed.[4] The Cambridge Examination, having started very much in the wake of the other, was bound to have been on a smaller scale and no doubt the large number of failures in summer 1858 had deterred a number of possible candidates from offering themselves in the winter.

The first report of the Cambridge Syndicate seems in many ways parallel to the first report of the Delegacy. In the Preliminary Examination much criticism was levelled at the English grammar

---

[1] *Del. Local Exams., First Annual Report* (1858), p. 17.
[2] *Local Examinations Syndicate, First Annual Report* (1859). This was decided by a Grace of 19 March 1858. The regulations for 1859 are contained in the first bound volume of reports.
[3] See pp. 103–4.
[4] There were eight original Cambridge centres: Birmingham, Brighton, Bristol, Cambridge, Grantham, Liverpool, London, Norwich.

and the English history, the latter of which seemed to have been got up out of 'meagre handbooks'. The arithmetic was well done so far as the application of well-known rules was concerned but boys showed little ability to enunciate them. The English section was taken by candidates who had done little special preparation for it or had relied on their preparation for the Preliminary Examination. The best work done was in classics, especially in translation into English. The mathematics on the other hand showed imperfect preparation and suggested defects both in the methods of teaching and in the books used by the teachers. In modern languages, as in classics, the translation was the best part of the work, the French being better than the German. The scientific subjects attracted very few candidates.

The publication of the first series of results stimulated further widespread public discussion and comment in the press.[1] Much was written about the large numbers of failures in the Oxford Examinations. One particular stumbling-block was the Preliminary Examination. The *Morning Star* quoted the sad case of 'a young gentleman from Brixton, who had previously matriculated with honours at the London University and is one of the few candidates who took double honours in languages and mathematics at Oxford' who had been plucked 'for failing, if we are informed rightly, to draw from memory a correct map of Africa'. Complaints were made that many of the candidates were much too young and not fitted for an external examination at all, that the standard of the teachers was very low and that in many cases they were in the hands of parents who did not know good education from bad. If so many had failed among the elite who had taken the examination, it was asked, what must the rest of the pupils in middle-class schools be like? The *Educational Times* took the line that the universities had tried to do too much and that, although many boys had been fairly rejected, the programme had been far too ambitious; as one correspondent wrote, boys of fourteen had been put through an ordeal 'which twenty years ago would not have been required for a B.A. degree in Oxford itself'.[2] When the Manchester educationalist Canon Richson presented the prizes and certificates won on the

---

[1] For a series of extracts from the newspapers see *Educational Times*, vol. XI, pp. 221–7 (October 1858). The quotation from the *Morning Star* of 9 September is on p. 222.

[2] *Educational Times*, vol. XI, p. 251 (November 1858).

Oxford Examination in that city, he expressed the disappointment which had been felt in Manchester about the results of the examination, more particularly that the centre had not gained a single first-class certificate.[1] One perennial subject of argument raised its head very early on: did the new examinations lead to the neglect of the average boy in the interest of the few who could be pushed into high success? Here the earliest evidence, like all the later evidence, was conflicting. One headmaster, Hudson of Bristol Grammar School, definitely said that the duller boys would be neglected, that boys would be overworked and that, since grammar-school staffs were very small, the preparation for the examinations would fall into the hands of private tutors.[2] J. S. Howson of the Liverpool Collegiate Institution thought that private tutors might be under a temptation to push the clever boys, but that in a large school it would not be practically convenient to do this and that, on the contrary, the examinations would have a very beneficial effect on the training of boys who would not enter for them at all.[3] In fact they were exerting a very useful influence on standards all round. It is interesting to compare with these outside opinions the views of H. J. S. Smith of Balliol, one of the Oxford examiners of 1858, on the first examination. He mentioned the stringency of the Preliminary Examination but thought that this was a necessary precaution to ensure that the foundations were well and truly laid. In mathematics, both senior and junior, the rate of success had been low, though on the credit side he had a special word for the high standard of the English section in the Senior Examination, which perhaps fitted in well with the curricula of non-classical schools.[4]

Smith also remarked in his survey that it would have been far better for the two universities to have a common examination, a point which was to be raised in many quarters, though in the end unification proved impossible to achieve. The need seems to have been particularly felt among supporters of the Locals on Merseyside[5] like J. S. Howson, who urged the importance of harmonizing

[1] *Manchester Guardian*, 15 September 1858.
[2] *English Journal of Education*, vol. XII, n.s., pp. 297–302 (July 1858).
[3] *Transactions of Social Science Association, 1858*, pp. 241–9.
[4] *Ibid.* pp. 211–20.
[5] The Liverpool Committee suggested to the Delegacy early in 1859 that each university should examine at midsummer in alternate years (Del. Local Exams., Minutes 3 March 1859).

the two systems.[1] At the Social Science Congress of 1859 Nicholas Waterhouse, local secretary for both examinations at Liverpool, reviewed the workings of the examinations in Liverpool, where the number of candidates examined and of certificates gained had been exceeded only in London. Almost all the candidates had come from a small group of schools. The Cambridge Examinations had appealed particularly to the sons of professional men, the Oxford Examinations to the sons of merchants and tradesmen. Of the two the Oxford had proved the more popular, and a much greater proportion of the Cambridge candidates were juniors since they were allowed to present themselves up to sixteen years of age. Like Howson, Waterhouse thought that the system was establishing itself soundly; changes which he wished to suggest were the partial assimilation of the two systems, while preserving a choice of examiners and subjects, the conferring of a degree with a higher requirement than the existing A.A. and the adoption of the Cambridge system of examining religious knowledge.[2]

By the New Year of 1860 opinion among schoolmasters was moving strongly in the direction of assimilation. In October 1859 a memorial had been sent both to the Syndicate and to the Delegacy asking that the two universities should so arrange matters that there might be only one annual examination at each centre. Among the signatories were Barry Gifford and Howson among prominent headmasters, Joseph Payne, C. H. Pinches and H. S. Turrell, leading members of the College of Preceptors, and James Templeton, one of the Exeter pioneers.[3] The same group held a meeting in January 1860 at the Society of Arts in the Adelphi and passed a series of resolutions. The most important of their suggestions were that there should be only one examination in each year on the basis of Oxford and Cambridge taking seniors and juniors in alternate years; that the religious knowledge examination be held on the Cambridge pattern; that the age for juniors be fifteen; and that a title be given to seniors, the exact title used to be settled by the universities themselves.[4]

[1] 'The Co-operation of Oxford and Cambridge in Local Examinations and the assimilation of their schemes', *Occasional Papers on University Matters and Middle-Class Education* (1858 and 1859).

[2] *Transactions of Social Science Association, 1859*, pp. 437–8. Waterhouse says that 326 candidates had been examined and 136 certificates gained. Most candidates had come from 11 grammar, 7 modern public and 23 private schools.

[3] Del. Local Exams., Minutes, 20 October 1859; CUA Guard Book 57.1, no. 9.

[4] CUA University Papers 1858–60, no. 1110.

The Delegacy and the Syndicate took very quick cognizance of the schoolmasters' initiative. On 7 February 1860 the Delegacy conferred with a deputation from Cambridge including Philpott, the Master of St Catharine's, and H. J. Roby, the Cambridge secretary, and agreed with them a common policy.[1] The most important suggestion put forward was that only one examination per year should be held at each centre. This examination should be held in the summer and the universities should examine alternatively north and south of a line to be drawn (say) from the Wash to the Severn. The advantages to the schools of avoiding a double examination, one in June, the other in December, with all the resulting administrative complexities, are obvious enough and from the school point of view the change was clearly desirable. If this was to be achieved, however, the systems of the two universities would need to be altered in two major respects – the age limit for juniors and the title for seniors. Here the Cambridge Syndicate was prepared to recommend changes to bring their examination into line with Oxford. The first of these would be a reduction in the age limit for juniors; the second, and far the more controversial, the adoption of a title. Here the Syndicate expressed the view that great value was attached by many people to the Oxford A.A. and that it was of primary importance for the success of the proposed arrangements with Oxford that some title be adopted, though this need not necessarily be the same as that used by the sister university. The Syndicate's recommendation consequently was that candidates who passed the senior Examination be allowed to call themselves Associate of Cambridge (A.C.).

Just as in 1857 the fat was in the fire. Richard Shilleto, the great classical coach put the issue into verse:

> Pray vote for a title – the title's A.C.
> It means ASS. CAM. Ask Oxon. Ox won't disagree
> So Academies all throughout England will be
> With the Sister Academies one family.[2]

When the report of the Syndicate was discussed, Philpott and Roby, who had been engaged in the negotiations with Oxford spoke in favour

---

[1] For the following see Del. Local Exams., Minutes 7 February 1860; CUA Guard Book 57.1, no. 17 [a report from the Syndicate on the schoolmasters' memorial].

[2] CUA, University Papers 1858–60, no. 1216.

of the title, while J. W. Donaldson was again prominent in opposition,[1] urging that a title could not be given where residence was not involved and that the proposed step would need the permission of the Crown.[2] Nor were the pamphleteers silent. On one hand it was claimed that Cambridge opinion had been almost unanimous against the title in 1857 and that there was no reason to change the attitude which had been taken up then.[3] On the other the theologian J. B. Lightfoot urged that to refuse the title would put Oxford even further ahead of Cambridge and that it would be folly not to seize the chance afforded by Oxford's willingness to co-operate.[4] Most probably Lightfoot and those who thought like him felt that Cambridge, whatever the original rights and wrongs of the question, was negotiating from a position of weakness and that she could not afford to stand out against her stronger rival. However, the Senate decided for independent action. On 8 March 1860 the Grace proposing a reduction in the age for juniors passed: the Grace proposing the title of A.C. was defeated by 69 votes to 33.[5]

So Cambridge re-affirmed its original decision and the co-operation movement foundered. With different policies about the title it was difficult to see how the proposed sub-division of the country between the two bodies could be effected. On 2 November 1860 the Delegacy considered a letter from the vice-chancellor of Cambridge enquiring about a joint programme for the examination of June 1861. It was then decided, in the light of Cambridge's refusal to give a title, to reconsider the proposed division of the country into two and to consult the local committees about it.[6] On 13 November an official letter was sent to the Syndicate pointing out all the difficulties and stating that the Delegacy would have no objection either to examining alternately with Cambridge or to examining itself every year, according to the wishes of the local committee and provided the examination were held by both universities in the summer.[7] The answer from Cambridge a few days later pointed out 'that difficulties which they (the Syndicate) had not

[1] See pp. 82–3.
[2] CUA Guard Book 57.1, no. 18.
[3] *Ibid.* nos. 19, 20, 22. This point of view was taken by John Roberts of Magdalene and by H. R. Luard, later registrary of the university.
[4] *Ibid.* no. 21. *The Report of the Syndicate appointed to regulate the Examination of Students not Members of the University.*
[5] CUA Guard Book 57.1, no. 23.
[6] Del. Local Exams., Minutes, 2 November 1860.
[7] *Ibid.* 13 November 1860.

been led to expect have arisen to diminish the prospect of the proposed co-operation between the two Universities'.[1]

In their third annual report the Syndicate explained that the difference in policy over the title had been fatal to the scheme.[2] The idea of closer co-operation was to be brought forward later, but nothing came of it. The opportunity offered in 1860 was not to arise again. The failure of the collaboration scheme marks in fact, the end of the foundation period in the history of the Locals. After ten years or so each examining body had formed its own tradition and preferred to go its own way. Cambridge was soon to strike out in new paths, in particular the inspection of schools and the opening of the examinations to women, and by the end of the sixties had made remarkable advances. Meanwhile the Oxford Delegacy had been riven by controversy over the examination in religious knowledge, a struggle which used up a great deal of energy and led to an inconclusive result. Year by year, the machinery of the examinations worked steadily on, and a picture can gradually be built up of the papers set, the standards demanded, the criticisms voiced. In the middle of the decade, too, the enquiries of the Taunton Commission throw a good deal of light on what had been achieved and on what still remained to be done.

[1] Del. Local Exams., Minutes, 16 November 1860.
[2] *Local Exams Synd., Third Annual Report* (1861), p. 3.

5

THE EDUCATION OF WOMEN

The collaboration scheme had failed despite the activity of many schoolmasters in promoting it. Another problem which was to attract further public attention to the Locals was that presented by the examination in religious knowledge at Oxford. The two universities had both included such an examination in their programmes, but, characteristically, each had approached it in a different way. At Oxford the examination rested on a definite basis of Church of England doctrine. It had to be accepted or rejected as a whole at the free choice of the parent or guardian, and it originally carried with it no inducement in the form of marks since the results achieved made no difference to the candidate's position in the list.

At Cambridge the examination was not of an exclusively Anglican character, and it counted for marks alongside other subjects. All candidates had to study the Scriptures, but the study of the Church formularies was left entirely optional. As Temple wrote to Robert Scott, 'they make their religious examination non-church and then press everybody in it. We make ours church and leave it quite open.'[1] Very few boys chose not to present themselves, and the scheme was generally successful. The fact that the records say very little about the matter is evidence that the scheme worked, and the people who mention it do so with approval.[2] Since the marks gained counted towards a certificate, there was an obvious incentive to conform. Since almost everyone believed that education should be based on Christian principles, there was a constant demand for biblical studies, provided that controversial points of dogma could be avoided. Cambridge seemed to have squared the circle, to have made the best of both worlds by satisfying Dissenter and Churchman alike.

---

[1] *Memoirs of Archbishop Temple*, vol. I, p. 131, n. I.

[2] Nicholas Waterhouse, the local secretary, pointed out that at Liverpool not a single parent had objected to his son taking the Cambridge Examination (*Transactions of the National Association for the Promotion of Social Science, 1859*, pp. 438–9).

At Oxford the Locals subject entitled 'The Rudiments of Faith and Religion' became entangled in the religious discords of the time. In an age when the university was ceasing to be an exclusively Anglican institution, the 'Rudiments' examination was yet another battleground between the liberals and those like E. B. Pusey who were always alert to maintain the supremacy of religion in education and to combat the forces of infidelity. The standards set in the Locals were never orthodox enough for Pusey and his friends. On the other hand they were too distinctively Anglican to satisfy many of the schools with which the Delegacy had to deal. The result was a long drawn-out university wrangle which dragged on from 1860 to 1865, and ended in an unsatisfactory compromise. The full story is of great interest, though it would take too much space to tell it here. After 1865–6 controversy died away, though the general concept survived that only Churchmen could obtain complete success in the whole Oxford Examination since the religious paper in its complete form was open only to them. A general impression of illiberality was the natural result, an impression which only too many people throughout the country were anxious to regard as characteristic of the University of Oxford. Pusey had said in 1864 that, although he did not wish the university to go back on its decision to examine boys of a different faith, 'I think that very probably it might have been better had we, in the first instance, confined ourselves to the examination of members of our Church'.[1] His argument was logical, consistent with his whole career, even courageous, but it was simply not in harmony with the requirements of the time. The examinations had been created for the middle class, and a large and vocal proportion of that class were Dissenters. Oxford itself was soon to lose its exclusively religious character. Only seven years after Pusey's remarks – in 1871 – came the abolition of all religious tests. To enforce a religious requirement on the schools was to move against the general direction of opinion in the country.

It is noteworthy too that, throughout the whole Oxford controversy of 1860–5, no attempt was made to find out the opinion of the schools on a subject of great importance to them. The examinations themselves had arisen out of close contacts between the universities and the schools, and every creative step in their history was to be

[1] From a paper in Pusey's hand, Pusey House MSS, Chest A, drawer 3. This is very probably a prepared speech delivered in Congregation on 21 April 1864.

the result of a partnership between the two in which each showed itself responsive to the needs of the other. The 'Rudiments' controversy had been fought out as a matter of internal university politics, one of the issues dividing theological parties in Oxford at a period of great intellectual tension. This may have been inevitable, but it probably did no good to the standing of the Oxford Examinations in the country at large. After the 1860s there was a check to the expansion of the Oxford Locals while the Cambridge Locals went ahead fast. The evidence certainly suggests that Oxford residents, more particularly the Hebdomadal Council, were showing themselves insensitive to the needs of parents and of schoolmasters in a field where the university could not afford to ignore what its clients wanted.

The first important advance made by the Cambridge Syndicate was the introduction in 1862 of a plan for the examination of schools as opposed to the examination by centres of individual candidates. The idea of examining whole schools had, as we have seen, already been raised at Cambridge in 1857, though it had not been pressed, perhaps because at the time the difficulties were felt to be too great.[1] Many of the writers of the time felt that the examination of individual pupils was not enough; what was needed was a system which should combine it with the inspection of schools and sometimes with the certification of teachers as well. If then these activities – examination, inspection, certification – could be combined in the hands of a single agency there would be much greater security for educational advance. In the early days of St Mark's Training College, Derwent Coleridge wrote that the examination conducted by Her Majesty's Inspector 'justifies the hope which I have ventured to express as to the probable benefit of an efficient inspection, – severe and impartial as coming from without – appropriate and helpful, as agreeing with that which is within'.[2] A decade later the Manchester educationalist Canon Richson wanted to extend inspection to the endowed schools and to private schools as well if they were ready to accept it, while 'Periodical Public Examinations' should be held adapted to the requirements of schools of different types.[3] The same ideas

[1] See pp. 84–5.
[2] *National Society, Thirty-Third Report* (1844), p. 77.
[3] C. Richson, *The Agencies and Organization required in a National System of Education* (1856), pp. 12–13.

affected the reports of both the Taunton Commission (1868) and the Bryce Commission (1895), being frequently linked in the latter part of the century with the idea of a general school leaving examination on the lines of the German *Abitur*. Such a leaving certificate was in fact established in Scotland in 1888. The elementary schools too were dominated for a generation after the Revised Code of 1862 by the idea of examining by stages. Grants were paid to the schools partly on the result of a general examination carried out annually by Her Majesty's Inspector.

Thus the interest shown at Cambridge in the examination and inspection of schools was linked with much wider currents of educational opinion. In September 1859 Robert Potts, Secretary of the Cambridge centre for the Local Examinations and a well-known writer of mathematical textbooks, wrote to E. H. Bunbury, secretary of the Statutory Commission which was engaged in making new statutes for the colleges and the university, urging that the commissioners should frame a statute enabling the colleges to provide stipends for inspectors of schools. In this way the Universities of Oxford and Cambridge might undertake the inspection of both endowed and private schools, a measure which, in the case of endowed schools, might be required by the Court of Chancery. If this were done, Potts argued, the effect on the schools would be very beneficial and both the numbers and the standard of attainments of the men entering the university would be raised.[1] Academics who were interested in the schools, then as now, usually had at the back of their minds the hope that the universities would be stimulated by the more efficient management of the schools. This connection between examination and inspection and what the Victorians called 'university extension' must be re-emphasized later. The immediate interest of Potts' letter of 1859 is that it bridges the gap between J. P. Norris' ideas of 1857[2] and the report of the Local Examinations Syndicate in March 1862:

that it would be an advantage to many schools if the Syndicate were authorized by the Senate to entertain applications for the appointment of one or more persons who should examine the scholars of the school that makes the application, and should make a report of the results of the examination to the Syndicate, it being understood that all the expenses attending on the appointment of the Examiners and on the Examination should be borne by the school.

---

[1] CUL Add. MSS 4251: 1125 (5 September 1859).   [2] See p. 84.

A Grace based on these recommendations passed the Senate on 27 March 1862.[1] Four schools were examined under the new regulations in the first year – Brewood Grammar School, Newcastle under Lyme Grammar School, Stone Grammar School and the Guild Hall School, East Dereham. In all cases the number of boys examined was fairly small, varying from seventy-two to twenty-five. The ages ranged from eight to seventeen years.[2] The report for 1864 shows that the number of schools inspected had risen to nine. The subjects in which these nine schools were examined show the type of curriculum which might have been expected from the fact that the Locals appealed not to the classical schools but to the schools of the second grade. All nine schools took religious knowledge, English and mathematics and, all except one, Latin. French, examined in six schools, was more popular than Greek, examined in four. Drawing followed in three schools with German, chemistry and book-keeping each taken in one.[3] The growth of this side of the Syndicate's work was steady and impressive. In 1872 twenty-five schools were examined containing 1,800 boys and 700 girls.[4] By that date Cambridge still had the field to itself. The Oxford Delegacy did not advertise a similar scheme until 1876 and in that year examined only one school.[5]

The Cambridge figures for 1872 which have been quoted above contain totals for both boys and girls. In the decade since the examination of schools had begun both universities had opened their schools examinations to women, the most important step, after the original foundation, in the whole history of the Locals. In the sixties the claims of women to fuller self-development were being voiced far more loudly than before. Efforts were being made by Madame Bodichon and others to enlarge the opportunities for employment open to them. John Stuart Mill, elected for Westminster in 1865, raised the subject of women's suffrage in the House of Commons. In 1865 Elizabeth Garrett (Mrs Garrett Anderson) qualified as a doctor and opened in the following year the hospital which now bears her name. During the same decade the *Transactions of the*

[1] *Local Exams. Synd., Fourth Annual Report* (1862), p. 10; CUA Guard Book 57.1, no. 27.
[2] *Fifth Annual Report* (1863), pp. 7–8.
[3] *Sixth Annual Report* (1864), pp. 9–11.
[4] *Fifteenth Annual Report* (1873), pp. 7–8.
[5] Del. Local Exams., Minutes, 20 November 1875, 10 May 1876; *Nineteenth Annual Report* (1876), p. 17.

Social Science Association, an important organ of progressive opinion, which was very sympathetic with the women's movement, contained many papers on women's education. In 1862 the association held a discussion on granting university degrees to women after a paper on the subject had been read by the philanthropist Frances Power Cobbe; her proposal was, she says, received with 'universal ridicule'.[1] On later occasions the cause of women's education was advocated by the philanthropist Mary Carpenter, by Dorothea Beale of Cheltenham Ladies' College, and among the men by J. P. Norris and by F. D. Maurice who had been active in the work for twenty years already.[2]

One of the most interesting and vigorously expressed of these demands for the better education of upper-class and middle-class women, published in the association's transactions for 1864, was written by Emily Davies.[3] Miss Davies was the sister of John Llewelyn Davies, a member of Maurice's circle and active in the causes, the education of women among them, to which Maurice was devoted. She was a friend and supporter of Elizabeth Garrett and had herself for some years been active in promoting women's interests generally. In 1862 she became interested, as a result of the discussion by the Social Science Association of Miss Cobbe's paper on degrees for women which has already been mentioned, in the possibility of opening the Local Examinations to girls. If this were to be done, it would mean a memorial or petition to the universities:

> This agitation [she wrote to a friend in July 1862] is hateful work, but it becomes clearer every day that incessant and unremitting talking and pushing is the *only* way of gaining our ends. I stop sometimes and ask whether the ends are worth such horridly disagreeable means, and if one had only a personal interest in the matter, I am sure it would be impossible to persevere. But we are fighting for people who cannot fight for themselves, and as I believe, directly working towards preserving women from becoming masculine in a bad sense.[4]

In October 1862 Miss Davies formed a committee of which she became secretary, the members of which were mostly connected

---

[1] *D.N.B.: Transactions and Sessional Proceedings of the National Association or the Promotion of Social Science, 1862*, pp. 339–42.

[2] *Ibid. 1864*, pp. 404–12; *1865*, pp. 268–91; *1869*, pp. 351–64.

[3] 'On Secondary Instruction as relating to Girls', *Transactions of Social Science Association, 1864*, pp. 394–404.

[4] Barbara Stephen, *Emily Davies and Girton College* (1927), pp. 83–4.

with the Social Science Association. In her evidence to the Schools Inquiry Commission she related that the first step they had taken was to ascertain the views of the existing Local centres in order to find out whether their proposals would do harm to the education of boys. Some of the centres refused to express an opinion but the conclusion of these preliminary enquiries was rather favourable than otherwise.[1] Among those who helped was T. D. Acland who suggested the idea of a small pilot scheme, like his own Exeter Examination of 1857, and who brought the subject forward to friends at Oxford. It soon became clear, however, that there was no chance at Oxford for anything other than a scheme of examinations specially designed for girls which the committee were unwilling to accept.[2]

At Cambridge they were more successful. The local secretary, Robert Potts, was friendly, and Miss Davies' committee decided to approach the Local Examinations Syndicate. On 23 October 1863 the Syndicate considered the committee's request 'for copies of the Examination papers to be used in a private examination of girls, simultaneously with the Local Examination in London'.[3] The request was granted; the Syndicate appear to have been doubtful whether the venture would succeed though they were willing to permit the experiment.[4] Its strictly unofficial nature was however pointed out by Charles Gray, the secretary to the Syndicate, in a letter to *The Times* which also pointed out that the formal admission of girls to the examination had hardly been discussed.[5] The Syndicate was probably unwilling in any case to get too deeply committed to what must have seemed at the time a very hazardous venture. The women's committee were thrown into some confusion by what was evidently an unexpected success:

Our breath was quite taken away on Saturday [Miss Davies wrote] by receiving quite unexpectedly a favourable answer from the Cambridge Syndicate to our application. I fully expected they would politely get rid of us by saying it was 'beyond their powers'. It has thrown us into dreadful agitation. We have only six weeks to work up our candidates, and who can expect them to come up on so short notice? Do come to

---

[1] *SIC*, vol. v, pp. 233; 11208; 241: 11306–9.
[2] Stephen, *Emily Davies*, pp. 85–6.
[3] Local Exams. Synd., Minutes, 23 October 1863.
[4] *Transactions of Social Science Association, 1865*, pp. 357–62 (G. W. Hastings).
[5] CUA University Papers 1862–4, no. 725.

the rescue. We shall look unspeakably foolish if we have no candidates, after all, and people won't understand the reason.[1]

In fact all the difficulties were successfully overcome and eighty-three girls took the examination in London. As might have been expected from the poor condition of the girls' schools of the day the results were not very brilliant. No girl took up Latin or anything mathematical more advanced than arithmetic and even in that they were extremely weak.[2]

However a respectable number of girls had offered themselves, the examination had taken place, and it could not be dismissed as the chimera of a disordered feminist imagination. As an anonymous writer pointed out the experiment of December 1863 showed that the Locals system was admirably fitted for girls, its syllabus corresponded with those of the girls' schools and it was the only suitable examining mechanism in the field.[3] Nevertheless the whole idea of public and external examination of girls was a strange, even a ludicrous one. Its comic side to the mind of the time is illustrated by a mock examination paper written by 'Ainger M. A. (Trin. H.) and sold by Miss King at the Bazaar for the Peterboro' Training College', which has survived in the Cambridge University Archives. The humour, laboured as it now seems, is well enough illustrated by two of the questions:

Discuss the question of the best thing to do with the cold mutton, giving the respective theories of Miss Acton, Soyer, and Cre-Fydd.

Analyse, on Morell's system, the following sentence, pointing out the subject, predicate and object: 'Mr. Jones of Johns called and spent last evening with us, though he knew that papa and mamma were in London.' From your knowledge of the *subject*, what would you *predicate* as to his *object*?[4]

It must have seemed to many people in the 1860s that if girls were to sit examinations, cooking and flirting would be the most appropriate subjects of study. However Miss Davies and her friends, having tried their unofficial experiment, were anxious to go much further than that. In October 1864 the vice-chancellor of

---

[1] Stephen, *Emily Davies*, p. 88.

[2] *SIC*, vol. v, pp. 241–2: 11311–11318 (Miss Davies' evidence); see also J. G. Fitch, *Proposed Admission of Girls to University Local Examinations* (1865).

[3] *Reasons for the Extension of University Local Examinations to Girls* (Bodleian Library, G.A. Oxon. 8° 208).

[4] CUA University Papers 1864–6, no. 1358 (dated 17 May 1865). Morell's *Grammar* was used in the Cambridge Local Examinations.

Cambridge published a memorial with almost a thousand signatures asking that girls be admitted to the Locals and in the following month a Syndicate was appointed to consider whether girls might be examined in the same way as boys under the Grace of 1858.[1] When the Syndicate reported in February 1865, it recommended the adoption of the same system for girls as for boys. Examinations should be set in the same subjects for both since the Syndicate thought it inexpedient to introduce 'others which belong exclusively to female education'.[2]

When the report was discussed,[3] the secretary of the Local Examinations Syndicate, Charles Gray, said that London and several other centres had expressed a willingness to help in every way possible. The only centre which had objected was Liverpool, its grounds being that the examinations were not suitable for girls and that to open them in the way proposed would reduce their beneficial effect for boys. It is noteworthy that the views of the Liverpool committee were supported by so active and enlightened an advocate of the Locals as J. S. Howson.[4] Those who spoke against the measure in the discussion urged that to bring girls into an examination room would have an unfavourable effect on their characters and that it was undesirable to pit boys and girls against one another. That sturdy academic Conservative, E. H. Perowne of Corpus, thought that a lower class of girl would take the new examination and that it would be unfortunate 'to introduce a new element into one of the great corporations of the world'. The supporters included prominent figures like the chemist G. D. Liveing and the Liberal economist Henry Fawcett, their arguments being based on the double claim, firstly that girls' schools needed the stimulus and secondly that the candidates would suffer no harmful effects from the excitement of the examination. The advocates of the measure won the day but only by the tiny margin of five votes (56–51) and Miss Davies herself had expected defeat up to the very end.[5] G. F. Browne, later secretary to the Local Examinations Syndicate, looking back on these events in his old age, thought that the success of the measure was primarily due to the exertions of Thomas Markby, a private coach in the university,

[1] Guard Book 57.1, nos. 28–9.
[2] *Ibid.* no. 31.
[3] *Cambridge Chronicle*, 4 March 1865.
[4] The Liverpool memorial of February 1865 is in Guard Book 57.1, no. 30.
[5] *Cambridge Chronicle*, 11 March 1865.

who became secretary to the Syndicate in November of the same year.[1] 'It was a close contest', Markby had written to Emily Davies after the poll. 'I got votes enough to turn the scale first before going into the Senate House.'[2] The examinations were opened initially to girls for a period of three years. In May 1867 another grace placed the new arrangements on a permanent basis.[3] The comments in the Annual Reports of the three initial years shed an interesting light both on the girls' work and on the attitude of their examiners towards them. In 1865 126 girls took the examinations at six centres (London, Cambridge, Brighton, Manchester, Bristol and Sheffield). The examiner who presided in London wrote:

Everything went on quite regularly and quietly as at any examination at which I have been present. The girls seemed to take a great interest in it, and worked at their papers in a very businesslike way, and for the whole time allotted to them. I was quite struck with the easy way in which they bore the stress of the examination. I could not detect any flagging of interest in it, or any sign of weariness, or any ill effect upon them whatever.[4]

It is impossible for us in the mid-twentieth century to recapture this astonishment at the discovery that girls could surmount successfully the same problems as their brothers. It was generally agreed, too, that they did their work well but their strong and weak points were discovered to depart from the masculine norm. Their mathematics, though better than at the trial examination of 1863, was still poor. Very few of them took Latin and Greek. Their French and German was better, however, than the boys'. The report for 1868 says of their French that 'they appear to take a rational interest in the subject matter, which to the large majority of the boys is evidently a matter of absolute indifference'.[5] In English composition 'the best boys wrote with vigour and precision;

---

[1] G. F. Browne, *The Recollections of a Bishop* (1915), pp. 125–6. Markby was elected Secretary on 24 November 1865 (Local Examinations Syndicate, Minutes); see also T. Markby, 'The Education of Women', *Practical Essays in Education* (1868).

[2] Stephen, *Emily Davies*, p. 100. In this letter Markby gives the figures as 55–51. I have used the figures in the *Cambridge Chronicle*.

[3] 16 May 1867 (Grace Book Σ, fol. 195); Guard Book 57.1, no. 39.

[4] *Eighth Annual Report* (1866), p. 12.

[5] *Tenth Annual Report* (1868), p. 10.

the best girls with ease and vivacity'. The former were content to retail information derived from books or to describe mechanical processes. The latter were most successful 'when they endeavoured to trace their own intellectual phases, or to depict the trifling incidents of everyday life'.[1]

When Miss Davies was examined by the Taunton Commissioners she told them that an application had also been made to Oxford, but the feeling there was that, since Cambridge had decided to make the experiment, they might as well wait and see how it worked before making a decision.[2] In 1865 the Hebdomadal Council had refused to entertain the idea,[3] and it was not until the Cambridge Senate had decided to make the girls' examination permanent that the Oxford Delegacy petitioned the council to open their own examination to women.[4] Subsequently the Statute was changed and the Oxford Examination was thrown open to women in 1870.[5] Thus Oxford lagged some years behind Cambridge, and even there the new statute of 1865 had scraped through only by the narrowest of margins. In fact opinion on the opening of the Locals to girls was extremely divided. If there was doubt in the universities, there was reluctance among many schoolmistresses too. Many were impressed by the argument that the Locals were in the field and that the only sensible thing to do was to make use of what lay at hand. Many others however believed that the Locals system was too public and that it might foster among girls an undesirable spirit of emulation.

A writer in *The Times* described the girls' examination at the London centre and pointed out its advantages in providing a true test of girls' capabilities.[6] At first many parents had been deterred from entering their daughters both from fear of overwork and from fear that the class of competitors with whom they would have to associate would not be respectable. However, as the system developed, these difficulties were disappearing because of the excellence of the arrangements adopted. In the examination room two ladies, members of the local committee, were present, together with the examiner who was a married man. The examination itself had

[1] *Ninth Annual Report* (1867), p. 10.
[2] *SIC*, vol. v, p. 241: 11309.
[3] Del. Local Exams., Minutes, 4 February 1865; Minutes of Hebdomadal Council 1854–66, fol. 472 (20 March 1865).
[4] Del. Local Exams., Minutes, 8 June 1867.
[5] *Ibid.* 15 December 1869.
[6] 10 January 1868 (CUA University Papers 1867–83, no. 76).

lasted for six days but in fact every girl had had an interval of rest during this time. In the conduct of the business 'the utmost delicacy is observed ... publicity is entirely avoided, for in the Universities' report neither the names of the successful nor unsuccessful competitors appear. They are represented by the numbers which they are allotted to the candidates previous to the examination.' Both the author of this *Times* article and other articles in the press attributed both the winning over of the University of Cambridge and the successful administration of the examinations largely to Emily Davies herself.[1] In her own statements of the time she spoke and wrote enthusiastically of the experiment which she had done so much to launch. She was clear that the education of girls needed to be measured by a fixed standard and that the most appropriate way to achieve this was by extending the existing examinations to test girls' schools rather than by inventing some special standard which was supposed to be suited to them. Experience proved, she thought, the utility of examinations. 'It may be better even to cram than to leave the mind quite empty; and though the word has become, by perpetual interaction, closely associated with the idea of examinations, it is well to remember that it is quite possible for knowledge to be equally undigested, whether it has been got up for an examination or not.'[2] Already in the middle sixties she was looking forward to a higher examination for girls over eighteen.[3] To this further ambition we must return later; out of it grew the individual colleges for women at Oxford and Cambridge.

Miss Buss and Miss Beale, the two great headmistresses eternally linked in verse,[4] both gave evidence on examinations to the Taunton Commission. Miss Beale had told the Social Science Association that she was against the opening of the Locals to girls because the

---

[1] *The Museum and English Journal of Education*, vol. III (1866–7), p. 165. 'It is mainly to her personal influence that the University of Cambridge was induced to set on foot an important experiment in this direction; and it is to her skilful administration, and to the zeal and sympathy which she has shown in bringing the subject under the notice of school mistresses, that the very remarkable success of that experiment is mainly due.'

[2] *The Higher Education of Women* (1866), p. 146; see also 'On the Influence upon Girls' Schools of External Examinations' (1868), in *Thoughts on Some Questions relating to Women, 1860–1908* (1910), pp. 108–17; *SIC*, vol. v, pp. 240–1: 11302–3.

[3] *Higher Education of Women*, pp. 148–9.

[4] 'Miss Buss and Miss Beale/Cupid's darts do not feel./Oh, how different from us,/Are Miss Beale and Miss Buss!'

subjects were often unsuited for them and because the spirit of rivalry elicited was undesirable.[1] She told the commission that she was in favour of a central system of examination for both teachers and pupils linked with the inspection of schools, in fact the idea of examination, inspection and certification which has been discussed earlier in this chapter and which produced in the seventies the Oxford and Cambridge Joint Board for the public schools.[2] Miss Beale at Cheltenham Ladies' College was worried in the case of the Locals by the problem of class division which, as we have already seen, was one of the problems faced by the Syndicate and the Delegacy from their earliest days. 'The brothers of our pupils go to the universities', she told the commissioners. 'Now generally speaking, those who go in for the local examinations occupy a much lower position in the social scale, and our pupils would not like to be classed with them, but regarded as equal in rank to those who pass at the university.'[3]

Miss Buss, working in the different environment of the North London Collegiate School for Ladies, an important day-school in St Pancras, was an enthusiastic supporter of the Local Examinations. Her school sent up twenty-five candidates to the experimental examination of 1863,[4] and there survives in the archives of the school today an anonymous pamphlet putting the case for throwing the examination open to them on a regular basis.[5] The arguments ran naturally on much the same lines as those which have already been outlined. The curriculum of the examinations, it was claimed, fitted very closely with the work usually done in girls' schools if accomplishments such as dancing and practical subjects such as needlework were omitted. Nor was it really relevant to urge that a 'Board composed of husbands and fathers' would be a better examining body than the existing university organizations with their expert knowledge, even if it were possible to create such a Board at all:

It has not yet been proposed [wrote the author] to restrict girls to the use of feminine grammars and dictionaries, nor do we hear of manuals

---

[1] *Transactions of Social Science Association, 1865*, p. 285.
[2] See p. 234.
[3] *SIC*, vol. v, p. 730: 16129.
[4] *SIC*, vol. v, pp. 253–4: 11467.
[5] *Reasons for the Extension of the University Local Examinations to Girls*, n.d. [North London Collegiate School, Canons, Edgware].

of arithmetic and geography specially adapted to the female mind, and if boys and girls are learning common lessons from common school books, a common examination seems to follow as a matter of course. Scholarship and experience, rather than a minute acquaintance with the details of family life are surely the qualifications to be sought in an Examining Board.

So far as the arrangements were concerned, they had been carefully planned both to maintain the proprieties and to avoid any undesirable excitement. In fact there would be far less display 'than in the quasi-public examinations and concerts, common in ladies' schools, at which the parents and friends of the pupils are invited to be present'.

Miss Buss reinforced the same points in her evidence to the Taunton commission.[1] The girls' work, particularly in English and arithmetic, had been greatly stimulated. The parents had willingly accepted the new scheme. There was no danger of overstrain since the girls had accustomed themselves perfectly naturally to the examinations, nor was there any reason to worry about the effects of publicity on the school. The school's prize day reports, presumably drawn up by Miss Buss herself enforce the same conclusions. In 1871 it was said that:

the level of scholarship in the higher classes has been steadily rising since the University of Cambridge extended its examinations to girls. There can be little doubt as to the good effect of these Examinations on girls' education. To pass them requires attention to the really necessary elements of a sound education – good Arithmetic, Spelling, some knowledge of Grammar, History, Geography and French are surely essentials of instruction, yet the reports of the Schools Enquiry Commission clearly show that these branches, useful as they may be, are frequently neglected in girls' schools, for the sake of hours spent at the piano, or wasted over some feeble drawing. These University examinations have pointed out the defects of school instruction and have already largely helped to cure them.[2]

It would be tedious to quote the evidence of other ladies examined by the Taunton Commission which only repeats the views of Miss Davies and Miss Buss.[3] The assistant commissioners enquiring

---

[1] SIC, vol. v, pp. 253–4: 11467; 258–9: 11543; 262–3: 11597–9.

[2] North London Collegiate School, Prize Day Reports and Lists 1870/1880, report for 1871, fols. 22–4.

[3] SIC, vol. v, pp. 705: 15819–21 (Miss E. E. Smith); 629: 15090–5 (Miss M. E. Porter); 741: 16192–9; 746–8: 16254–64 (Miss E. Wolstenholme).

into the state of the schools in different parts of the country also reported that, though the examinations for girls had not yet advanced very far, they would be used much more in time and that there was a widespread desire among schoolmistresses to make use of them.[1] Nevertheless there were difficulties. T. H. Green, assistant commissioner for Staffordshire and Warwickshire, pointed out a great lack of interest in the education of girls and quoted the case of the head of a girls' school at Wolverhampton who had tried to form a class for the Cambridge Examinations, but her day girls, their parents being indulgent to them, would not stand the pressure.[2]

Clearly there was sometimes opposition from parents and friends.[3] There was the fear that the examinations would promote vanity and ostentation,[4] a fear which may sometimes have been genuine and on other occasions was a convenient excuse for avoiding a test which would have revealed ignorance and superficiality in the school work. G. W. Hastings, secretary of the Social Science Association, told the association in 1872 that he had persuaded the Malvern Committee to open their examinations to girls but that none of the girls in the many Malvern schools had entered. He had, he explained, taken:

the pains to see more than one of the schoolmistresses. To one lady of whose character and attainments he could speak with the highest respect, he pointed out the advantage the girls and the school would receive from the examination if she would avail herself of it; but she steadfastly refused, saying that no girl from her school should go into the examination, and she gave as her reason that no girl ought to go through anything that was public.[5]

Even those who wanted to submit girls to public examinations were not always convinced that they should use the same system as boys. J. P. Norris, whom we have met several times before, was very anxious that what he called 'one of the great discoveries of our day' should be extended to girls, but he thought that there should be a

---

[1] *SIC*, vol. VII, p. 71 (C. H. Stanton); vol. VIII, p. 54 (H. M. Bompas), p. 527 (J. L. Hammond); vol. IX, p. 312 (J. G. Fitch).

[2] *SIC*, vol. VIII, p. 249.

[3] See the evidence of Miss M. E. Porter, *SIC*, vol. V, p. 629: 15090–5.

[4] Miss Francis Martin, *SIC*, vol. V, p. 683: 15494–5.

[5] *Transactions of Social Science Association, 1872*, pp. 271–9 in a discussion of a paper by Miss Sheriff, 'What Public Provision ought to be made for the Secondary Education of Girls?'

separate system for them because men and women are different and need to develop in different ways.[1]

This argument was repeated over and over again in the history of women's education, for instance when women were claiming admission to university degrees. Directly opposed to it was Miss Davies' view that what the girls wanted was a fixed standard which was generally applicable to both girls and boys, not some arbitrary standard contrived solely for them. The Locals represented a programme of studies to which boys had already been working for a decade. They embodied moreover the prestige and the authority of the great Universities of Oxford and Cambridge. To women struggling to raise the educational level of their sex they seemed to offer exactly what they needed. For the first time women could in one field at least compete on equal terms with men. In 1873 a girl, Annie Rogers, daughter of the economic historian J. E. Thorold Rogers, headed the list of seniors at Oxford and, since there was nothing in the list to indicate her sex, received the offer of an exhibition which had been offered by Worcester College on the results of the examination![2] Clearly it could no longer be maintained that women's brains were of a different order from men's. If women could compete with men and beat them in fair competition, an educational and social revolution was in the making. The women's movement had scored an unspectacular but a far-reaching triumph. In the excitement women may have been forgiven for failing to notice that they were binding on themselves shackles which might later prove hard to be borne. From the contemporary standpoint it is easy to see the disadvantages of a rigid examination system; to many women of the sixties and seventies it represented not enslavement but freedom, freedom to develop their minds and their personalities.

Yet the Local Examinations went only part of the way towards meeting the women's problem. It was certainly something to train the pupils better. There remained the much greater problem of training older women, more particularly teachers, for the greatest single weakness of the girls' schools lay in their lack of a really competent teaching staff. All the women who were pressing for better educational opportunities for their sex were agreed on the

---

[1] Norris, *The Education of the People, Our Weak Points and our Strength: Occasional Essays*, pp. 161–71.

[2] Annie M. A. H. Rogers, *Degrees by Degrees: The Story of the Admission of Oxford Women Students to Membership of the University* (1938), pp. 3–5.

great importance of higher education, but they differed as to the best means of achieving their object. After the opening of the Locals to women in 1865 Emily Davies concentrated her efforts on the idea of a women's college. She looked forward to the time when they would be able to take degrees and in the meantime she wanted the system adopted in it to be the same as that which already existed for men. The new college was to be a dependency and eventually a part of the University of Cambridge. She was not deflected by the argument that there were parts of the existing Cambridge system which were imperfect and which it would be wise for women to alter or to avoid. To her mind the overmastering point was that it was only by submitting themselves to the same curriculum as the men that the women could establish their claim to the same educational treatment, that they could avoid the stigma of being fobbed off with the second-best.

As a result she and her friends were very much opposed to teaching or examining designed particularly 'for women', and were distinctly luke-warm towards the plans of the 'North of England Council for Promoting the Higher Education of Women', a body representing local associations in Leeds, Liverpool, Manchester, Newcastle and Sheffield. This body was formed in 1867 and was inspired by Miss A. J. Clough, later Principal of Newnham College. Its first task was to organize lectures for women, which were to be one of the main roots of the whole university extension movement. It also gave attention from the beginning to the establishment of an examination for women over eighteen years of age, more particularly as a test for teachers.[1] The original plan had been to ask university men to act as voluntary examiners but this was soon replaced by the more ambitious scheme of asking the university to act corporately, since the plan was supported by a number of influential men at Cambridge such as the theologians, F. D. Maurice and J. B. Lightfoot, the classical scholar B. H. Kennedy, the astonomer J. C. Adams, and Charles Kingsley.[2] Miss Davies on the other hand feared that the lectures would be merely second-best to her proposed college and distrusted the appeal made for the proposed new examination that it was in a special way womanly and adapted to women's needs. Her London committee voted that it could take

[1] B. A. Clough, *Memoir of Anne J. Clough* (1897), ch. 5.
[2] CUA University Papers 1867–83, no. 87, is an undated fly-sheet representing the ideas of this group.

no part in a proposed memorial to the University of Cambridge since special schemes of examination tended to keep down the level of women's education.[1] In May 1868 Miss Davies wrote to a friend in Cambridge that she and her associates were not opposing the scheme but were anxious only to keep out of it.[2]

However the North of England Council rallied impressive support for their proposals. In May 1868 the vice-chancellor of Cambridge published two memorials, asking for the establishment by the university of 'some recognized test of the capacity and attainments of women who desire to become teachers in families or schools'. The first of these came from the North of England Council and was signed by their president, Josephine Butler, best known as one of the leading opponents of the Contagious Diseases Acts, and their secretary, Anne J. Clough. The second was signed by seventy-four Masters of Arts, including, in addition to the men who have already been mentioned, a considerable number of other leading men in the university.[3] The projected scheme was then referred to the Local Examinations Syndicate for their consideration and they reported in October of the same year in favour of establishing an examination of a more advanced character suited to the greater age of the candidates.[4] When this report was discussed, Markby, the secretary to the Syndicate, emphasized how great was the demand for an examination of this type,[5] and the Grace establishing the new examination for women over the age of eighteen passed successfully on 29 October 1868.[6]

The first examination, held in July 1869, brought forward thirty-six candidates of whom twenty-four passed.[7] It was divided into six groups. The first of them, containing divinity, arithmetic, English history and English literature and composition was compulsory and, in order to obtain a certificate, one other group had to be passed as well. The voluntary groups were (B) languages, (C) mathematics, (D) logic and political economy, (E) natural sciences, (F) art and music. In this first examination almost all the successful candidates took group B and no one passed in Group E

[1] Stephen, *Emily Davies*, pp. 189, 191, 192.
[2] To Sedley Taylor, May 1868 (CUL Add. 6258, 37).
[3] CUA Guard Book 57.1, no. 40; see also Minutes of Local Examinations Syndicate, 22 May 1868.
[4] Guard Book, 57.1, no. 42.
[5] University Papers 1867–83, no. 171 (*Cambridge Chronicle*, 24 October 1868)
[6] Guard Book 57.1, no. 44; Grace Book Σ fol. 412.
[7] *Transactions of Social Science Association, 1869*, pp. 363–4 (F. W. H. Myers).

at all.[1] F. W. H. Myers of Trinity, describing this first examination to the Social Science Association, pointed out that several women had taken it who had no intention of teaching and who merely wished to have their knowledge tested.[2] Certainly, from whichever group of women it came, the demand was there. In 1870 there were 84 candidates, in 1871, 127. By 1877, 488 candidates entered.[3] In terms of numbers at least the Higher Locals had been a resounding success.

Here again Oxford acted more slowly than Cambridge, and eventually on rather different lines. The Delegacy appointed a committee in December 1872 to report 'on the Examination of Women with a view to action on the part of the University', but this committee reported in the following February that it was unable to agree.[4] No more seems to have been done for a year until the Hebdomadal Council received a memorial organized by J. E. Thorold Rogers asking them to admit women to the same examinations in arts as were held for undergraduates.[5] This was referred in the Michaelmas term of 1874 by the Council to the Delegacy with the request that they would consider 'an examination &c for girls and women who are more than 18 years of age, for the purpose of granting a Teacher's Certificate'.[6] Enquiries were then made of several prominent heads of girls' schools, including Miss Buss and Miss Beale, who were much in favour of the scheme but did not wish it to be limited exclusively to intending teachers. The Delegates recommended that the women's examinations should proceed according to the same pattern as the existing university tests and should therefore correspond to Responsions, Moderations and Final Schools. The subjects 'should include such kinds of learning as are peculiarly parts of women's education, as well as others, which may from time to time be recognized in the Schools of the University'.[7] A draft Statute was sent to the Council in March 1875[8] and the definitive Statute instituting the examinations for women was passed on 10 November 1875. It provided for a Preliminary

---

[1] *Cambridge Higher Local Examinations Class-Lists, 1869–1883.*
[2] See p. 118 above.
[3] *Cambridge Higher Local Examinations Class-Lists.*
[4] Del. Local Exams., Minutes, 7 December 1872, 8 February 1873.
[5] Rogers, *Degrees by Degrees*, p. 6.
[6] Del. Local Exams., Minutes, 21 November 1874.
[7] *Ibid.* 24 February 1875.
[8] *Ibid.* 11 May 1875.

Examination on the lines of Responsions, though without obligatory Latin and Greek, for a Pass Examination and for an Honours Examination.[1] These were first held in March 1877 at Oxford and Cheltenham, when twenty-six candidates sat of whom fourteen passed. Most of the girls sat the Preliminary Examination. There was only one candidate who took honours and who won a first class – Annie Rogers who had also triumphed in the Local Examination of 1873.[2] The report on the work suggests that French and German were the best subjects. In the Latin the grammar and set-books were better done than the prose and sentences. The algebra and arithmetic were satisfactory but the Euclid was done in a very confused and unintelligent way.[3]

Annie Rogers, the one candidate for honours in that very first examination, wrote long afterwards that this 'was an absurdly ambitious scheme for a Delegacy appointed to examine schoolboys and schoolgirls', and that it would have proved a failure but for the impetus it gave to Women's Halls of Residence.[4] In fact the Oxford Examination developed far more slowly than its Cambridge partner; in 1887 there were still only sixty-five candidates.[5] In both universities alike Women's Examinations, once they had moved beyond the school level, soon came to demand both teaching and residence if the work was to be carried forward. The movement which began by providing written tests of competence was quickly to broaden out into the foundation of residential colleges for women, parallel to the men's colleges which had already existed for centuries. It was to this field, as we have seen, that Emily Davies had transferred her efforts after Cambridge had thrown open the Locals to girls in 1865. The college, opened at Hitchin in 1869, was transferred to Girton near Cambridge in 1873. Miss Davies, resolutely progressive as she was in intellectual matters, was convinced that her students could not live a full and undisturbed life in Cambridge itself and had resisted sharply any attempt to bring the College into the town. Her policy remained quite adamant that the students should submit themselves to the same tests as the men. The first of them were permitted to take the Previous Examination in 1870, the

---

[1] Rogers, *Degrees by Degrees*, p. 7.
[2] See p. 118.
[3] *University of Oxford Local Examinations: Reports on Examinations for Women, 1877–1907*, Report (1877).
[4] *Degrees by Degrees*, p. 8.
[5] *Reports on Examinations for Women, Eleventh Report* (1887).

Tripos in 1873. Though the burden of elementary work necessary to pass the Previous Examination in Latin, Greek and mathematics imposed a heavy strain on them and left them with all too little time for the Tripos itself, she would make no concessions, even when in February 1873 all thirteen students in residence petitioned to be allowed to become candidates for the Tripos without passing the Previous Examination.[1] Her attitude towards the Women's Examination remained unyielding. In the very early days at Hitchin she became very worried by the ideas of the classical lecturer who had remarked to her:

that Greek was no use to ladies, and showing in other ways a narrow tone and yesterday I had a letter to say that in his teaching he did not intend to make any reference to the Cambridge curriculum, having devised one of his own which he considered superior ... It is curious to see how possessed he must be with the female idea. He suggests the Cambridge Examination for Women as the right thing for our students, having been devised especially for their class. About the best thing that can be said of this examination is that it is *probably* just a step above the Senior Local, i.e. about on the level of our *Entrance*. It was devised to suit struggling governesses, with no teaching, and no time for study except their evenings. But they and our students are alike females, and beyond this, Mr Clark fails to discriminate.[2]

In fact it seemed to her that the Women's Examination had made her task even more difficult by setting up another and inferior standard, and she was particularly worried in the early seventies by the appearance of a rival in Cambridge which grew out of the movement promoted by Miss Clough and Mrs Butler. In 1869 the philosopher Henry Sidgwick, a warm friend of women's education but not necessarily in agreement with all Miss Davies' ideas, took steps to organize lectures in Cambridge to prepare for the newly established Women's Examinations. The lectures began in the Lent Term of 1870 and as a result a number of students were attracted to Cambridge for whom Sidgwick, on his own responsibility, decided to establish a house of residence. Of this house in 1871 he persuaded Miss Clough to be the head.

The ideas of Sidgwick and his friends were in many ways different from those of Miss Davies. The house of residence, which was to become Newnham College, had grown out of the demands of

---

[1] Stephen, *Emily Davies*, pp. 277–8.
[2] *Ibid*, p. 217.

the Women's Examination and in its curriculum in the early years remained very closely connected with that examination. Whereas Miss Davies thought it a badge of inferiority Sidgwick considered it a better course of preliminary study than the Previous and was very anxious not to impose compulsory Latin and Greek on the girls. In the early years many Newnham students worked for the Higher Local Examinations only and those who went on to the Tripos normally did so by that route rather than by the Previous Examination. Whereas Girton constrained its students to complete their course within the period prescribed for men, Newnham allowed its members a longer period since most of them had never received any proper education preparatory to a university course. There were other differences too: the founders of Newnham wished to provide education at a lower cost than at Girton and they disliked the formal connection established in the Girton constitution with the Church of England.[1] These differences between the colleges gradually disappeared as they grew stronger and as the range of women's studies widened, but they were important in the early days and they make it easy to understand Miss Davies' fears of what seemed to be a dangerous rival. The whole contrast between the schools of thought represented by Miss Davies and Miss Clough is a very interesting one, and it brings out many of the difficulties experienced by the pioneers. Miss Davies' attitude, from the point of view of a century later, seems ultra-cautious and that of the North of England Council and its successors far more practical and flexible. She was, of course, primarily concerned with the whole question of women's status rather than with education in itself. It is difficult now to recapture her fear that women would be palmed off with the second best. It is not difficult to appreciate the courage and determination with which she held on to the principle which she believed to be fundamental.

By the late seventies a number of women had taken University Examinations at Cambridge, though this had been done entirely informally by arrangement with the examiners. There was no security that this would be allowed and there was a real danger that, if opinion among examiners hardened against the practice which had recently grown up, very serious damage might be done to the cause of women's education. The eventual goal for women could only be the full degree; if it was premature to ask for that, there were

---

[1] B. A. Clough, *Memoir of Anne J. Clough*, pp. 152-4, 174-6.

strong arguments for claiming that the examinations at least might be put on a definite basis. The initiative came not from Girton and Newnham themselves, but from Mr and Mrs W. S. Aldis of Newcastle who, on their own initiative, got up a memorial asking for the admission of women both to University Examinations and to University Degrees, which collected more than 8,500 signatures. This move was stimulated by the success of a Girton student, Miss C. A. Scott, who in the Mathematical Tripos of 1880 was known to have been equal to the eighth wrangler, and the Aldis memorial was followed by a number of others. Though both the women's colleges viewed this move with some hesitation, they were forced by it to take some action themselves, though Miss Davies declined the suggestion made by Sidgwick that the two colleges should act together. Sidgwick thought that it would be premature to ask for degrees and wanted merely to have the existing examination arrangements regularized. Miss Davies, as we have already seen, disliked the Newnham practice of presenting candidates for the Tripos who had not precisely fulfilled the university conditions and was very anxious to avoid any plan which might lead towards the dreaded special examinations for women. Consequently the Girton College memorial explained that their students had complied exactly with university regulations and asked specifically that women should be given the B.A. degree. The Lectures Association, the controlling body of Newnham, explained that their practice had been to require their candidates to take the Higher Locals rather than the Previous, and asked that the entry of women to the University Examinations might be put on a more formal basis.

A Syndicate, appointed in June 1880 to consider the various memorials, reported in December 1880.[1] It refused to recommend that women be admitted to degrees, but recommended that they be admitted to the Previous and Tripos Examinations, and suggested that they be qualified for the latter not only through the Previous Examination itself, but also through an honours certificate in the Higher Locals provided that it included passes in languages and mathematics. The debate on the proposals raises issues beyond the scope of this study and will not be examined in any detail here. It is

[1] *Cambridge University Reporter* (1880–1), pp. 193–218 gives the report of the Syndicate and the various memorials mentioned. See also Stephen, *Emily Davies*, pp. 322–4; Clough, *A. J. Clough*, pp. 183–9.

however relevant to mention that one speaker in the discussion on the report pointed out how deeply the university had already involved itself in the business of examining girls. 'In the Local Examinations', he said, 'it examined among the seniors three times as many girls as boys, and in the Higher Local Examination almost all the candidates were women. The reason of this was that the girls' schools had no standard but that of the University.'[1] Into such a mighty tree had the little shoot planted in London at Christmas 1863 grown. Despite many doubts and fears there was to be no halt to the growth. The principal Grace based on the report of the Syndicate passed the Senate on 25 February 1881 by 398 votes to 32.[2]

'The victory just won', wrote James Stuart, the pioneer of the university extension movement, to Miss Davies, 'is indeed a magnificent one.' From her point of view there was gall in the potion because the special exemption from the Previous which enabled women to escape from learning Latin and Greek was preserved. No Girton student, however, was permitted to make use of the option. The university had still to arrange how the new system was to be operated. Clearly some permanent control must be instituted and the Syndicate on Women's Education turned to the Local Examinations Syndicate for help. They declared their readiness to co-operate and when the Women's Education Syndicate made its second report in March 1881, it recommended that the entire management of the Women's Examination should be placed in their hands.[3] Though very few votes had been cast against the Graces of February 1881, there were people who believed that they were of doubtful legality since the university had no power under its statutes to admit women to Tripos Examinations. This school of thought proposed that an interpretation of the Statutes on the point be obtained from the chancellor. The supporters of the Graces in their reply urged among other arguments that if they were *ultra vires*, so was everything which had been done since 1858 to extend the work of the university to persons other than its own members.[4] Finally the proposals of the Women's Education Syndicate passed

---

[1] *Camb. Univ. Rep.* (1880–1), p. 371 (T. J. Lawrence).
[2] *Ibid.* p. 391; Stephen, *Emily Davies*, pp. 325–6.
[3] *Camb. Univ. Rep.* (1880–1), pp. 415–16; Local Exams. Synd., Minutes, 12 March 1881.
[4] *Camb. Univ. Rep.* pp. 415–16, 440–2 [Second Report of the Syndicate and discussion of this], 447–9, 507–10 [Memorials giving the views of the two sides].

without a division on 5 May 1881.[1] It was to be many years before women were to be fully admitted to Cambridge Degrees, but at least they could now measure themselves against the standard. In 1887 a Girton student came out at the top of the Classical Tripos, ahead of all the men; in 1890 a Newnham girl came out above the senior wrangler. Academically there were no heights which a woman could not scale. An intellectual revolution had taken place since the debates of 1865 on opening the Locals to girls, when they had won their case by so narrow a margin. The fact that the university had entrusted the management of the Women's Examination to the Local Examinations Syndicate was a permanent reminder of the very small beginnings from which such an important movement had grown. Later events had been far more spectacular but the opening of the Locals had been the crucial stage in the whole process. After that one advance had followed logically from another.

At Oxford events followed a broadly similar course though there were certain important differences of detail. The collegiate instruction of women got under way rather later than in Cambridge. In 1878 the Association for the Higher Education of Women in Oxford (familiarly known as the A.E.W.), which undertook responsibility for the education of women students, was founded and in the following year the first two halls, Lady Margaret and Somerville, were opened. Very soon the question of the admission of women to University Examinations was raised by the Master of University College (J. F. Bright) who, at the annual meeting of the association in 1882, suggested that the time was coming to apply for this 'on the ground that the standard of the Delegates' Examination was found by experience to be not generally valued or recognized'.[2] Once again, as at Cambridge, a separate Women's Examination was found to lack prestige; the only thing which would really count in the outward world, it was argued, was a university certificate. The association then decided to confer with the Delegates of Local Examinations which, after considering the practice at Cambridge under the regulations of 1881 and at London and Durham where women were already admitted to degrees, resolved to petition the

---

[1] *Ibid.* p. 533.
[2] *Association for the Higher Education of Women in Oxford: Reports 1879–1920* [Bodl. Lib.], *Report* (1884). This report tells the story of the opening of the University Examinations; see also Rogers, *Degrees by Degrees*, pp. 15–16.

Hebdomadal Council 'to introduce a Statute opening all the Honour Examinations of the University to Women'.[1] The Council on this occasion refused to move and, even after the A.E.W. Committee had organized a petition, it again refused to take any action. Finally the matter passed Council by a narrow majority and a Statute was presented to Congregation in the Lent term of 1884 which permitted the Delegates of Local Examinations to use Honour Moderations and the Final Schools of mathematics, natural science and modern history. The battle was more hardly fought than in Cambridge. The Statute passed Congregation only narrowly (107–72). 'The opponents', said the A.E.W. report for 1884

determined to fight once more in Convocation: and the Easter recess was enlivened by a voluminous controversy in the 'Guardian' and elsewhere, in which many of our friends [and one or two of our adversaries] did us good service. The Committee drew up a paper containing a full statement of our case, and sent a copy to every member of Convocation. When the day came, our friends appeared to the number of 464 against 321 on the other side. The Statute was carried by 143, a finally decisive result. (29 April 1884.)[2]

From the ultra-conservative viewpoint the controversy was enlivened by a sermon preached by Dean Burgon in New College chapel entitled 'To Educate Young Women like Young Men – A Thing Inexpedient and Immodest'![3] The Oxford arrangements of 1884 differed in a number of ways from the Cambridge arrangements of 1881. No reference was made to residence, no intermediate examination was prescribed. Nor were the University Examinations in general thrown open to women; permission was limited to those Schools which corresponded with the Delegacy's already existing Women's Examinations.[4] Gradually the number of Schools open to women was increased until in 1894 all the remaining B.A. Examinations were opened and all newly established Honour Schools were to be available to them.[5] As each barrier came down, the same course of action had been followed. The A.E.W. Commit-

---

[1] Del. Local Exams., Minutes, 15 May 1883.
[2] The words in brackets are in the proof; they are omitted in the final version of the report.
[3] Pusey House Pamphlets, no. 5041.
[4] *Oxford A.E.W. Report* (1888).
[5] *A.E.W. Report* (1894); Rogers, *Degrees by Degrees*, p. 23.

tee had first approached the Delegates of Local Examinations which had then brought the matter before Council. Just as at Cambridge, the mechanism by which the higher education of women at Oxford operated bore the marks of its origins in school examinations. By the end of the century the examination of girls and girls' schools had expanded very rapidly. In December 1878, 6,435 candidates took the Senior and Junior Cambridge Locals, of whom 2,480 were girls. The senior girl candidates in fact considerably exceeded the senior boys in number (997 to 626),[1] and the predominance of girls in the senior examination continued to grow. In December 1898 there were 15,941 candidates of whom 6,451 were girls; there were 1,414 senior girl candidates to 801 boys.[2] The figures for the Cambridge Higher Locals, as the Women's Examination had come to be known, had increased in the same way. The original 36 candidates of 1869 had become 741 in 1879, 1,118 in 1897–8.[3] In 1897 the parallel Oxford Examinations for women over 18 attracted 199 candidates.[4] As a conclusion to this survey of women's education, it will be interesting to consider the work done in girls' schools of several different types. The first example will be the North London Collegiate School of which Miss Buss was headmistress. The second will be St Mary's Hall, a school for clergymen's daughters at Brighton, founded by the Evangelical leader Henry Venn Elliott. The last will be two girls' high schools, one in Leicester, the other in London.

The North London Collegiate, as we have already seen, had been well represented among the candidates at the first examination in December 1863. The school's report for 1870 explained the advantages of an external examination as setting a standard both higher and more impartial than that of an examination taken within the school itself. When a girl's age was suitable and her parents did not object she was sent in for the Cambridge Examinations. Since these had rigid age limits, a girl who had been ill or whose

---

[1] *Twenty-First Annual Report* (1879), p. 3.

[2] *Forty-First Annual Report, Camb. Univ. Rep.* (1898–9). These figures are not exactly comparable with those for 1878 since they include the Preliminary Examination for candidates below the junior level (see *ibid.* p. 682).

[3] *Camb. Univ. Rep.* (1898–9), pp. 126–7. The 1897–8 figures cover two examinations, December 1897 and June 1898.

[4] *University of Oxford Local Examinations: Reports on Examinations for Women, 1877–1907, Twenty-First Annual Report* (1897).

education had been neglected was sent in for the College of Preceptors' Examinations for which age limits did not apply. The comment in the report for 1871 that 'the level of scholarship in the higher classes has been steadily rising since the University of Cambridge extended its examinations to girls' has already been noted.[1] Thereafter the headmistress's reports record the steady development of the system. In 1872 the Regent's Park centre was formed. The examination would thenceforth be held in the school itself and 'the fatigue and expense of going to the London University' be saved.[2] In the following years Miss Buss announced that 'most of the extra prizes offered in connexion with the Cambridge Local Examinations came to our centre'.[3] In 1874 many girls in the middle of the school had been entered for the Preceptors' examinations, and more than half the whole school was working for a recognized public examination.[4] Examining in girls' schools sometimes presented an all-male Syndicate with peculiar problems. The school had been in touch with G. F. Browne, the Cambridge secretary, about the possibility of holding examinations in subjects which the Locals did not normally cover like domestic economy. Browne, a confident man, was not to be deterred by such difficulties, and replied, 'Such a subject as "Domestic Economy" would not naturally fall within our range, but no doubt a common-sense man with a syllabus before him could examine in it. Or he could hear an oral lesson given by a teacher.'[5] By 1876 girls were presenting themselves for the Locals a whole year younger and there was therefore a class at the top of the school which had passed Senior Cambridge and was working for the London University Women's Examination.[6] The policy of the school was considerably affected in later years by the opening to women of London University Degrees. The majority of girls continued to take the Cambridge Examinations, but a number took the London Matriculation and Intermediate Arts and others the Preceptors' Examinations.[7] 'Our practice', Miss Buss told her governors in 1891, 'has been

[1] See p. 116.
[2] North London Collegiate School: Headmistress's Reports to Governors, vol. 1 (1871–85), fol. 28 *bis*.
[3] *Ibid*. fol. 42 *bis*.
[4] *Ibid*. fols. 49–51.
[5] N.L.C.S., Headmistress's Reports to Governors, vol. 1, fol. 71.
[6] *Ibid*. fol. 95.
[7] *Ibid*. vol. 1, fols. 163 *bis*–164; Prize Day Reports and Lists, 1881–1894, fols. 152–4 (1888).

therefore to use the public Examinations of the Cambridge and London Universities for the purpose of a school external examination.' 'Since our scheme was passed', she remarked in the same report, 'nothing less than a revolution in the education of girls and women has taken place.'[1]

Miss Buss' school was, of course, one of the leading girls' schools of the day, and educationally very much at the centre of things. It is therefore interesting to compare the impact of external examinations there with their effect at St Mary's Hall, a small school with a very markedly religious atmosphere.[2] In their report for 1872 the trustees explained that they had for the first time applied to the Cambridge Syndicate for an examiner in order to discover 'what position this prominent school occupies amid the advancing requirements of the age and in comparison with the more recent institutions and appliances for educational objects'.[3] The same examiner, Arthur Holmes, fellow of Clare, came to both in 1872 and 1873; his remarks were on the whole complimentary, though he had some faults to point out, particularly, it appears, in arithmetic and French. In 1873 one girl presented herself 'for the Cambridge Local Examination of Women, and passed with much credit in most of the subjects; but, failing in one, awaits her certificate at the next trial'.[4] Thus far the trustees had merely arranged an internal examination conducted by the Syndicate under the arrangements sanctioned in 1862.[5] To allow the girls to sit publicly for the Local Examination was a more adventurous step. The report for 1875 explained that this step would be taken if parents wished it, since it had been warmly recommended by many friends of the school. Most of their girls would become governesses and the Cambridge Certificate would be valuable to them in their later work. The difficulty clearly was that the public examination would need special preparation. The trustees were prepared to try, though with some reluctance; 'they believe, that in the case of private families there will be found a preference for the qualifications of high character, well-regulated temper, and ability to train the minds

---

[1] Headmistress's Reports to Governors, vol. II, fols. 253 bis–256.

[2] The following remarks are based entirely on *St Mary's Hall, Brighton Reports, 1838–97*, a volume in the possession of the school kindly lent to me by the present headmistress.

[3] *Reports 1838–97*, Thirty-Sixth Report (1872), pp. 5–6.

[4] *Thirty-Seventh Report* (1873), p. 6.

[5] See p. 106.

of children, over the technical acquisitions to which the certificates testify'.[1] The experiment was successful since six girls passed, one of them with honours, though even after this success the trustees were still concerned about the need for preparatory study and thought that the expediency of taking the Locals had not been fully established.[2]

The reports of examiners sent down by both the Syndicate and the Delegacy give a very clear idea of the work done in the school and the results obtained. As might have been expected, a good deal of attention was given to religious knowledge and good results were obtained in it. In addition to this subject the Cambridge examiner of 1879 examined fifty-two girls in the top four classes in Shakespeare's *Merchant of Venice*, English grammar, English history, geography, arithmetic, physical geography, Greek history, composition, French and German. The comments in general were favourable and a great improvement had been made since the previous year.[3] Another Cambridge report of 1885 mentioned with approval that the course of study had been extended to include some science and to give more prominence to German and mathematics and to Latin, which had not earlier been examined. The written work was good, though the spelling all through the school was weak. The papers in the English subjects were well done, apart from the geography where there was a great want of accurate knowledge. The Shakespeare play studied was *The Tempest* and the papers on it were 'written, I should judge, much more *con amore* than any others I received'. The languages examined were French, German and Latin. The report on the last-named suggests that it had in earlier years been rather neglected, though the work was now being more thoroughly done. Both French and German were well taught in general, though the older girls reading *Les Femmes Savantes* had never entered into the spirit of the play ... 'its humour was lost upon them, and the work was bound to be very dreary'. The knowledge of German was rather elementary but it was taught as a class subject halfway through the school and not merely to a few girls. The elementary arithmetic was satisfactory, though less skill was shown in dealing with any problem, however simple. The work in science was commented upon favourably.

---

[1] *St Mary's Hall Reports, 1838–97, Thirty-Ninth Report* (1875), p. 6.
[2] *Fortieth Report* (1876), pp. 5–6.
[3] *Forty-Third Report* (1879), pp. 6–8.

Form VI answered a paper on heat, and botany was taught to the lower forms; 'the younger children learning it by means of simple reading books of a conversational character. I was pleased to find that it is made no mere matter of long scientific names, &c., but of actual observation, comparison of specimens.'[1] A later Oxford Examiner of 1893 mentioned object lessons given to the younger children, one of these dealing with molluscs. On this occasion the lower classes were examined *viva voce*, as well as the written examination taken by the older girls. The examiners commented on the thoroughness of all the work, though the range might sometimes be limited. 'I should say', wrote one of them, 'that the average of intellectual capacity is not high, but I consider the results attained very creditable. It seemed to me that throughout the School a very large amount of sound and conscientious work was being done.'[2] The range of examinations taken at St Mary's Hall was similar, though the number of candidates was far smaller, to that of the North London Collegiate. In 1893 girls were successful in London Matriculation, the Cambridge Higher Locals and the Oxford Senior and Junior Locals.[3]

The information available in the St Mary's Hall and the North London Collegiate School reports shows the effect of examinations on a small and a large girls' school over a considerable period of time. The final example consists of two single reports, one of 1896 on the Wyggeston High School for Girls at Leicester, the other of 1899 on Aske's School for Girls, Hatcham, South-East London.[4] Both these schools probably aimed at a level rather below that of St Mary's Hall. They followed a basically similar course covering scripture, the English subjects, mathematics, French and German. The senior girls at Wyggeston also took Latin. At both schools 'the kindergarten' is mentioned; at Wyggeston this side of the work included clay-modelling and games. At both schools there were drill exercises in addition. At Wyggeston the mathematical work was thoroughly done; the standard at the top of the school covered in arithmetic 'vulgar fractions, compound interest, present worth and the easier part of a question on stocks', in algebra a paper up to progressions, in Euclid the first four books. In both schools some

---

[1] *Forty-Ninth Report* (1885), pp. 8–11.
[2] *Fifty-Seventh Report* (1893), pp. 7–11.
[3] *Ibid.* p. 12.
[4] For the following see Public Record Office, Ed. 27/2430 (Wyggeston High School for Girls, Leicester), Ed 27/2990 (Aske's School for Girls, Hatcham).

science was done; lessons are mentioned on the silkworm, on physiography, on 'science measurements', and particularly on botany, 'each pupil (at Hatcham) having a leaf or a flower to dissect as she studied the Teacher's description'. At Wyggeston much attention was given to geography and the girls drew excellent maps. The history was more uneven; some excellent work was shown up but there were weak and confused answers as well. At Hatcham the history teacher sometimes poured out too much information 'without [its] being always sufficiently questioned back again from the pupil'; however care was taken to look up the sites of battles and other geographical references on small maps with which all the girls were provided. The French and German lessons too were well managed. At Wyggeston the French grammar and translation were, except in the top form, better than the composition, a state of affairs very commonly noted in examiners' reports. Only the top form was examined in elementary German with good results. Latin was studied only in the top two forms and very little time was allowed in the time-table for it. Consequently Form IIa had not mastered its work; Form I Lower 'failed almost completely in turning English sentences into Latin and shewed great weakness in grammar'; even Form I Upper did disappointing work in composition and no girl could render an easy sentence into oratio obliqua. In both schools household subjects were not neglected. At Wyggeston careful attention was given to sewing. At Hatcham the examiner saw a lesson in cookery, 'the Teacher questioning the girls well at the same time that she was practically illustrating her subject. And in the afternoon of the same day I saw the same class, in aprons, endeavouring to prove, by each of them making a gooseberry pie, that they had profited by their morning's lesson.'

The examiner at Hatcham described in his report how he had carried out his task. After attending prayers he had been taken round to all the class-rooms, beginning with the kindergarten, by the headmistress, who had introduced him to all the form mistresses. 'After this', he wrote, 'I went about, time-table in hand, to the different rooms, as I pleased me, hearing lessons given in many subjects, observing the behaviour of the pupils, and forming my opinion as to the general state of the school.' It would have been unthinkable fifty years earlier for a girls' school to throw itself open to inspection by a man in that way, and the transformation which this suggests is an eloquent tribute to the achievement of the Locals in bringing girls' schools out of their isolation, and launching them firmly into the main stream of educational advance. There were of course many other reasons why the education of women progressed so fast during the second half of the nineteenth century, and examinations could be a straitjacket as well as a stimulus. Even at the time, as we shall see later, their advantages and disadvantages were keenly debated.[1] Yet what the girls' schools needed above all was an external standard to which they could work and without this it is difficult to see how they could have advanced at all. The influence of the Locals had been felt from the modest high schools like Hatcham and Wyggeston to the new colleges at the universities, and because this was so, they were one of the most important levers in raising the whole level of women's education throughout the country.

[1] See p. 247.

6

SECONDARY SCHOOLS AND THEIR STUDIES

While the broad questions of religious affiliation and of women's rights which have been considered in the last chapter were attracting public attention, the internal development of the Locals went steadily on. The character of the examinations was gradually established as year succeeded year and the Delegacy and the Syndicate each created its own tradition. Something has already been said about the first results of 1858[1]. Though a few changes of detail were adopted, the general pattern remained unchanged during the ensuing twenty years. The major changes were in scale not in form, and here, as has already been noted, the outstanding feature was the remarkable growth at Cambridge. The Oxford Delegacy, which had begun as so very much the senior partner in the whole concern, was aware as early as the middle sixties that the change was taking place; in its Minute Book there is a note for the meeting of 3 November 1866 which mentions:

Cambridge increase which may be due to lower standard
freedom in Divinity
age of juniors
time of year
length of Exam
readiness to make Centres.

By that time, of course, the influx of girl candidates had hardly begun to operate. The Cambridge figures speak for themselves. At the first examination in December 1858 297 juniors and 73 seniors appeared. In December 1878 the total number of candidates was 6,435; that is 626 senior boys and 997 senior girls with 3,329 junior boys and 1,483 junior girls. In 1858 there were 8 centres; in 1878 there were 93 centres for boys and 81 for girls.[2] The changes in the financial position of the Syndicate were equally striking. The accounts for the first year showed a deficit of £40; the candidates' entry money amounted to £383, the examiners' fees and expenses

[1] See pp. 94–7.
[2] *Local Exam. Synd.*, *Twenty-First Annual Report* (1879).

to £310 and the printing bill to £89.[1] The Oxford secretary had
£150 per annum from the beginning; the Cambridge secretary was
not voted a salary of £50 per annum until 1864, though he had
earlier had an allowance for a clerk.[2] In November 1874 the
secretary's salary was raised from £400 to £600 per annum;[3] for
purposes of comparison it is worth noting that professorial salaries
in the eighties ranged between £700 and £850. By the mid-sixties
the Syndicate was beginning to accumulate a small balance, which
grew so fast that in February 1873, £1,500 Exchequer Bills were
purchased.[4] The distribution of the Syndicate's income in 1874
was as follows: of the sums collected in entrance fees, thirty and a
quarter per cent went to superintending examiners, forty-five per
cent to examiners in the various subjects, twelve per cent to the
secretary and clerk, eight per cent to printing – 'in all 95%, leaving
5% or nearly £210 clear and all Higher £414 and schools £40
clear – £664 in all less 65 gratuities'.[5]

In 1870 the fees paid to thirty-three examiners totalled £960
and to forty-six superintending examiners at centres £665. This
meant in most cases during the sixties payment of between £20 and
£30 to individuals examining in the major subjects and £10 to £15
to those examining in the minor.[6] In 1873 the Syndicate adopted a
report on the remuneration of their examiners which followed the
principle, already used for some years, of payment by weight on a
scale adjusted for the relative difficulty of examining in different
subjects. On this scale the cheapest subjects were arithmetic at
9s. 6d. per lb and algebra and English composition at 10s. Religious
knowledge, English literature, geography and history scored 12s.,
and linguistic subjects the highest of all – modern languages 17s.
and classics 18s. In all cases the examiner was to be paid to the
nearest multiple of £2 10s. on the appropriate scale. The presiding

---

[1] *First Annual Report* (1859).
[2] Minutes, 29 November 1864.
[3] Local Exams. Synd., Minutes, 1 December 1874.
[4] Minutes, 12 February 1873.
[5] A note in Minute Book 1 in G. F. Browne's hand-writing [for Browne see
p. 165]. This, the earliest Minute Book of the Syndicate, begins on 11 December
1862. It is labelled 'Non-Gremial Syndicate' and was started by Secretary Gray.
This was used as the official book until about 1867 and was then used as a rough
book until the late '70s. Minute Book II, also labelled 'Non-Gremial Syndicate'
begins in January 1866 and was started by Secretary Markby. This was used until
May 1886. Thereafter the Minute Books run in chronological sequence.
[6] All these figures come from notes in Minute Book 1.

examiners at centres were to receive £15 out of which they had to pay their railway and hotel expenses; if they were resident in the neighbourhood, they received £10 only.[1] Some of the secretary's notes show that presiding examiners sometimes created problems. At the London Girls' Centre an M.A. had been assisted by two ladies, one of whom was Miss Davies. The secretary noted: 'Mr Holmes believes that two M.A. and one lady will work much better.' Presumably Holmes thought that a woman would co-operate with another man better than with another woman! There is a wealth of administrative frustration in the terse notes, 'B. Anningson made every possible mistake in envelopes', 'Mr Moxon told boys A and B didn't matter.'[2]

Less detailed information is available about the financial position of the Oxford Delegacy, though smaller numbers and a less innovating spirit naturally meant that expansion was far slower than at Cambridge. The 750 junior and 401 senior candidates of 1858 had grown to 1,665 junior and 665 senior in 1878.[3] This grand total of 2,330 is rather more than one-third of the Cambridge candidates for the same year. In the early eighties the Oxford entries were actually falling; in 1883 they numbered only 1,845 when Cambridge had risen to 8,290.[4] This decline must be connected with the fact that severe criticisms of the Oxford Examination were being expressed in the educational press of the day. A writer in the *Journal of Education* pointed out that the time of year was inconvenient and that the set-books and question-papers were often unsatisfactory. He reserved his heaviest fire for Sallust's *Jugurtha*, remarking that 'the present writer, who has gone through the experience, not easily forgotten, of taking a class of boys in a second-grade school, of ages between fourteen and sixteen, through Sallust's interminable vagaries on the subjects, now of Africa and now of Roman politics, fails to see one single argument for the particular course adopted by the University authorities'.[5] The *Educational Times* noted that the Delegacy had at last taken action by arranging that there should in future be two examinations, one

---

[1] Minutes, 3 May 1873.
[2] Minute Book 1.
[3] *Del. Local Exams., First Annual Report* (1858); *Twenty-First Annual Report* (1878).
[4] *Oxford, Twenty-Sixth Annual Report* (1883); *Cambridge, Twenty-Sixth Annual Report* (1884).
[5] *Journal of Education*, vol. IV (1882), p. 214.

in June and another in July, and by allowing parents to decline the religious examination without stating that their objections were on conscientious grounds.[1] Whatever the justice of these complaints there is no doubt of the serious financial effects of a shrinking market. In 1882 the Delegacy adopted a new system of payments to examiners, based on an initial payment of three guineas for setting a paper, together with a reduced rate per set of answers. On this basis, using the 1881 entries, the payments to examiners would have been reduced from £1,325 to £1,198.[2] However this system itself did not last very long. In November 1883 the Delegacy considered the report of another committee which, in view of the fact that a considerable loss on the Women's Examination was expected to produce a small deficit, recommended that the payment for setting a paper be discontinued and that the payments to superintending examiners be reduced from 10 guineas to seven guineas. They also suggested that the University Press be asked to reduce the charges for paper and printing and that efforts should be made to get marks into the secretary's hands more rapidly after each examination. The greater part of the committee's recommendations were immediately adopted by the Delegates.[3] Clearly the key-note of the financial situation at Oxford in these years was retrenchment rather than expansion.

At the end of the first quarter-century then, the Cambridge Locals were in a much more prosperous condition than their Oxford partners. However the resemblances between the two are far more striking than the differences, and they can be discussed here together. The Delegacy and the Syndicate were confronted by very similar problems; similar too were the judgments passed by their examiners on the candidates, judgments which throw a very interesting light on the work done in the schools of the time. The examining work of both bodies brought them into close connection with the various plans which were put forward to improve middle-class education. From the very beginning examining was regarded as an important type of 'extension' work, as an almost missionary activity which would both raise the standards of the schools and bring forward a more numerous and a better trained group of

[1] *Educational Times*, vol. xxxvi (July 1883), p. 195.
[2] Del. Local Exams., Minutes, 8 March 1882.
[3] Minutes, 7 November, 4 December 1883.

entrants for the universities themselves. One form of 'extension' work which was very much in people's minds at the time was the training of teachers. In 1868 both the Syndicate and the Delegacy were approached by the Scholastic Registration Association with a request that a teacher's examination might be established. The Delegacy decided that it was not prepared to consider any such step 'in view of the approaching Report of the Schools Inquiry Commission, and pending the whole question of University Extension now under consideration'.[1] It clearly looked at the time as if the whole organization of secondary education was in the melting pot, and nothing was done. Nine years later the chemist G. D. Liveing put forward another proposal to the Syndicate that the Higher Local should include 'an examination in the principles and practice of Paedagogy'.[2] From the very beginning of the Women's Examinations, of course, the intention that they should be useful to women who were going to teach had been very much in everyone's mind.

One of the primary purposes of the Locals had always been to prepare able boys for Oxford and Cambridge who would not otherwise have had the opportunity to get there. Most of this side of the work will be discussed later in connection with local centres and the scholarships which they were sometimes able to award. Something, however, was done by those Oxford and Cambridge colleges who made awards on the results of the examinations. Of the two groups the Oxford colleges seem to have been the more generous. As early as 1867 Balliol, always a pioneer in a new development, were offering five exhibitions of fifty guineas tenable for four years to seniors obtaining the highest places in the general list, with three more exhibitions to be offered in 1868. In 1868 too Worcester were offering three or four exhibitions of £55.[3] In 1874 and 1875 Balliol and Worcester were still offering exhibitions, though a smaller number – Balliol, two of £40 for four years and Worcester one at least of £70 for four years. In addition Merton offered one of £80 for five years.[4] At Cambridge, colleges appear to have been less inclined to help. In 1872, after the question had been considered by the Syndicate, and the Manchester local committee had petitioned that colleges might be persuaded to take some action, a

[1] Del. Local Exams., Minutes, 18 February, 28 March, 9 May 1868; Local Exams Synd., Minutes, 30 April, 22 May 1868.
[2] Local Exams. Synd., Minutes, 19 November 1877.
[3] Del. Local Exams., Tenth Annual Report (1867), p. 9.
[4] Local Exams. Synd., Minutes, 26 November 1875.

generous offer was made by St John's. Two sizarships would be given:

with £20 a year added to each for two years, to the most distinguished candidates in each of the three years 1873, 1874, 1875, one to the boy who is first among those who receive the mark of distinction both in Pure and in Applied Mathematics, and the other to the boy who is the first among those who receive the mark of distinction both in Latin and in Greek (seniors).[1]

St John's went on offering these exhibitions, but its example was not followed by other colleges. In 1875 the Syndicate, impelled to take action by a fall in the number of boys as senior candidates, agreed to make enquiries about similar awards at Oxford and to ask members to bring the subject before their respective colleges. When the secretary reported to the Syndicate on his enquiries at Oxford, he explained that the Master of Balliol and the tutor of Worcester had given 'a very good account of the men to whom their exhibitions had been given for several years past'.[2]

Certainly the Locals brought forward able men who would never have gone to the university without the stimulus they provided, though it would be very dangerous to argue that, because a boy did well in them and then went on to Oxford or Cambridge, he would not have gone to the university otherwise. Some certainly were brought into higher education only by this means. Browne, the erstwhile Cambridge Secretary, claimed long afterwards in a debate in the Lords: 'I was personally concerned in saving at least three future senior wranglers, all of them of unusual mark even for senior wranglers, from their loss to their career. For one it cost three fights, in three successive years, to prevent the promising boy from going into an ironmonger's shop as an apprentice.'[3] There are a few more pieces of similar evidence. An author in the sixties mentions the son of a Devonshire tradesman in the village of St Mary Church who stood first in mathematics in the Locals of all the candidates in England and was thereby encouraged to go to Dublin University, where he was gaining the highest honours.[4]

[1] Local Exams. Synd., Minutes, 12 December 1872.
[2] Minutes, 10, 26 November 1875.
[3] *178 Parl. Deb.* 4th Series 1533–9; see also G. F. Browne, *The Recollections of a Bishop* (1915), p. 176.
[4] J. Mason Coxe, *Middle Class Education: A Letter to the Rt. Hon. the Earl of Devon* (1865), p. 10.

Many years after the first Oxford Examination the distinguished lawyer Edward Clarke told the candidates at a London prize-giving that in 1858 he had left school for a year or two and was in his father's business. He took the Oxford Examination and came out first in it. 'He was therefore', he said 'entitled to call himself the first Associate in Arts ever made by the University of Oxford. He remembered, as if it were the previous day, going with *The Times* in his hand, to tell his dear old schoolmaster of the success he had obtained, and the pleasure and shouting of the boys in the school.'[1]

This type of argument is however unsatisfactorily subjective; the only firm evidence which can be provided is to list the exhibitions which were awarded on the Locals and to review the subsequent careers of some of those who won them. The first point to make is that in some parts of the country there was little or no hope of a boy getting any help to carry his education further. Fortescue commented to Brereton in the sixties that Norfolk was stony ground for the Local Examinations and that the schools were suspicious of them.[2] No doubt the onset of agricultural depression, which was so keenly felt there, made things even worse. In 1882 Canon Hinds Howell, who had been secretary of the Cambridge Locals for almost twenty-five years, commented at a public enquiry in Norwich:

We have exceedingly clever boys who have distinguished themselves, and who coming from the class they do – many of them sons of tradesmen, farmers and artizans – would be greatly benefited if they could have attached to their schools just what Mr Tancock and Mr Pinder desire to have attached to theirs; that is, some means of getting to Oxford or Cambridge. I have constantly had to correspond with parents who have asked me 'Is there no means of helping my son to a scholarship?' and I have had to reply 'None whatever'.[3]

The scholarships founded in connection with the Locals were comparatively few in number. The first was the Albert scholarship founded by a public subscription of £1,000 at Liverpool in memory of the Prince Consort. It was first awarded in February 1863; the candidates were required to have been educated within seven miles of the Liverpool Exchange; the scholarship was awarded for three years by the Cambridge Syndicate and the scholar was required to

---

[1] *Educational Times*, vol. XXXIII (December 1880), p. 302. Clarke was made solicitor-general and knighted in 1886.

[2] Fortescue to Brereton, 7 June 1866.

[3] *Norfolk Chronicle and Norwich Gazette*, 28 October 1882 (reference supplied by Dr F. E. Balls).

become a member of the University of Cambridge.[1] It was fitting that the pioneer step should be taken by Liverpool which had from the beginning shown such a keen interest in the examinations. In 1866 two scholarships were founded by subscription in Staffordshire in memory of Edward, first Lord Hatherton, a Whig politician who had been Lord Lieutenant of the County. These scholarships, worth £50 a year for three years, were to be tenable at either Oxford or Cambridge and were to be awarded alternately on the results of the two Local Examinations.[2] Later awards of the same type at Oxford were the Abbott scholarships for the sons of clergymen[3] and the Dyke scholarship for boys from Somerset, Devon and Cornwall.[4] According to the 1898 regulations the Delegacy themselves were offering four scholarships for one year, £30 to a senior boy and girl, £10 to a junior boy and girl, while the Non-Collegiate Delegacy also offered a £50 exhibition to seniors.[5]

Many centres gave prizes to distinguished candidates, though these were honorific rather than valuable,[6] and, much more important, some of the public schools awarded exhibitions to Locals candidates under fifteen. The proposals for these scholarships were outlined at a meeting between a group of heads including Thring of Uppingham, Moss of Shrewsbury, Bell of Marlborough and Wickham of Wellington and the Delegacy in November 1882, at which G. F. Browne was also present. The boys were to be put forward by the Delegacy as exceptionally distinguished in the Locals and must be in need of financial assistance to meet the cost of a public-school education. The scholarships were to be awarded for two years only with the prospect of renewal if progress and conduct were satisfactory. They should be of sufficient value to reduce the cost per boy to £25–£30 per annum and the right of recommendation was to go alternately to Oxford and Cambridge unless the schoolmaster preferred to confine himself to one or other

[1] CUA, Guard Book 57.1, no. 32; *Local Exams. Synd., Fifth Annual Report* (1863).

[2] *Del. Local Exams., Ninth Annual Report* (1866), p. 13; Local Exams. Synd., Minutes, 17 November 1866.

[3] Del. Local Exams., Minutes, 15 December 1870.

[4] *Ibid.* 29 October, 11 November 1879, 18 February 1880.

[5] *Oxford Local Examinations 1885–1901: Regulations.*

[6] E.g. among many examples Oxford (*Prize Fund for Candidates examined in Oxford at the Local Examination, 1864* (Bodl. Lib. G.A. Oxon 8° 208); and Wolverhampton. (CUA, University Papers 1820–67) has an interesting notice about the Wolverhampton prize-giving of 1867.

university.[1] The *Journal of Education*, announcing the scheme in the spring of 1883, said that seventeen schools had offered such scholarships and commented: 'This is the best stroke of work that the Headmasters' Conference has yet done.'[2] From the Oxford regulations, however, it appears that only two or three schools offered these scholarships each year; for instance in 1885 Tonbridge offered an award of £67, Uppingham £90 and Wellington of the same amount though it was provided that the boy would be boarded and educated for £10 if he were the son of a deceased officer.[3]

No details can be discovered about the subsequent careers of these boys who won scholarships to public schools because they are nowhere named. Quite a lot can be said, however, about the undergraduates who went up to Cambridge with awards gained in the Locals; indeed many of them, especially the Liverpool contingent, were very able people. If the Syndicate reports are analysed for twenty-five years from 1863, when the Albert scholarship was first awarded, nineteen boys are named as either Albert or Hatherton scholars together with a few of the sizars of St John's whose names happen to be given.[4] Three of these either cannot be traced in Venn's *Alumni* or the identification is uncertain.[5] Most of the remaining sixteen went to St John's, probably because of the sizarships awarded by the College in the Locals. Of that total of sixteen, four gained first classes at least, three more became fellows of colleges, one at Oxford to which he had removed as an undergraduate; another two became professors in other universities. Two more Albert scholars, A. R. Forsyth, senior wrangler and later Sadleirian Professor of Pure Mathematics, and Sir Donald Macalister, vice-chancellor and chancellor of the University of Glasgow, were men of very considerable distinction. Probably not all the sixteen would have been especially poor boys, though one of the Hatherton scholars was the son of a butler. Macalister's case, however, is almost a copy-book example of the claims made by the advocates of the Locals. He was one of the large family of a Highland Scot who was a publisher's agent. He had been intended for business, but when he was fifteen he did so well in the Oxford Locals that

---

[1] See papers on the subject in Del. Local Exams., Minute Book, 1877–1904.
[2] *Journal of Education*, vol. v. p. 129 (1 April 1883).
[3] *Oxford Local Examinations, 1885–1901: Regulations.*
[4] For the sizarships at St John's awarded on the Locals see p. 141.
[5] The following details come from J. A. Venn, *Alumni Cantabrigienses*, Part II (1752–1900).

he was advised by his headmaster to try for the university. During his last three years at the Liverpool Institute he paid his fees by scholarships and eventually won the Albert scholarship and the St John's sizarship together with another local exhibition. He also gained exhibitions at Balliol and Worcester but preferred to go to Cambridge. He was senior wrangler and first Smith's prizeman in 1877.[1]

There is no information available to provide a parallel study of Oxford award-winners, but an interesting vignette of one of the Oxford scholarships is provided in a speech by Acland at the Bible Christian College at Shebbear. One of the boys, H. W. Horwill, had won the Dyke scholarship. Acland explained that his chief rival had been a boy named Thomson of Kingswood and the trustees had had great difficulty in deciding – Thomson, for instance, had passed in the rudiments of faith and religion and Horwill in holy scripture only. Finally they chose Horwill who was two years the older of the two and would not have another opportunity to sit, whereas Thomson could have two more attempts. Horwill was planning, it may be noted, to go to Oxford as an 'unattached student'.[2]

It is a remarkable fact that, within a very few years, the influence of the Locals was being felt in British possessions overseas. Examinations proved eminently suitable for export, and by the end of the century the overseas work of the Cambridge Syndicate was of great importance. In 1898, the fortieth anniversary year, there were 36 colonial centres and 1,220 colonial candidates, one of whom was placed highest among the senior boys.[3] Indeed the overseas centres had a history in 1898 almost as long as that of the Locals themselves. In the annual report for 1862 the Syndicate mentioned that an application had been received for an examination in Trinidad. The arrangements had not been fully settled but there appeared to be no insuperable difficulties in the way.[4] Early the following year the secretary wrote to the Oxford Delegates in very encouraging terms.[5]

[1] E. F. B. Macalister, *Sir Donald Macalister of Tarbert* (1935), pp. 11 ff.

[2] *Intermediate Schools on a Confessedly Religious Basis* (Exeter, 1882).

[3] *Local Examinations of the University of Cambridge, 1858–1898* (a leaflet prepared for English Education Exhibition, London, January 1900).

[4] *Local Exams. Synd., Fourth Annual Report* (1862), p. 8.

[5] Del. Local Exams., Minutes, 7 February 1863. The letter is dated 30 January 1863.

We arranged with the folk at Trinidad to send out the papers of questions to the Governor, who undertook to be responsible for their proper distribution; and he named to us the Inspector of Schools as the most proper person to superintend the examination while in progress and to seal up the papers and send them over to us at the close of the examination. The results are to be published in a second edition of our class lists, as they can hardly be ready for the first edition.

No arrangement has been made for examinations in Natal, but our Syndicate agreed to do for them as much as for the people of Trinidad.

The Syndicate and the Delegacy had been in touch with one another because Oxford had also received a similar request from Natal. A committee of the Delegacy reported that such an extension of their work would be perfectly practicable and it was agreed that the Hebdomadal Council should be asked to get the Statute establishing the Delegacy amended, so as to cover the Natal application.[1] It is not clear from the records whether any Natal candidates were sent in. The Syndicate successfully examined ten candidates in Trinidad in 1863, partly as the annual report explained 'by the great assistance rendered by the Governor of the Colony, and the gentleman he appointed to superintend the examination; and partly, by the courtesy of his Grace the Secretary of State for the Colonies, the Duke of Newcastle, who permitted the Examination papers to be sent in *sealed* parcels to the Governor through the Colonial Office'.[2]

Those ten candidates of 1863 in Trinidad were the first of the mighty army who were to sit Cambridge Overseas Examinations during the ensuing century. During the next ten or twelve years growth was slow. In 1869–70 approaches were made about an examination in Natal, and in October 1870 the Syndicate decided to extend its examinations to that colony.[3] Favourable replies were given to requests for centres at Prince Alfred College, Adelaide[4] (October 1871), in Mauritius[5] (February 1873) and in Wellington (New Zealand) and George Town (Demerara)[6] in November 1874. In the last case, since the application came from a congregationalist minister, the Syndicate clearly felt that it must be cautious and the

---

[1] Del. Local Exams., Minutes, 6 December 1862, 7, 13 February 1863.
[2] *Local Exams. Synd.*, *Sixth Annual Report* (1864).
[3] Minutes, 16 November 1869, 25 March, 24 October 1870.
[4] Minutes, 30 October 1871.
[5] Minutes, 12 February 1873.
[6] Minutes, 11 November 1874.

secretary 'was instructed to require the appointment of a representative local committee'! By this time the needs of the colonial centres were affecting the whole time-table of the Syndicate's work; in 1875 it was decided that the papers for December must be prepared before the end of the Easter Term so that the parcels for the colonies might be sent in September and early October.[1]

There is little sign of any similar interest in overseas examining in the papers of the Oxford Delegacy. In March 1874 they considered a request for an examination in Nassau (Bahamas) and agreed to hold one if the governor desired it and time permitted.[2] The following year, however, it was decided that, although an exception might be made for Nassau on this occasion since negotiations had already begun, 'it is inexpedient for the Delegacy to undertake Examinations out of the United Kingdom'.[3] Other requests were however considered from time to time. In November 1874 the Delegacy declined a request that they should examine candidates in Albany (U.S.A.).[4] Two years later, on the application of the philologist Max Müller, they agreed that certain papers might be taken by a young lady living in Germany on the understanding that she would not in any case receive a certificate.[5] In general, the Delegacy's policy in this, as in other fields, was conservative, and Cambridge was left to head the field overseas.

Although such questions as teacher-training, college exhibitions and overseas centres were of importance at the time and are of great interest today, the records of the Delegacy and the Syndicate concentrate largely on the day-to-day working of the Locals themselves. Marks had to be harmonized and adjusted; schoolmasters angry at unsuitable set-books or difficult question-papers had to be pacified; examiners had to be kept up to the mark or removed if they fell below it; local committees had to be encouraged or chided; care had to be taken to see that some schoolmasters did not take unfair advantages and that some candidates did not cheat. The greatest problem in large-scale examining is to ensure that the marks given by different examiners and marks in different papers are consistent with one another. In modern practice elaborate measures are taken to see that these aims are achieved. Clearly the pioneers appreciated

[1] Minutes, 11 May 1875.
[2] Del. Local Exams., Minutes, 7 March 1874.
[3] Minutes, 20 November 1875.
[4] Minutes, 7 November 1874.
[5] Minutes, 26 April 1876.

their importance. When the very first examination was being planned at Oxford, it was suggested that a special committee be set up to communicate with examiners and to receive their reports, so as to ensure 'the general consistency of the examination as a whole, and ... its adaptation to the age of the candidates, and to the great variety of the systems under which they may have been respectively educated'.[1] A few years later the Syndicate was appointing committees, one to revise the total marks in the various subjects with power to alter them if necessary and another 'to devise a better method of checks to insure accuracy in the conduct of the examinations'.[2] Unfortunately the surviving records give no details of the methods by which this was to be done, though there are numerous examples of the difficulties which occurred when it was not done.

The theory was unimpeachably stated in a letter which the secretary of the Delegacy was instructed to write to examiners in 1873.[3] Papers were to be framed in accordance with the regulations; they should be adjusted both to the age of the candidates and to the time available, they should be of such length that an excellent candidate could answer them thoroughly; there must be sufficient elementary questions for average candidates. Naturally things did not always work out like that. The papers were generally set by academics with little knowledge of school-work, and in the earlier years schoolmasters were neither well organized nor vocal, though this changed very markedly in the last decade of the century after the foundation of the Incorporated Association of Headmasters in 1890.[4] A much earlier example of pressure from the schools is a trio of resolutions considered by the Syndicate in 1874, which emanated from the Association of the Masters of the Endowed Schools of Warwickshire, Worcestershire, Shropshire and Staffordshire.[5] The association urged that the pass subjects in senior mathematics had been made much more difficult so that boys of only average mathematical ability were deterred from taking the subject. They also recommended that candidates in this section should be able to satisfy the examiners by passing in Euclid Books

---

[1] Del. Local Exams., Minutes, 29 April 1858.
[2] Local Exams. Synd., Minutes, 29 November 1864, 11 May 1865.
[3] Del. Local Exams., Minutes, 15 March 1873.
[4] See p. 246.
[5] Local Exams. Synd., Minutes, 28 April 1874.

I to IV and in algebra to quadratic equations inclusive, and that the algebra paper should be divided into two parts, the first part only being regarded as indispensable. So far as junior candidates were concerned, the association urged that a 'consistent regard should be paid to the proficiency that may be fairly expected of boys under 16 years of age'.

When actual mistakes occurred examiners' decisions had sometimes to be reversed. In 1873 the Delegacy was put to a good deal of trouble over the marking of the history paper in the Preliminary Examination for senior candidates. After complaints had been received from the chairman of several local committees, an enquiry was made, and it was decided that of the 58 unsuccessful candidates, 48 would have passed if the marking had not been far too severe. Finally, after consulting the examiner in senior history it was decided that candidates should be allowed to pass in the preliminary paper, who had obtained 16 marks at least.[1] When things went wrong in this way efforts were usually made to see that similar mistakes did not occur on future occasions. In January 1876 the Syndicate was led, as the result of an error in the junior algebra paper, to consider 'the propriety of requiring all examiners to attend the meeting for the revision of the examination papers as well as that for the final entering of the marks in the mark book of the Section to which they belong'.[2] A year later, in order to secure more careful revision of questions, it was agreed that a copy of each paper should be sent to each examiner at least a week before the meeting to revise the papers.[3]

One perpetual source of trouble was the set-books in modern languages, which were sometimes considered to contain unsuitable passages. In 1873 the Syndicate set up a committee to consider the issue of expurgated editions.[4] Two years later the secretary reported that he had received many complaints about the French and German books published by the Pitt Press and that letters had also appeared in the *Standard* about them.[5] In 1876 the Syndicate had withdrawn Alphonse Karr's *Autour de mon Jardin* and had received a letter of complaint from the headmaster of Framlingham College

[1] Del. Local Exams., Minutes, 15, 22, 29 November 1873.
[2] Local Exams. Synd., Minutes, 28 January 1876.
[3] Local Exams Synd., Minutes, 26 February 1877.
[4] Minutes, 3 December 1873.
[5] Minutes, 10 November 1875. The *Standard* is mentioned in a note in Minute Book 1.

about *Die Harzreise*.[1] In 1871 a complaint was received about Goethe's *Egmont* which had been set as the verse subject for seniors, though it was decided to retain it.[2] Goethe's works were again causing trouble in 1875 when the editor of the school text expressed unwillingness to remove one or two lines from *Hermann und Dorothea*. Here, however, the Syndicate would make no concessions and minuted 'that the subjects would not be considered a satisfactory one for the purposes of the Local Examinations if the lines were not removed'.[3] Even the withdrawal of an unsuitable book did not always end the trouble. At Oxford the Delegacy on one occasion decided to introduce a new book for junior French since some undesirable passages had been found in the old one. This led to complaints from several schoolmasters about the change and it was decided to give candidates the option of taking either book.[4] A more novel reason for a change was forced upon the Syndicate in 1870 when the book originally chosen for junior French had to be given up, 'being difficult to obtain in consequence of the siege of Paris' or as the draft minutes say more picturesquely, 'being locked up in Paris'.[5]

Relations with local centres and with schools sometimes needed care and diplomacy. There could be real problems of interpretation: for instance, in 1870 the Syndicate considered a request from the Brighton centre that certificates might be given to three boys who had passed in the preliminary section and two other sections but had not obtained a sufficient aggregate of marks. The request was declined on the ground that the requirement to satisfy the examiners on the whole result of the examination was more important than the subsidiary requirement of passing in particular papers.[6] It was clearly a constant problem to ensure that local committees made adequate arrangements for the conduct of the examination and provided proper supervision while it was going on.[7] The difficulties which could occur can be seen from a complaint

[1] Minutes, 15 July, 11 October 1867.
[2] Minutes, 23 February 1871.
[3] Minutes, 26 November 1875.
[4] Del. Local Exams., Minutes, 24 October 1868, 6 February 1869.
[5] Local Exams. Synd., Minutes 2 December 1870. The draft minutes are in Minute Book 1.
[6] Local Exams. Synd., Minutes, 3 June 1870. The letter addressed to the Brighton centre is in Minute Book 1.
[7] Minutes, 21 November 1870, 3 May 1872; *Eighth Annual Report* (1866), p. 2.

by girl candidates at Manchester that they had been unable to do the English grammar paper properly as the result of 'the confusion which prevailed in the examination room, due to a ball having been held in the room on the previous night'. It was decided that the Syndicate could do nothing since the local committee ought to have taken steps to prevent the confusion which had ensued.[1] This was rather hard on the candidates perhaps, but the case does show the vital importance of the local committees in the management of the examinations.

Relations between the local committees and schools and the authorities at Oxford and Cambridge centred on the presiding examiners, and there were sometimes difficulties. One Cambridge centre where difficulties can be sensed was Huddersfield where, as the Syndicate noted in 1875, the principal of the Collegiate School had made a speech in which he described the examiners appointed by the Syndicate as comparatively young and in-experienced men.[2] Two years later there was further trouble there about candidates copying from one another. When trouble arose with presiding examiners it sprang either from unpunctuality or from giving out the papers at the wrong time. After the 1875 examination the Syndicate had to apologize to the Birmingham committee which had reported that the presiding examiner was one and a quarter hours late on one of the mornings of the examina-tion, the examiner himself admitting that he was an hour late.[3] A year or two earlier the secretary had been instructed to look into a report that at one important centre the previous year the presiding examiner had given out the Saturday's papers on the Friday. If this proved to be so, the examiner was to be told that the Syndicate did not wish him to seek re-appointment for the current year.[4] No details are given in the Minute Book of the offences which led the Master of Stroud Grammar School to refuse to pay the fee for Mr Finlaison's examination of his school. The Syndicate decided to pay Finlaison out of their own funds and not to employ him again in any capacity, resolving that the claim on the school should be waived 'in order to be rid of a very disagreeable subject'.[5]

[1] Minutes, 14 March 1872.
[2] Minutes, 26 November 1875.
[3] Minutes, 28 January 1876.
[4] Minutes, 11 November 1874.
[5] Minutes, 24 October 1876.

Such unpleasant problems as these represent, of course, but a tiny fraction of the hundreds and hundreds of harmonious transactions between the authorities, their examiners, and the schools and candidates. Sometimes it was the latter class which created the problems in the form of candidates who cheated and schoolmasters whose behaviour was not straightforward. In fact there were comparatively few of either class. The Delegacy decided in 1861 that no certificates should be given to any one of four candidates who had been caught copying.[1] Five years later the annual report of the Syndicate mentioned thirteen junior candidates who had also been detected.[2] The Syndicate had to consider two more cases after the 1876 examination. One was at the Totteridge Park centre where most of the candidates came from one school and where copying had already been detected on an earlier occasion. The Local secretary was informed that if any more cases were discovered the Syndicate would cease to hold an examination at Totteridge Park. The second case was at Huddersfield where, as we have seen, there had already been some friction with a local headmaster. In December 1876 the secretary of the Syndicate received an anonymous letter purporting to be from a Huddersfield candidate saying that copying was general there. A telegram was sent to the presiding examiner who detected two boys in the act of asking questions of their neighbour. It was then discovered that the writer of the letter was an assistant master who was about to leave the school from which the candidates came, and who named some of the alleged offenders to the presiding examiner. Presumably some spite or motive of revenge lay behind the assistant master's action. Eventually it was concluded, after enquiries had been made, that the papers of the accused candidates did not show any signs of unfair assistance, though two boys were rejected, one for asking his neighbour a date and the latter candidate for again passing the question on to the next boy (though the second boy was rejected in one subject only). Probably as a result of these cases the Syndicate decided that the index numbers of any candidates rejected for copying should be inserted at the end of the class lists.[3] A much more unusual type of offender was the man who wrote to the Syndicate in April 1870 saying that in December 1862 when he

[1] Del. Local Exams., Minutes, 15, 24 July 1861.
[2] *Local Exams. Synd., Eighth Annual Report* (1866), pp. 1–2.
[3] Local Exams. Synd., Minutes, 3, 26 February 1877.

had obtained second class honours, he had copied from his neighbour in the French, history and catechism papers. It was decided to cancel his honours certificate and to give him an ordinary certificate instead.[1] There is no clue as to what made the man confess an offence more than seven years after it had taken place.

The Syndicate rarely had trouble with headmasters, and the few cases which occurred were usually connected with the examination of schools. In 1871 the secretary was instructed to write to the editor of the *Liverpool Courier* about a false statement which had appeared in his paper about honours obtained in the examination by pupils of Alston College.[2] Later the same year a letter of rebuke was sent to the Master of Trinity School, Stony Stratford, who had printed the examiner's report on his school with the omission of paragraphs containing criticisms. The secretary was instructed to tell masters that if examiners' reports were printed they must be given in full.[3] A more complex case occurred a few years later when an examiner obviously felt that a headmaster was using the machinery of the Syndicate's examination to give a false impression of the achievements of his boys.[4] The head, Dr Cranage of the Old Hall School, Wellington, Salop, had applied for a re-examination of his school. At the beginning of the year Cranage circulated an extensive programme of work in accordance with which the examiners were asked to set their papers. The examiners reported that a considerable part of the work was not attempted by the boys, that it was Cranage's practice to circulate the programme and the question papers with the report, and that in his view the system was a bad one. Cranage complained that this report was unnecessarily damaging, and the Syndicate eventually decided on a compromise, decreeing 'that if Dr Cranage abandoned the circulation of the programme and examination papers, the report might be so far modified as to deal with the actual performance of the boys'.

Many of these reports of the examination of schools have survived, and some of them will be considered later as they form a very valuable source of material on the operation of the Locals. Even more valuable is the complete set of the annual reports of the

---

[1] Minutes, 4 May 1870.
[2] Minutes, 13 March 1871. The ensuing examples are all from Cambridge because Oxford did not advertise any scheme of school examinations until 1876.
[3] Minutes, 27 November 1871.
[4] Minutes, 9 May 1877.

Delegacy and the Syndicate beginning in 1858 and 1859 respectively. There are few better sources of information about the academic work of the schools for which the Locals catered, broadly the 'second-grade schools' of the Taunton Commission Report which aimed to take their pupils up to about the age of seventeen. The mass of criticism and comment contained in the annual reports is bulky and difficult to analyse. Some years were good, others bad, some examiners were kindly, others the reverse, but an attempt has been made in the ensuing paragraphs to build up a composite picture of the candidates' work for the first twenty years or so, studying it according to the main subject divisions of the school curriculum. There are a few general comments which apply to all subjects alike. The early Oxford reports stressed the improvement which the examination had effected in the work of the schools; in 1863 reference was made to a marked raising of the standard both in the preliminary subjects and in literature and mathematics.[1] Naturally this could not continue indefinitely, and three years later the Oxford report commented that the level had now settled down and that no great changes either for better or for worse were to be expected.[2] The great difference in performance between candidates from different centres was often stressed, and the natural conclusion pointed out that 'such a difference can only arise from good teaching in one case and bad teaching in the other'.[3] Another contrast which was often brought out by the Cambridge examiners in particular was the marked difference in performance between boys and girls. The former tended to be much better at mathematical subjects generally; the latter were much better at French; the difference again must have reflected the strong and the weak points of their schools. The girls were thought to be better at expressing themselves than the boys, though it was a rather backhanded compliment to remark, like the Cambridge examiner in religious knowledge in 1869, that 'it was curious to observe how in many cases a girl in answer to a question about which she evidently knew nothing, could nevertheless cover a sheet of paper with very fairly expressed English conveying no information whatever either right or wrong!'[4]

[1] *Del. Local Exams.*, *Sixth Annual Report* (1863), p. 5.
[2] *Del. Local Exams.*, *Ninth Annual Report* (1866), p. 3.
[3] *Local Exams. Synd.*, *Twentieth Annual Report* (1878), p. 5.
[4] *Local Exams. Synd.*, *Eleventh Annual Report* (1869), p. 8.

The Oxford reports pointed out on many occasions the excessively routine nature of the teaching and the prevalence of cramming without much concern for relevance or independent thought.[1] However there is no sign that the examiners were self-critical enough to consider how far this was a natural result of the system of written examinations or even how far their papers were arranged so as to reduce the evil to the smallest possible dimensions. Another frequent cause of complaint was the number of candidates who entered for subjects of which they were really quite ignorant. 'It is evident', wrote the Oxford examiner in 1872, 'that many candidates offer for Examination subjects in which they cannot have any reasonable expectation of passing; that they do not take pains to understand the drift of the questions put before them, and that they waste time in writing answers of which they are wholly ignorant. The Delegates wish to discourage the practice of offering a variety of subjects with which the candidates are very slightly acquainted.'[2] The Syndicate noted at about the same time that with the rapid increase in the number of Cambridge candidates the percentage of failures had greatly increased, partly because many of their teachers had no previous experience of the standard required.[3] An increasing proportion of failures was not necessarily a bad thing if it meant that schools were not merely selecting a few bright boys but were sending in whole classes. The critics of the Locals in the early days had been particularly severe on the bad results of sending in only a few boys from each school. The Syndicate mentioned several times during the seventies that this was becoming far less common and that the examination was being used far more as a test of the whole school. To do this, it was claimed, was to provide much more incentive to really careful teaching of all the boys.[4]

All candidates both at Oxford and Cambridge had to take the preliminary subjects, and, although after the first few years they ceased to be a stumbling block as they had been at the beginning, they remained fatal to the chances of many candidates. The figures varied from year to year, but in 1878 22·8% of Oxford seniors failed in them and 8·7% of juniors.[5] At Cambridge in the seventies

[1] *Del. Local Exams.*, *Twelfth Annual Report* (1869), p. 3.

[2] *Del. Local Exams.*, *Fifteenth Annual Report* (1872), p. 4.

[3] *Local Exams. Synd.*, *Thirteenth Annual Report* (1871), p. 5.

[4] *Local Exams. Synd.*, *Nineteenth Annual Report* (1877), pp. 6–7; *Twenty-First Annual Report* (1879), pp. 14–15.

[5] *Del. Local Exams.*, *Twenty-First Annual Report* (1878).

there is constant reference to the weakness of the girls in arithmetic, the subject which had been so fatal to them in the trial examination of 1863.[1] The trouble arose, the examiners thought, from defective teaching and obsolete textbooks.[2] In the early days there are numerous references both at Cambridge and at Oxford to the connection between the standards of the Preliminary and of the Civil Service Examinations; for instance the Cambridge examiner of 1859, Mr Headlam of the Civil Service Commission, reported that the juniors who had passed in arithmetic would be able to pass for offices where elementary arithmetic only was required, whereas many seniors who had passed would not be able to succeed in departments requiring a knowledge of vulgar and decimal fractions.[3] As the years went on, however, these references to the Civil Service and to the standards achieved by pupil-teachers drop out of the reports. Presumably the connection between the Locals, the Civil Service Examinations and the training of teachers which had been so strongly felt in the pioneering days was much less strongly felt once the Locals themselves had developed their own traditions.

The comments on separate subjects can be divided between the languages (ancient and modern), mathematics with a little science, and the English subjects. Languages meant primarily Latin and French. The earliest Cambridge reports take a favourable view of the classical papers, commenting that the unprepared Latin was done by seniors 'as well as it would be done by the average of Freshmen at Cambridge'.[4] This was perhaps no very exalted claim to make, but the early Oxford reports strike a wise note of caution. The report for 1859 pointed out that in all languages candidates were pushed on too fast;[5] the result, said a later report, was to produce 'showy Examination papers' but not 'sound scholarship'.[6] If the examiner's criticisms are to be believed, the method of teaching Latin and Greek used in the schools was to prepare very carefully the set-book, often by learning it by heart in translation. The result was that although the candidates knew their book in a mechanical fashion they had no real understanding of the structure

[1] See p. 110.
[2] E.g. *Local Exams. Synd., Fourteenth Annual Report* (1872), p. 7.
[3] *Second Annual Report* (1860), pp. 3–4.
[4] *Local Exams Synd., Third Annual Report* (1861), p. 6.
[5] *Del. Local Exams., Second Annual Report* (1859), pp. 4–5.
[6] *Eighth Annual Report* (1865), p. 8.

of the Latin language nor any idea of how to apply the rules of accidence and syntax to translating an unseen passage or to composing from English into Latin. The Oxford report of 1872 said of the senior Latin: 'the questions from the accidence were with marked exceptions answered well, and Candidates whose Latin writing had presented every monstrosity of formation and every violation of every "concord" were able to write down the perfects of the verbs asked for with an accuracy that surprised me. Their power of memory evidently outstripped that of observation.'[1] Candidates often had a good mastery of the grammatical rules but had neither the understanding to apply them nor any real practice in writing the language. In 1877 forty-five and a half per cent of the Oxford juniors failed to pass in Latin and lacked the most elementary knowledge of the language.[2]

The Cambridge reports tell much the same story, though they put even more emphasis on the candidates' sheer ignorance of the grammar. The severest criticisms were reserved for the juniors; in 1864 their translations were 'an unconnected tissue of words';[3] the following year their compositions ignored the most elementary rules and were eked out with French and German words.[4] In 1872 over half the juniors who took Caesar failed to pass in it; the examiner commented that 'it frequently happened that a passage was translated with remarkable accuracy by a candidate who showed in his next answer that he had not mastered even the elementary rudiments of the language'.[5] It is only fair to point out, however, that in the same year the senior Latin was well prepared and carefully done. In 1874 the Syndicate decided that candidates would not be allowed to pass in Latin, Greek, French or German without a fair knowledge of the accidence of the language, a rule which led to many failures in the December Examination of that year.[6] In 1878 candidates were required to attempt a passage of unseen translation, which revealed that many of them had no experience in translating at sight and could not even make use of the vocabulary given.[7] However the reports for the later seventies suggest that

[1] *Del. Local Exams., Fifteenth Annual Report* (1872), p. 9.
[2] *Twentieth Annual Report* (1877).
[3] *Local Exams. Synd., Seventh Annual Report* (1865), p. 8.
[4] *Eighth Annual Report* (1866), p. 7.
[5] *Local Exams. Synd., Fifteenth Annual Report* (1873), p. 11.
[6] Minutes, 22 May 1874; *Seventeenth Annual Report* (1875), p. 7.
[7] *Twenty-First Annual Report* (1879).

tightening up the requirements did gradually produce better work, and the general impression given by them is that some of the worst weaknesses were being overcome. The remarks about the French and German are very similar to the remarks about the Latin. In French the girls were on the whole better than the boys.[1] Many of the boys' answers were simply worthless; they had little idea how to translate a piece of easy French and their ignorance of the grammar defeated their attempts at composition; in 1868 the examiners commented, even among the better scholars of the seniors, on 'a ludicrous ignorance of grammar or indifference as to spelling. In their composition parlez, parlé, parlais, parlaient, etc., seem to be looked upon as convertible terms to be used with impartiality.'[2] Towards the end of the seventies the standard of French, like that of Latin, seems to have been going up, but the compositions still tended to be mere strings of words joined together without any regard for grammatical rules and the examiners suggested that the root of the trouble was the failure of the schools to set regular written exercises.[3]

The mathematical reports provide some of the sharpest contrasts between different candidates and centres. The standard of teaching in some schools was very defective and many boys and girls entered who had no hope of passing because they had never mastered the rudiments of the subject. When the Oxford report of 1872 speaks as follows of the junior mathematics, it was voicing a general opinion: 'One candidate states apologetically that he has "only been learning Algebra for three months, and has not been allowed to give more than two hours a week to it". This is probably only one out of some hundreds of instances in which sufficient attention has not been bestowed upon this subject to warrant any expectation of success.'[4] A few years later the Oxford reports again complained that far too many candidates aimed simply at a minimum which was thought to be sufficient for passing; if, in consequence, the standard was slightly lowered one year, there was a general deterioration the year following since teachers gauged

---

[1] *Fourteenth Annual Report* (1872).
[2] *Eleventh Annual Report* (1869), p. 9.
[3] *Twentieth Annual Report* (1878), p. 11; *Twenty-Second Annual Report* (1880); *Camb. Univ. Rep.* 1879–80, p. 495. The Twenty-Second and ensuing reports of the Syndicate are printed in the *Reporter.*
[4] *Del. Local Exams., Fifteenth Annual Report* (1872), p. 13.

the standard of lowest requirement very exactly.[1] The Cambridge reports put much emphasis on the inferiority of the girls' work to that of the boys. Though in the first official examination of girls in 1865, they made a good recovery from the debacle in arithmetic of the first examination of 1863,[2] there were plenty of complaints later. In 1872 only six per cent of the girls obtained half marks in the arithmetic paper of the preliminary subjects; the unsuccessful failed through 'inaccuracy in the earliest rules; confusion of arrangement, contrasting most unfavourably with much of the boys' work and undoubtedly the result of careless teaching; and lastly, the use of obsolete and inaccurate methods to be attributed to the employment of bad text-books'.[3] In the previous year the junior girl candidates for the same paper had been cautioned 'against wasting time in the embellishment of their papers with superfluous lines and coloured inks'![4] Not many girls entered for the mathematics papers proper, but of those who did some achieved good results.[5] On the boys' work the general comment is often made that they had not been taught the principles of the subject properly, so that, for instance in their Euclid, the use of definitions was much too inexact and slapdash.[6]

The natural sciences can be discussed briefly because comparatively few candidates offered them. Indeed it is remarkable that from the very beginning both Local Examinations offered a full range of scientific papers at a time when science had certainly not become a regular part of English school work. A few statistics show the numbers involved. At the 1878 examination at Cambridge for senior boys 461 took pure mathematics and 167 applied mathematics. 92 took theory of chemistry, 49 practical chemistry, 21 statics, 38 heat, 30 electricity, 15 zoology and 11 botany. Of the senior girls, on the other hand, considerably more took zoology (79) and botany (177) than pure mathematics (76); 962 senior girls took French.[7] The Oxford figures for 1877 are similar though

---

[1] *Twenty-Third Annual Report* (1880), p. 14; *Twenty-Fourth Annual Report* (1881), p. 13.

[2] *Local Exams. Synd., Eighth Annual Report* (1866), pp. 9–10.

[3] *Local Exams. Synd., Fourteenth Annual Report* (1872), p. 5.

[4] *Thirteenth Annual Report* (1871), p. 6.

[5] *Fifteenth Annual Report* (1873), p. 14.

[6] *First Annual Report* (1859), pp. 9–10; *Second Annual Report* (1860), pp. 6–7; *Del. Local Exams., Tenth Annual Report* (1867), p. 7.

[7] *Local Exams. Synd., Twenty-First Annual Report* (1879).

chemistry was rather less prominent among scientific subjects.[1] The first Oxford report commented that chemistry was the only scientific subject much taught, that the physics stood at a decidedly lower level, and that in natural history there were hardly any candidates.[2] The complaint made in this first year that the scientific knowledge of candidates came entirely from books and that hardly any practical work had been done was to be echoed over and over again in later reports. The Oxford report of 1863, looking back over the first six years, commented that the level of the scientific work had actually declined. Since the requirements of the examination had been devised to exact a real test of knowledge, the schools had naturally concentrated on teaching languages and mathematics rather than science because they had the staff and equipment for one and not for the other.[3] Such candidates as there were learnt their textbook by rote and when they performed experiments, described not what they saw but what they thought they ought to have seen. This comment from the Cambridge report of 1872 is characteristic:

The papers of a majority of the boys abound in references to theories of chemistry while they show ignorance of the commonest chemicals and the simplest experimental laws. They draw no distinction between matters of theory and of fact, and even refer to theory by the way of proof of the experimental facts on which the theory is founded. The boys have been taught to manipulate chemical equations and they use them freely as a substitute for thought, evolving by means of them practical absurdities which a small acquaintance with chemicals would have led them to avoid.[4]

The great difficulty, of course, was that there was as yet no properly trained group of science teachers at work in the schools, and until such a group had been created, no real improvement could be expected.

The English subjects are the last major group which remains to be discussed. In English itself, history and geography a common criticism was constantly expressed – that candidates learnt their

---

[1] According to the Twentieth Annual Report (1877, Oxford) 315 seniors took mathematics, 47 electricity, 49 chemistry, 60 physiology, 14 geology and mineralogy. The Oxford figures do not distinguish boys from girls.

[2] Del. Local Exams., First Annual Report (1858), p. 16.

[3] Sixth Annual Report (1863), p. 5.

[4] Local Exams. Synd., Fourteenth Annual Report (1872), p. 15.

work quite uncritically and poured out their knowledge without much consideration for the relevance of what they were writing. The early Oxford and Cambridge reports point out that there was little systematic teaching of English grammar in the schools, though the Cambridge report for 1862 suggests that the introduction of Morell's *English Grammar* as a definite textbook in the examination had achieved an improvement.[1] Candidates' essays often came under attack for diffuseness and lack of arrangement, stemming again from the fact that they had received little instruction at school in how to organize their ideas on paper. The Oxford examiners even considered that essays had been prepared and learned by heart before the examination. 'On one subject', wrote the report of 1873, 'which seems to have been guessed in this way, I had whole essays apparently ready made; and on other subjects elaborate fragments, entirely off the point, were sometimes introduced as so much good material which should not be lost.'[2] In the papers on Shakespeare and other set-books the same type of teaching showed itself in the comparative neglect of the text and a very elaborate study of the notes given in the school edition. Candidates tended to learn the notes with mechanical accuracy and to be both vague and verbose when they got away from the shelter provided by this type of information; the senior Shakespeare papers, said the Cambridge report of 1876, 'give evidence of being the result of an inaccurate study of the notes in the Clarendon Press edition'.[3] In this subject too many of those who entered showed very little knowledge; usually the girls did better than the boys.

History and geography, like English, suffered from too much time spent in cramming small manuals and too little devoted to oral explanation by the teacher. In the mid-twentieth century, when history masters and mistresses are often criticized for teaching too much, it is interesting to note that their predecessors were criticized by the examiners of the 1860s and 1870s for teaching orally far too little. The method generally used at that time was to commit to memory as much as possible of 'the meagre and ill-arranged textbooks used in Schools',[4] books which often themselves

[1] *Fourth Annual Report* (1862), p. 6.
[2] *Del. Local Exams., Sixteenth Annual Report* (1873), p. 5; see also *Eighteenth Annual Report* (1875), p. 8.
[3] *Local Exams. Synd., Eighteenth Annual Report* (1876), p. 8.
[4] *Local Exams. Synd., Seventh Annual Report* (1865), p. 8

contained many errors.[1] The result was that the same answers were produced in wearisome iteration by candidate after candidate; they learned names and dates but were often very confused about the relationships of the one with the other and had no knowledge of the events themselves. The bizarre result is outlined in the Oxford report on junior history for 1879:

> The Candidates write too much and too hastily, and do not appear to think of what they are writing about. About half of them confused the Civil War of the fifteenth century with that of the seventeenth, and give the career of Wolsey for that of Becket or vice versa. Another common mistake is to confound Lambert the Parliamentary general, with Lambert Simnel, the pretender. The special portion (that of the civil war of the seventeenth century) was done better than the general questions, but here the Candidates constantly quote some phrases from the manual in which they have learnt the subject.[2]

One reason for the poor performance was, as the above extract makes clear, the very long time-span covered by the paper. The examiners were asking too much from boys under sixteen, however serious the boys' faults might appear.

In the geography papers the results of the methods used in the schools were that the subject was learned as an academic exercise without much reference to the physical characteristics of the earth or to the economic and political circumstances of modern nations. Candidates did not understand the difference between latitude and longitude;[3] they were unable to use the terms 'east' and 'west' correctly;[4] they filled in outline maps with rivers going over the highest range of mountains.[5] During the political storms of the mid-seventies over the Eastern Question the Oxford examiner noted that the majority of candidates considered the Suez Canal to be a 'scientific discovery',[6] and the Cambridge Examiner commented that 'the amount of ignorance shown of Turkey was striking, considering how much attention has been recently attracted to that country'.[7] The demands made by the examiners on candidates in

---

[1] Del. Local Exams., Nineteenth Annual Report (1876), p. 6.
[2] Twenty-Second Annual Report (1879), p. 8.
[3] Local Exams. Synd., Seventeenth Annual Report (1875), p. 12.
[4] Twentieth Annual Report (1878), p. 8.
[5] Eighteenth Annual Report (1876), p. 8.
[6] Del. Local Exams., Eighteenth Annual Report (1875), p. 9.
[7] Local Exams. Synd., Twentieth Annual Report (1878), p. 7.

these subjects were in some ways very great; the extent of the ground to be covered meant that cramming was unavoidable. Nevertheless the very force of the criticisms levelled at the teaching of the English subjects shows that they, like the natural sciences, had not yet been fully absorbed into the system of school instruction.

7
THE EXAMINERS AND THE EXAMINED

At the end of the seventies, when both the Delegacy and the Syndicate came of age, they were undertaking important new responsibilities through the growth of extension lectures to adults. The pioneer had been a young fellow of Trinity College, Cambridge, James Stuart, who gave a series of lectures to mixed audiences in northern towns in 1867. In 1873 the University of Cambridge gave the work official recognition and a syndicate with Stuart as secretary was set up to manage it.[1] When he resigned in 1875, he was succeeded by G. F. Browne, secretary of the Local Examinations Syndicate. It was natural at the time that both lectures and examinations should be regarded as part of the 'extension' work of the university, and in May 1878 the Local Examinations Syndicate voted in favour of a recommendation that the two syndicates for lectures and for examinations should be united.[2] A Grace passed the Senate in June of the same year,[3] and Browne became secretary of the United Syndicate. At Oxford events took a different course. Oxford had been slower than Cambridge in entering the field of extension lecturing, and there the Local Examinations machinery was used from the first. In December 1877 the Delegacy agreed at the request of the Hebdomadal Council, to undertake the work of lecturing and teaching in the large towns, and on 29 May 1878 A. H. D. Acland, son of the joint founder of the Locals, was appointed secretary for lectures.[4] His successor chosen in 1885, was M. E. Sadler (Sir Michael Sadler), later a prominent authority on the history and organization of education. When in 1892 a separate extension delegacy was set up, the Delegates for Local Examinations voted him their thanks for 'his unwearied, self-denying and successful efforts in their behalf'.[5] During these years the lecture-work loomed very large in men's minds. It is interesting

---

[1] W. H. Draper, *University Extension: A Survey of Fifty Years, 1873–1923* (1923), pp. 8–20; James Stuart, *Reminiscences* (1912), pp. 154ff.
[2] Local Exams. Synd., Minutes, 10 May 1878.
[3] CUA Guard Book 57.1, no. 81.
[4] Del. Local Exams., Minutes, 6 December 1877, 29 May 1878.
[5] *Ibid.* 21 May 1885, 3 November 1892.

to note that when a presentation was made to G. F. Browne in 1893 after he had left Cambridge, much more emphasis was placed by the speakers on the achievement of the extension lectures than on the Local Examinations themselves.[1]

Browne had been secretary of the Syndicate from 1870 to 1892 and his successor, J. N. Keynes, held office for almost as long a period (1892–1910). At Oxford secretaries came and went with much greater frequency until the appointment of H. T. Gerrans in 1887.[2] It is possible indeed that the long reigns of two such able men as Browne and Keynes may account for much of the success of the Cambridge Examinations during the latter part of the century. Browne was a Yorkshireman who had gone up to Catharine Hall, a college of which he later became a fellow, and who had also been for a short time an assistant master at Glenalmond. He was elected Secretary of the Local Examinations Syndicate in March 1870 after a keen contest in which he was chosen after three scrutinies and then only by the casting vote of the vice-chancellor.[3] For the next twenty years Browne was at the very centre of university affairs. He had already been proctor in 1867–9 and was to serve again in 1877–9 and 1879–81. He was the first editor of the *University Reporter*, first published in October 1870, and he held that office for twenty-one years. In 1874 he was elected to the Council of the Senate and three years later became Cambridge secretary of the Statutory Commission of 1877–81. In a quite different field of work, his election in 1887 to the Disney Chair of Archaeology was a recognition of his work on ancient inscribed stones. No wonder that when he had left Cambridge in 1892 for a canonry of St Paul's, the Master of Trinity, H. M. Butler, remarked in a speech at a presentation ceremony that 'Canon Browne seemed to be constitutionally omniscient with regard to the affairs of the University; he knew everything that had been done by every Syndicate, and the part played by every leading man, and he was at the service of anyone who asked him for advice. He was also struck with the essential fairness of mind which characterized every piece of advice that he

---

[1] CUA University Papers 1884–95, no. 644. The meeting was held at Peterhouse on 29 April 1893.

[2] The succession of Oxford Secretaries in these years is as follows: 1870 S. Edwardes (succeeded J. Griffiths); 1880 G. E. Baker; 1885 J. S. Lockhart; 1887 H. T. Gerrans.

[3] There is a note of the voting in the Minute Book of the Local Examinations Syndicate. The vice-chancellor was Edward Atkinson, Master of Clare.

gave.' Another speaker on the same occasion made the same point
with greater pungency: 'Some of them on the Council knew, or
thought they knew, something about one or two things, but Canon
Browne seemed to know something about everything, and, what
was more, he knew it right too.'[1]

Clearly Browne was a very able administrator with remarkable
powers of hard work. His detailed care for what went on in the
Syndicate is illustrated in the following story. A few years ago a
mirror was taken down in a cloak-room in the old building in Mill
Lane. Behind the mirror, written on the plaster were the words
'Put the mirror here GFB'.[2] His relationship with the Syndics
seems to have been an extremely happy one on both sides. When he
left Cambridge they recorded their appreciation of his ungrudging
service, wisdom and forethought, tact and courtesy, and added
that by these qualities 'he inspired confidence in his management of
one of the most important branches of Cambridge work to a quite
exceptional degree'.[3] As a man Browne was a curious mixture of
acuteness, warm-heartedness and self-importance. As an old man,
after his retirement from the see of Bristol, he wrote a very enter-
taining autobiography.[4] In the preface he tells the story of a once
popular preacher who was publishing a book of sermons and who
found that the proofs suddenly dried up. The printer, explained
that he had run out of his stock of 'capital I' and was having some
more cast. Browne went on to explain that, although the supply
of 'capital I' had not run out for his book 'an indecent amount of it
has been used'.[5] He perceived his own weaknesses correctly. He
could be very self-satisfied; for instance, some of the stories in his
book display him as the wise man who foresaw all the difficulties
and always found the right answers to tricky problems. He wrote
to Keynes, his assistant and successor, in 1896 that he was being
told on all sides that the clergy and laity of the diocese of London
would have elected him to the bishopric at the recent vacancy if
thay had had the power.[6] Yet he also had the insight to see his own
limitations; a few days after the letter just quoted to Keynes, he

[1] CUA University Papers 1884–95, no. 644. The second speaker was James
Porter, Master of Peterhouse.
[2] This story was told me by the present general secretary, Mr T. S. Wyatt.
[3] Local Exams. Synd., Minutes, 16 March 1892.
[4] *The Recollections of a Bishop* (1915).
[5] *Ibid.* p. v.
[6] CUL Add. 7562 [J. N. Keynes' correspondence], 22 November 1896.

wrote again saying that he had no ambition in the ordinary sense, and going on: 'The talk about Canterbury and London, which very freely connected my name with those vacancies, made me ask myself a curious question, am I *able*, or only *ready?* And the answer was, "only ready". And that won't do for a really big place.'[1]

To balance the self-importance Browne had two admirable redeeming qualities. He was a man of complete integrity who bore no malice, and he was very warm-hearted. He played an active part in the politics of the university, borough and county of Cambridge on the Conservative side. H. M. Butler, as we have seen, commented on his fairness of mind. Browne fought hard, but he fought in the open and there was no meanness about him. His friend, Henry Bradshaw the university librarian, remarked, about a book Browne had written, on 'the total absence of what we call here [in King's] little vipers',[2] and the same point might be made about Browne's public life. He was on very friendly terms with Keynes, whose political views were very different from his own. When Browne went to Bristol in 1897, he wrote: 'If you are proud of being my successor, every visit I make in Cambridge sends me back more proud to be credited with having had a hand in you; it is delightful to me to hear you so much and so widely praised and to know how completely it is deserved.'[3] He was on equally friendly terms with one of the most prominent of Cambridge Liberals, the classical scholar Henry Jackson. On one occasion when there had been some misunderstanding between them over the contentious question of compulsory Greek, Browne wrote: 'I have not the slightest idea of trying to persuade you that I was right. But it would break my heart to think you could suppose I employed a trick or went a hair's breadth beyond what from my point of view was right and just.'[4] It is not surprising that Browne was liked and respected in the many circles into which his varied activities brought him.

His successor, J. N. Keynes, was perhaps a less colourful figure but he was also a man of very great ability in several fields, making a name for himself as a logician and an economist as well as an administrator. He and his family had in fact a far longer connection with Cambridge than Browne. In 1910, after nearly thirty years

[1] Add. 7562, 24 November 1896.
[2] Browne, *Recollections of a Bishop*, p. 228.
[3] CUL Add. 7562, 14 August 1897.
[4] CUL Add. 4251: 162, 3 November 1891.

with the Syndicate, he became registrary of the university and he lived in the town until his death in 1948. His wife, Florence Ada Keynes, whom he married in 1882, had been one of the earliest Newnham students. She lived to the great age of ninety-seven, dying in 1958. She was active in local affairs, serving as mayor in the borough in 1932–3, and she wrote in her old age a charming book of historical studies about Cambridge.[1] Their sons were Geoffrey Keynes, surgeon and bibliophile, and John Maynard Keynes, fellow of King's and Britain's most prominent twentieth-century economist. The main facets of Neville Keynes' personality and interests stand out clearly enough from his papers.[2] His examination scrapbook, which will be used later,[3] shows that he had a sense of humour. He managed for many years to combine both academic and administrative work. When he took his Sc.D. in 1891, the historian J. R. Tanner wrote to him expressing his pleasure that 'your non-official work is to receive recognition in a formal way: your official work is so heavy, that there is all the greater glory attaching to your other achievements'.[4] A few years later in 1895 Keynes was offered a chair of economics in the University of Chicago. In declining the office he wrote: 'as time goes on I find myself taking a more and more active part in the practical administration of the university, and my ties with various departments of its work are too strong to be broken'.[5] He had been elected to the Council of the Senate in 1892 and rapidly became one of the central figures in university administration, 'dear hewer and drawer of Agenda and Graces', as he was addressed by one vice-chancellor a decade later.[6] This side of his work reached its climax with his election as registrary in succession to J. W. Clark in 1910. Keynes also maintained the active concern for women's education which had been shown by his predecessors Browne and Markby and which formed one of the strong traditions of the Syndicate. When his appointment to succeed Browne was made known, the Mistress of Girton wrote in her congratulatory letter: 'You know to how great an extent we are dependent on the thoughtfulness and

---

[1] *By-Ways of Cambridge History* (Cambridge 1947, 2nd edn. 1956).

[2] His diary is in the possession of his daughter, Mrs A. V. Hill. I have not seen it.

[3] See p. 186.

[4] CUL Add. 7562, 11 June 1891.

[5] *Ibid.* (Keynes to J. L. Laughlin of the University of Chicago, 8 January 1895).

[6] *Ibid.* E. A. Beck of Trinity Hall, 27 January 1905.

courtesy of the Secretary to the Syndicate and it was with the greatest possible pleasure that I heard you were to be Prof. Browne's successor in the post.'[1] It was in this period that the two examining bodies acquired settled homes of their own. Browne had done his work in two sets of rooms in St Catharine's, the college of which he was a former fellow,[2] until in 1883 he gave up his college work and had no further right to rooms there.[3] It was then necessary to find a site for a building. Two were considered, one in Guildhall Place and one in Mill Lane, and eventually the second was chosen. The building there was designed by W. M. Fawcett and the first Syndicate meeting was held there in November 1886.[4] At Oxford about the same times the Delegacy worked in the Clarendon Building,[5] and an independent home was acquired about a decade later than at Cambridge. In November 1895 the Delegates agreed to ask the Hebdomadal Council to put at their disposal 'a vacant piece of ground situated near the south-west corner of the New Examination Schools' for a new building to be designed by T. G. Jackson. The new offices were opened in 1897.[6]

Between 1878 and 1898 both the Oxford and the Cambridge Examinations had continued to grow rapidly. In 1878 Cambridge had 6,435 candidates; in 1898 15,941.[7] The comparable figures for Oxford are 2,330 and 9,136, in fact a much faster relative growth than Cambridge.[8] The institution in the nineties of the Preliminary Examination for younger candidates had led to a great increase, accounting in 1898 for 5,256 of the Cambridge total and for 5,522 of the Oxford. The Delegacy had discussed the question of an

[1] *Ibid.* E. Welsh to J. N. Keynes, 3 June 1891.
[2] Local Exams. Synd., Minutes, 1 December 1874. The rooms faced Queens' Lane (see letter from Browne to J. W. Clark (CUL Add. 5066 f. XL).
[3] Minutes, 17 November 1883.
[4] Minutes, 17 November, 1, 8 December 1883; 1, 15 February, 19 March, 9 May, 12, 27 November 1884; 28 February, 14 March, 22 May, 24 October 1885; 16 November 1886; and CUA Guard Book 57.1, nos. 117, 121.
[5] Del. Local Exams., Minutes, 6 December 1888, 7 December 1893.
[6] Minutes, 21 November 1895, 4 November 1897 (when the Delegacy agreed to pay £36 per annum for 1897–8 to the curators of the schools for heating the building).
[7] *Local Exams. Synd., Forty-First Annual Report* (1899); *Camb. Univ. Rep.* (1898–9), p. 681; see also p. 136. These figures do not include the Higher Locals.
[8] *Del. Local Exams., Forty-First Annual Report* (1898).

examination 'of a standard below that of the junior Examination' in March 1894 and had referred the matter to a committee.[1] In May it was decided to ask the Hebdomadal Council to introduce a new Statute, 'the maximum age for Honours being fourteen'.[2] When the first Oxford Preliminary Examination was held in 1895, 1,416 candidates offered themselves. About one half of these came from the lower forms of schools already connected with the Delegacy, the other half from schools where no such connection had existed. The Oxford revising examiners in their report expressed their satisfaction that the new examination was likely to prove very useful, but pointed out that care must be taken that too great a difference was not created between the preliminary and the junior grades.[3]

Cambridge was only a little behind Oxford in making similar plans. A sub-syndicate was appointed in July 1894 to draft a report to the Senate. This report, adopted in October,[4] pointed out that there was a demand for an examination of a more elementary character, partly as a result of the institution at grammar schools of County Council scholarships for boys from elementary schools. This development – the germ of the whole modern system of state-supported secondary instruction – was in its first beginnings only in the nineties, but it is noteworthy that it was beginning as early as this to have an effect. As early as 1882, in fact, the Syndicate had been asked by the committee of the Newcastle School of Science and Art to examine scholarship boys from the elementary schools at a lower fee.[5] In 1891 the Syndicate examined for the first time for scholarships given by the County Councils of Kent and Norfolk.[6] No candidate in the Cambridge Preliminary was to receive honours who was over fourteen years of age. The compulsory subjects were to be arithmetic and dictation; the voluntary included religious knowledge, English, English history, geography, Latin, French, Euclid, algebra, elementary mechanics, elementary physics, elementary botany and drawing. The Grace for establishing the new examination passed the Senate on

---

[1] Minutes, 1 March 1894.
[2] Minutes, 24 May 1894.
[3] Del. Local Exams., *Thirty-Eighth Annual Report* (1895), pp. 2–3.
[4] Local Exams. Synd., Minutes, 30 July, 23 October 1894; CUA Guard Book 57.3, no. 219.
[5] Local Exams. Synd., Minutes, 25 October 1882.
[6] *Thirty-Fourth Annual Report: Camb. Univ. Rep.* (1891–2), p. 669.

22 November 1894. The first examination was announced for December 1895, when 3,905 candidates presented themselves.[1] In establishing a third-grade test both Oxford and Cambridge had moved very successfully into a field hitherto occupied by the College of Preceptors, though it may be doubted whether it was educationally desirable to hold public examinations for such a very young age-group. Another new project of the same period – for a commercial certificate – probably reflects the demand of the time for skilled labour. The plan was however unsuccessful, and had to be given up. In 1887 the London Chamber of Commerce had established an examination for commercial certificates, and the idea was also taken up by the Oxford and Cambridge Board.[2] The Syndicate received several requests for something similar, and in February 1888 adopted a report recommending that an examination be established for candidates of about seventeen years old whose education had been on commercial lines.[3] The report passed the Senate in March 1888; in the first examination for the new certificate forty-nine candidates entered of whom only eight passed, and the examiners' comments on the papers were very unfavourable.[4] Oxford also set papers in commercial subjects from 1888,[5] though just as at Cambridge few candidates appeared and the standard was low. In consequence of this Oxford discontinued the examination after 1892,[6] and Cambridge after 1894.[7] The Syndicate explained in a report to the Senate that sufficient candidates of seventeen years old had not appeared, and that they were unwilling to encourage specialization in commercial subjects at an earlier age. Other attempts were made in the nineties to broaden the scope of the work. In 1895 the Delegacy adopted a scheme for

---

[1] *Local Exams. Synd., Thirty-Eighth Annual Report: Camb. Univ. Rep.* (1895–6), p. 581.

[2] See *Educational Times*, vol. XL (December 1887), pp. 467–8; *Journal of Education*, vol. XVI (1 January 1894), pp. 17–19.

[3] Local Exams. Synd., Minutes, 24 December 1887, 22 February 1888. The report is in CUA Guard Book 57.2, no. 161. There were 4 compulsory sections: I Letter-writing, précis, shorthand; II Arithmetic and algebra; III Geography, English history; IV Modern languages, and 4 voluntary: political economy, English literature, elementary physical science, geometrical and mechanical drawing.

[4] CUA Guard Book 57.2, no. 172.

[5] *Del. Local Exams., Thirty-First Annual Report* (1888).

[6] Minutes, 3 December 1891; *Report of Revising Examiners* (1892).

[7] Local Exams. Synd., Minutes, 6 November 1894; CUA Guard Book 57.3, no. 222.

the training of teachers and two years later established a standing committee.[1] At Cambridge teacher-training lay in the hands of another syndicate established in 1879. A plan for a diploma for external students was also mooted there but this was rejected by the Senate in May 1898, its opponents fearing that it would be confused with the Cambridge Degree.[2]

Apart from the steady growth of the centres in Britain, there was during the nineties a marked expansion of the centres overseas, which the *Cambridge Review* celebrated in verse.[3]

> 'Though Roman legions ruled the world,
> Though Britain's thunderbolts are hurled
> At monarchs in Ashanti plains;
> The Locals Syndicate preside
> O'er realms more gloriously wide,
> Broad as the sky are their domains
> Black babes or yellow, brown or white,
> Cram manuals from morn to night
> No hue from culture now refrains;
> The infant startles from his cot,
> His bottle and his bed forgot,
> To moan aloud the name of K*****

Oxford had by 1898 established a few centres overseas,[4] but this was mainly a Cambridge development. In 1898 there were 1,220 Cambridge colonial candidates.[5] The first had been examined in 1863. By 1880 the total was only about 100. By 1890 this had grown to almost 400 and had multiplied three times during the nineties.[6] The problems of overseas centres tended to be more dramatic than those of the home centres. In 1898, for instance, the Syndicate examined charges by a headmaster in British Guiana that the presiding examiner there had behaved with partiality. Since they considered these charges unfounded they threatened to refuse to admit the headmaster's pupils to their examination unless the

[1] Del. Local Exams., Minutes, 7 November 1895, 4 February 1897.
[2] CUA Guard Book 57.3, nos. 245, 245a, 247–53; *Victoria County History of Cambridgeshire*, vol. III, p. 268.
[3] 28 November 1895 (from J. N. Keynes's Commonplace Book, see p. 186).
[4] Natal (Del. Local Exams., Minutes, 13 February 1884, 19 December 1885, 26 May 1887); Hong Kong (Minutes, 2 February 1888); Sierra Leone (2 December 1897).
[5] See p. 145.
[6] From a chart in the possession of the Local Examinations Syndicate. This was probably prepared for the English Education Exhibition of January 1900.

charges were withdrawn.[1] Certainly no home centre had to face the difficulties which beset the Gold Coast in the same year. The papers had not arrived home punctually to be marked, and the acting colonial secretary wrote to explain the delay. At the time of the examination the acting director of education was seriously ill and soon afterwards died. The acting colonial chaplain therefore conducted the examination and himself died very shortly afterwards. No trace of the papers could then be found and all hope was given up until a clerk accidentally came across a key in a pigeon-hole. This opened a box in which 'some of the church things' were kept and in this box were the missing papers. A curious vignette of the problems of examining in 'The White Man's Grave!'[2]

It is fortunately possible to give a good deal of information about the Cambridge Examinations in Jamaica, one of the large colonial centres.[3] The Locals were first held in Jamaica in 1882, almost twenty years after they had been first held in the West Indies in Trinidad.[4] The initiative had been taken by Dr Phillippo and the governors of the Institute of Jamaica who assumed the responsibility of conducting the enterprise. In the first year there were fifteen candidates. The new venture had its set-backs. On the first day of the first examination there was a disastrous fire in Kingston. Three years later the crown agents made a mistake in despatching the papers and the examination had to be held half-way through the Christmas holidays, so that about fifty per cent of those who had entered actually competed. However these initial troubles were successfully overcome and in 1887 an independent local committee was set up. The governors of the Institute of Jamaica announced that they would be unable to give further financial support, and in 1888 a small grant of £10 a year towards expenses was made by the colonial government.[5]

In 1890 38 boys and 12 girls entered of whom 30 boys and 7 girls

[1] Local Exams. Synd., Minutes, 26 January, 27 April, 19 October 1898.

[2] Local Exams. Synd., Minutes, 27 April 1898.

[3] I have seen the Minute Book (1887–1911) of the Jamaica Centre through the kindness of Mr K. Crooks, Cambridge Local Examinations, Kingston, Jamaica. The extracts from the Jamaican press were sent to me by Miss Glory Robertson of the West India Reference Library, Institute of Jamaica, Kingston.

[4] See p. 146 for the first Trinidad Examinations.

[5] For the early days see Gall's News Letter, 29 June 1893, 18 December 1895; for the withdrawal of support by the Institute and the government grant see Jamaica Minute Book, 10 November 1887, 21 January, 16 August 1888.

passed.[1] By 1898 [by which time the Preliminary Examination had considerably increased the total number of candidates everywhere] the entries had risen to 348 of whom 231 were successful.[2] In that year 10 senior boys won first-class honours, one of whom, F. C. H. Powell of Potsdam School, came out top in the whole examination and won the prize of £12 awarded by the Syndicate. In 1898, in fact, Jamaica accounted for about one-quarter of the total overseas entry. In 1891 the Jamaica committee decided to award prizes to the best senior and junior boys and girls, and in 1893 they decided to hold a public prize-giving.[3] In 1892 the government announced that the Jamaica scholarship of £200 a year for three years, first awarded in 1881, would be given on the result of the Senior Locals instead of, as before, on London Matriculation.[4] In 1894 the scholarship was awarded to A. W. Levy who had taken a first class in the Senior Local in 1892 and 1893, and who had also won a sizarship to St John's.[5] F. C. H. Powell, who had topped the Cambridge list in 1898, won it in 1900.[6] In 1892 the committee expressed great interest in holding the Higher Local Examination, which had not hitherto been held at a colonial centre, in the island.[7] One candidate, Miss A. C. J. Hollar of the Barbican High School, presented herself in 1896, and the government made a special grant towards the expenses of her examination. She passed successfully in the third class in mathematics, psychology, English history and constitutional history.[8]

The story of Cambridge examining in Jamaica is one of considerable success, both in quality and in quantity. It may be concluded here with the highly-coloured encomia of a local journalist:

As we visited the Collegiate Hall on Monday, the opening day of the Examinations, we were most favourably impressed with the intelligent and, as a rule, calm, composed, and collected countenances of the candidates. Some had been there before and exhibited a sublime stoicism

---

[1] Minute Book, 22 November, 1890, 18 April 1891.

[2] Minute Book, 8 October 1898, 6 May 1899.

[3] Minute Book, 18 April 1891, 22 April 1893.

[4] Minute Book, 6 December 1892. This decision caused much controversy; see *Daily Gleaner*, 9 January, 24, 30 March, 1, 5, 10, 12, 14, 24 April 1893; see also *Handbook of Jamaica* (1892), pp. 378–9; (1893), p. 315; (1895), p. 313.

[5] Jamaica Minute Book, 22 April 1893, 21 April 1894; J. & J. A. Venn, *Alumni Cantabrigienses, 1752–1900*.

[6] Minute Book, 28 April 1900.

[7] Minute Book, 23 April, 1 October 1892.

[8] Minute Book, 19 October 1895, 18 January, 11 April, 3 October 1896.

or sang froid which even if it may have been to some extent factitious or assumed did good service in exciting a spirit of daring imitation and not unhealthy emulation in the breasts of the less experienced tyros. On looking upon this interesting assemblage of young Jamaicans of every colour, creed and class – all met on equal terms to compete not only with one another but with the youth of their own age in the Mother Country and throughout the whole British Empire, we reflected with infinite pleasure on the fact that in no colony or country in the world save under the benign folds of the British Union Jack could such a spectacle of true fraternity and equality be witnessed.[1]

The examiners' reports for the last twenty years of the century do not add very much to the picture which was given in the last chapter. It is possible however to give a more detailed account of the work of a few selected schools, seen through the eyes of the examiners who visited them. No sets of reports on the examination of schools have survived in the records either of the Delegacy or of the Syndicate. Many still exist, however, in the charity commissioners' files in the Public Record Office or in a printed form in school registers and reports, and from these sources a selection has been made to illustrate the work done in various types of school. Of the examples which will be used here one comes from Trent College, Nottingham (1874), a newly established proprietary school, and two come from old grammar schools, Queen Elizabeth's, Darlington (1888) and Emanuel School, Wandsworth (1891). These will be followed by a consideration of the work of the Locals over a much longer period in two west-country schools, Tavistock Grammar School and the Devon County School at West Buckland, founded by J. L. Brereton, which took a very active interest in the Locals from very early days.

The Trent College report of 1874 was made by two examiners sent by the Syndicate: one, S. S. Lewis, took divinity and languages, the other, Ernest Temperley, took English subjects and mathematics. The sixth and fifth forms with the two divisions of the modern school containing in all about 150 boys were examined chiefly by papers. The lower school of 70 boys was tested orally. The small boys answered well in geography, English history and elementary arithmetic. They read some elementary French exercises with fair success and wrote neatly in their copy-books. Their answers in English grammar were less satisfactory 'owing

---

[1] *Gall's News Letter*, 18 December 1895.

probably to the subject having been taught in a manner too advanced for the age of the pupils'. The upper forms did good papers in divinity, especially in catechism. Their Latin grammar and translation was generally good; only nine boys were examined orally in the *Medea* but they translated and parsed it well. The French paper on the set-book was fairly well answered, but – a familiar complaint – 'the conversational sentences, set for translation into French, elicited very few attempts, and scarcely any that were successful'. In mathematics the standard of the arithmetic was good, though in both algebra and Euclid many boys had no more than an elementary knowledge. Few of the boys knew much about Euclid's third and fourth books and even in the first and second there were many who wrote out propositions entirely from memory with the result that they got them wrong. The history and geography were competently done. In English the paraphrasing was much better than the previous year. The English grammar was well answered except for the parsing which showed a lack of understanding of the relations between the words of a very simple sentence. In the *Merchant of Venice* a few boys sent up interesting answers but the general average was not very high.

Lewis also made some general remarks about the condition of the school. He noted with approval the appointment of an additional master, though this had been counter-balanced by a rise in the numbers to 220 from 200 the year before. Already the existence of the boys' libraries was a very valuable feature of the school; it would be equally valuable to establish a reference library for the masters with books on the various subjects taught in the school. Several other improvements in the arrangements were noted. Private locker-rooms for the boys had been installed. Wood-carving had been introduced as a pastime when the weather was too bad to allow out-of-door exercise; apart from its intrinsic interest this 'will bear prompt and pleasant fruit in the decoration of the chapel, which is now fast rising to completion'. The examiner concluded with a warning to parents to encourage their boys to excel in 'school-*studies*' rather than in 'school-*sports*'. The warning may have been justified, for the immense growth of organized games in English schools and universities during the last quarter of the nineteenth century was to effect a revolution in English education which had many harmful effects.[1]

[1] Pusey House Pamphlets, no. 71681; *Trent College School Lists, 1874*, pp. 8–14.

The reports on Queen Elizabeth's, Darlington (1888) and Emanuel School (1891) are rather different in their nature. At Darlington the higher classes had taken the Local Examination and the lower were examined either on paper or orally. At Emanuel the average age was lower. The 251 boys in the school were divided into seven forms, the average age of which varied from $14\frac{1}{2}$ to $10\frac{1}{2}$.[1] The whole of the fifth and sixth forms at Darlington, a total of 37 boys, had been entered for the Local Examination in December 1887, 10 as seniors and 27 as juniors. Of these 16 had passed and 16 obtained honours, 2 boys gaining first classes. The general level was high in all subjects, and the examiner professed himself very well satisfied. 'Having regard', he remarked, 'to the fact that the candidates were not selected boys specially prepared, but the whole of the two higher classes of the school sent up bodily on their past year's work, the results achieved were in my judgment in the highest degree praiseworthy and such as any school might be proud of.' The younger boys were examined in Latin, French, English subjects, arithmetic and algebra; one form also took Euclid and a few boys offered Greek and German. The general verdict on their work was also favourable, though many boys had taken little trouble with their English grammar and there was a good deal of inaccuracy in the mathematical papers. In general, however, the elementary part of the curriculum was studied with great thoroughness and a good foundation laid for the higher classes.

The boys offered for examination at Emanuel were at the same level as the junior boys at Darlington, and they took the same subjects with the addition of chemistry. Here the examiner was more critical. Since boys had been promoted into higher forms only a short time before the examination, there was a wide variation of standard within the forms themselves. Furthermore, at the top of the school, too much was being attempted. The French and Latin set-books had been read through only once without time for revision, and in algebra also more had been attempted than the boys could really assimilate. 'It can hardly be expected', the examiner wrote, 'that boys of $14\frac{1}{2}$, with a rather heavy curriculum, should be able to reach a Latin Prose standard.' The comment has often been made that the schools tended to push boys on too fast

---

[1] For the following paragraph see Public Record Office, Ed. 27/975 (Darlington Examiners' Reports, 1874–91; Ed. 27/3391 (United Westminster Schools Examiners' Reports, 1886–1902).

and to neglect the elementary work. Darlington seems to have avoided this pitfall, Emanuel to have fallen into it. It may be added on the credit side that the examiner at Emanuel thought very well of both the theoretical and the practical chemistry. On the extra-curricular aspects he also spoke well of the services in the School Chapel and of the boys' drill. 'They were put through different formations in admirable style. The marching was very steady, and the exercises were done in excellent time and with a very pleasing effect'.

The examples which have so far been taken refer to individual school examinations only; fortunately the records of two Devon schools, Tavistock and West Buckland, enable us to make a survey of a much longer period. Tavistock Grammar School was closed in 1888 on the retirement of the headmaster, the Reverend E. Spencer, formerly fellow and lecturer of Sidney Sussex College, Cambridge, who had been there since 1853.[1] During his reign the school regularly sent in candidates for the Locals with very creditable results. In 1861 a report on the school defined the course as comprising 'Latin, Greek, Divinity, English, Mathematics, French, Book-keeping, Surveying, Chemistry and Physics taught by Lectures and in the Laboratory'. Classics were voluntary but most of the boys took Latin. The school had taken first, second and third class honours in the Oxford and Cambridge Middle-Class Examinations, one of its boys being the only candidate distinguished by Cambridge for proficiency in chemistry in December 1860. The school was small – about 100 in number – and its candidates therefore not very numerous, though they achieved the best results of those examined at the Truro centre. In the Cambridge Examina-tion of 1867 three senior boys took first classes; in 1874 two boys got First-Class Honours in the Oxford Junior Locals out of four boys sent in; in 1884 the school carried off ten honours, including every first-class, out of the twelve honours won at the Oxford Truro centre, and three years later the headmaster pointed out that, although during the past few years they had sent in between thirty and forty candidates, they had never had a failure. Many of the better boys clearly went on to larger schools, like A. M. Mantell who did very well in the Oxford Junior Examination of 1874, then

---

[1] The following paragraph is based on a volume of 'School Records, 1839–1888', lent to me by the kindness of Mr H. A. Davies of Tavistock Grammar School.

went on to the Military Department of Cheltenham College and eventually passed out first from the Royal Military Academy, Woolwich.

The Tavistock example shows a school using the Locals for its better boys exclusively; West Buckland was the pioneer in using them as a general examination for all boys at the appropriate level in the school. The Devon County School at West Buckland as we have seen was the child of J. L. Brereton.[1] The school had been opened in 1858 to improve the education of farmers' sons, and Brereton had appreciated from the beginning that, although the Locals had developed on different lines from his own original scheme, they could be used to promote the welfare of the new school.[2] Two boys were sent in for the Oxford Examination in 1860 and a few more in 1861 and 1862. In October of the last named year a local committee was formed and arrangements made with the University of Cambridge to hold an examination at West Buckland in December 1862, the first time that an examination had been held exclusively for one school. Contrary to the usual practice of the time no selection was made; all the boys of the first and second classes were sent in on the argument that, although a few selected candidates would have achieved better results, it was much better for the school to enter the whole of the upper classes. Brereton told the Taunton Commission two years later:

the head master ... after consultation with me, determined to try how many he could send in. I am bound to say for him that he at the time urged that he might lose some credit, that his cleverer boys might not distinguish themselves as much as they would if he confined his preparation for these examinations to them; but he quite agreed with me that it would be very desirable to try whether whole classes could not be sent in.[3]

Two seniors and seven juniors were successful out of sixteen who entered and five more boys took the examination successfully who were over age to obtain certificates, but who had special permission to sit the papers.[4] The Syndicate in its report[5] commented on the

[1] See p. 52.
[2] J. L. Brereton, *Principles and Plan of a Farm and County School* (Exeter, 1858); *Education as connected with Agriculture* (1864).
[3] *SIC*, vol. v, p. 126: 10199.
[4] For the examination of 1862 see *Devon County School Register* (July 1863), pp. 9–14. The register was lent to me by the kindness of the headmaster.
[5] *Local Exams. Synd., Fifth Annual Report* (1863), p. 3.

enterprise shown by the school; entering the whole classes was the best way to improve school work, though it made the number of unsuccessful candidates appear large. During the next fifteen years West Buckland kept up a very high level of performance, though it fell on hard times later on.[1] In 1864, 1865 and 1866 it passed the highest number of candidates of any school in England at the Cambridge Examination. In 1873 Frederick Temple, who had returned to Devonshire as Bishop of Exeter, pointed out at the School speech day that half the school had taken the Cambridge Examinations the previous December, and that of those sent in seventy per cent had passed and twenty-five per cent had obtained honours:

This is the clearest proof [the Bishop said] that any school can give of the substantial soundness of the education that it bestows. I do not know whether it is absolutely the only school in the Kingdom that sends in boys in that way, but certainly, it is the only school in the country that sends in anything like that proportion of boys, and, I may add, it is the only school in the country that passes that proportion of its scholars.

In 1874 T. Stone, 'a bona fide Somersetshire farmer's son', as Fortescue exulted,[2] was the top junior boy in England of the 2,230 examined by the Syndicate.

Fortescue, in writing to Brereton about the boys' achievement, mentioned that he had called at the school to congratulate Thompson the headmaster and to shake hands with young Stone. He had also promised an *Araucaria* tree to plant in front of the school in remembrance of Stone's feat. In 1867 he had already presented the boys with a large cricket tent to commemorate their successes. At West Buckland the examinations and the visitors they brought with them seem to have provided much of the variety and excitement of the school year; in this remote part of the country other events must have been somewhat scarce. The first Cambridge examiner of 1862 had also planted a tree in front of the school.[3] When the Oxford examiner, Mr Curgenven, came in 1865 a supper was given to the boys who had been examined, after which he made a speech and offered a prize to be given on the results. When the headmaster had responded suitably, the whole school went into the dining hall,

---

[1] The following details are all taken from the *Devon County School Register*.
[2] Fortescue to Brereton, 9 March 1875. These letters are at Homerton College, Cambridge.
[3] *Devon County School Register* (July, 1863), p. 10.

'and the rest of the evening was spent in singing, the Rev. F. H. Curgenven presiding at the piano-forte'.[1] The following year the presentation of the Cambridge certificates was followed by the annual competition on the cricket-ground for the West Buckland sheep-shearing prizes.[2] Certainly the Devon County School authorities made examinations and prize-givings more festive occasions than they are today.

In the School Register too is preserved a unique document, a description of an Oxford Locals Examination written by a boy, R. L. Hodges (Class II).[3] His account runs as follows:

The Oxford Examination was held in our schoolroom. A small table is placed about the middle of the room in front of the desks, at which the person who comes to conduct the Examination sits. The boys who under-go the Examination sit at the desks about a yard apart from one another, so that they cannot look over each other's papers or take any unfair advantage. When the Examination begins, the person who comes to conduct it reads out the rules of the Examination and the cautions against copying, &c. He then gives out some paper to each boy for him to write his answers on, and a paper of questions on the subject the boys are to be examined in, and tells them the time allowed for the paper and says he will speak five minutes before the time is up. [The different subjects are described.]

If a boy has used all the paper given him by the Examiner for his answers, and requires more, he holds up his hand and calls out his number, when the person who conducts the Examination immediately attends to him.

The Examination generally lasts nearly a week, as the boys can hardly ever do more than three or four subjects in a day. At the end of each day the papers of the boys, that is their answers, are sent off to Oxford, where they are duly examined, and each boy who passes receives a Certificate to that effect.

These reports give a very clear picture of the contacts between the examiners and the schools. In their day-to-day work the examining bodies had to deal with many requests and criticisms. Most of these were fair and reasonable enough, though some of them, as we shall see, were curious in the extreme. There

---

[1] *Ibid.* (July 1865), p. 4.
[2] *Ibid.* (July 1866), p. 11.
[3] *Ibid.* (July 1864), pp. 13–14.

was naturally a good deal of correspondence about forming centres:

I regret to say [wrote one headmaster to Keynes] that my efforts to resuscitate the Camb Local in Burnley have been unsuccessful. Matters educational in the town are still unsettled, but next month the buildings in connection with the Gram: Sch: extension will be begun, & when they are completed I hope another effort will be made to bring in a high-class exam like the Camb Local again. But this year at all events there will be no chance of it.[1]

Another headmaster asked for extra time to pay examination fees since parents were very slow in paying their sons' school fees, 'and I cannot afford to sue people'.[2] The headmaster of the Intermediate School at Pembroke Dock applied for an independent centre since his pupils had to make a journey by ferry and train to Haverford West, and the parents of girl candidates disliked the travelling.[3] Both the Delegacy and the Syndicate had to deal with accusations that the Crystal Palace was an unsuitable place for examinations, though the charges were not substantiated.[4] There might be an echo of a famous Victorian *cause célèbre* in a Cambridge minute that since the father of a girl candidate had been described on an entry form as 'R. C. D. Tichborne Bart', the title 'Bart' should be omitted on any certificate awarded.[5] Sometimes ill success led to hard feelings. In 1889 the Syndicate had to deal with charges made by the master of the Trade School at Keighley that in the previous December his better boys had been rejected and the weaker passed, so that 'the whole thing was regarded by the boys of the school as a lottery'. The Syndicate minuted – clearly with both surprise and horror – that no such experience had occurred within their recollection and that, if the feeling really was as stated by the master, they would be unwilling to examine at Keighley again. However, a satisfactory letter was received from

[1] J. Langfield Ward to Keynes, 29 April 1899. This and the following letters come from a small collection of correspondence at the Local Examinations Syndicate.

[2] G. N. Clark, headmaster of Borlase School, Marlow, to Keynes, 4 December 1899.

[3] T. R. Dawes to Keynes, 25 August 1896.

[4] Del. Local Exams., Minutes, 3 November 1880; Local Exams. Synd., Minutes, 27 October, 6 November 1880; 7 May 1881.

[5] Local Exams. Synd., Minutes, 20 October 1883. Arthur Orton, who had claimed to be Sir Roger Tichborne, had been sentenced to 14 years penal servitude for perjury in 1874. He was released in 1884; see M. C. F. Morris, *Yorkshire Reminiscences (with others)* (1922), ch. 15.

the chairman of the Keighley Institute, and so the matter was regarded as closed.[1]

Some of the difficulties with candidates and parents, though they must have been vexatious at the time, make amusing reading now. The most extraordinary case was that of J. A. Gregory, a music teacher at Southport, who arrogated to himself a number of impressive sounding degrees; as he wrote to Browne, 'so far as degrees at Camb. are concerned I just put as many to my name as I choose and defy either you or the devil himself.'[2] Gregory had taken the Higher Local in 1880, 1884, 1885 and 1886 without gaining a certificate. After his fourth failure he wrote to Browne, asking for information about the pass standard in French and German, describing the whole system of examination in languages as 'simply a swindle', and asserting that another candidate had passed in political economy by the use of a 'tip book' obtained through his vicar. This letter was followed by a series of letters and cards, in the course of which he described Browne as an 'infernal swindler' for retaining a stamped addressed envelope, and remarked that he did not 'recognize thieves & snobs as Reverends & Browne having retained the stamp enclosed for reply to a former letter is a thief & by a previous letter is a snob'. Gregory further claimed the return of his fees and expenses, amounting to £12 11s., in the examinations which he had taken unsuccessfully. Eventually, after the Syndicate had considered the matter,[3] he was brought in the spring of 1888 to withdraw his accusations. Two years later, however, after he had been making further trouble, Browne wrote to him, suggesting that his position in Southport would not be improved if proceedings were taken against him for sending offensive postcards, and this threat seems to have brought the correspondence to an end. He had not long before this sent Browne a prospectus of some new songs in which he described himself as 'Mus D (Oxon)'; it was therefore a nice touch on Browne's part to suggest that he might in future confine his attention to the Local Examinations of the University of Oxford!

[1] Local Exams. Synd., Minutes, 8 June, 12 October 1889. There was a rather similar dispute about an examination at Camberwell Grammar School in 1894-5 (Minutes, 27 November 1895).

[2] Gregory's correspondence with Browne and the Syndicate is in the papers of the Local Examinations Syndicate. The letters begin on 3 February and end on 9 April 1890.

[3] Local Exams. Synd., Minutes, 22 February, 3 March 1888.

A correspondence with an angry parent entered in the Oxford Minute Book for 1893 illustrates the splendid unreason to which the Victorians sometimes fell victim.[1] Mr W. B. Ellis had entered his daughter for the Junior Examination under the impression that it was to be held at 31 New Bond Street, the address of the local secretary's club, which had been entered in the regulations merely for forwarding purposes, since the secretary, Miss Hutton, was moving house. After the entry fee had been received Miss Hutton informed Mr Ellis that the examination would be held at Drapers' Hall, Throgmorton Street. He then replied that this was most inconvenient, that he would not have entered his daughter at all unless he had thought that she could be examined in New Bond Street, and he demanded either that the examination be held there or that the entry fee be returned, since he had been misled. After Gerrans, the Oxford secretary, had refused to take either course Ellis threatened legal proceedings. When the matter was considered by the Delegacy, Gerrans stressed that Miss Hutton, whom Ellis had described as a 'kind of wandering Jew', was the best Local secretary in the list who did her work with great tact and courtesy. As might have been expected, the Delegates supported their officials and refused to return the fee, though they expressed the hope that Miss Ellis might even yet present herself for examination at Drapers' Hall. There is no evidence, however, whether she did so or not.

Unsatisfactory presiding examiners were a fruitful source of trouble. They might be pompous, like the man about whom a local secretary wrote to Keynes as follows: 'The only thing for which we pray is – if we remain independent do not impose Mr Hermann on us again. We have borne with him twice, but a *third* attempt to put up with his consequential but inconsequent airs would result in an explosion not all pleasant to him. I cannot imagine how a person of such importance can be spared from the university with any chance of its survival.'[2] More common were the presiding examiners – and the local committees – who exercised no proper control, the most common result of this being an outbreak of copying among the candidates.[3] Trouble arose in this way at the Croydon boys'

---

[1] This correspondence with Mr W. B. Ellis is printed. It was considered by the Delegacy on 1 June 1893.

[2] W. J. Spratling to Keynes, 29 October 1898.

[3] See the case of copying at the Wellingborough centre (Local Exams. Synd., Minutes, 1, 15, 16 February 1884).

centre in 1890. The presiding examiner, J. J. Lias, had had a number of years' experience, though it is clear that matters had not always gone smoothly on earlier occasions.[1] It seems quite likely that at Croydon Lias was not properly assisted by the Local secretary and committee and he admitted to Browne that he got flurried in consequence and made mistakes. The scene in the examination room must certainly have been somewhat confused. When the vicar of Croydon arrived to assist in invigilating, he took offence because Lias did not interrupt the handing out of the papers to come and greet him. The vicar then retired in dudgeon to Lias' own desk from which Lias had to turn him out! The results of the general disorder were as might have been expected. When the subject examiner in Greek read his papers, he found several instances of copying among boys from Epsom College. When this was reported to their headmaster, the form was questioned and the boys confessed, though the headmaster urged, in palliation of their offence, that they had been allowed to crowd together while they were writing the paper and that they had not been made to turn their scripts face downwards as the regulations required. When December 1891 came round Lias was not employed again as a presiding examiner. He wrote in consequence several aggrieved letters to Browne, complaining that he had been given no notice that he would not be required and alleging that both his character and his capacity had been impugned. Browne noted on one of these letters: 'I did distinctly warn him that I felt such work did not suit him.' From the secretary's point of view it was almost equally embarrassing in such a case to give a full explanation or no explanation at all. T. R. Glover neatly summed up the difficulties which had unseated poor Mr Lias in verse:

> There's a pamphlet of Instructions to be read like Holy Writ,
> You may break the Ten Commandments but you must remember it;
> By a microscopic blunder might the Universe be wrecked,
> And 'the very greatest trouble is occasioned by neglect'.[2]

On one occasion the result of a Cambridge Examination led to a libel action. In January 1882 Browne was subpoenaed to give evidence in a case heard at Exeter Assizes before Lord Chief Justice

---

[1] The correspondence between Browne, Lias and T. N. Hart-Smith, headmaster of Epsom College, is in the papers of the Local Examinations Syndicate.

[2] 'A Local Centre (Cave Keynem)' in J. N. Keynes' Commonplace Book (Local Examinations Syndicate Papers).

Coleridge. Browne had himself inspected Kingsbridge Grammar School in South Devon in 1881. Fox, the editor of a local newspaper, had criticized the headmaster, Ranking, for withholding the publication of the examiners' report. In fact the governors had withheld it, and they agreed eventually that it should be read at a private meeting of governors and parents. Only four parents attended the meetings. One of them told the editor that the report was as bad as could be; another that it might have been worse. The editor then published an article, stating 'that the headmaster's ability had been tried and found wanting' and demanded his dismissal. The headmaster then sued for libel.[1] When the Syndicate discussed the matter, it decided that the secretary should resist production of the report on the general grounds of inexpediency.[2] In fact the plaintiff's copies of the reports for 1880 and 1881 were put in as evidence, so the question of the Syndicate's duty to produce them never arose directly, though Browne claimed in court that they were privileged communications, and that it would be fatal to the confidence of the schools in the university if their completely confidential nature could not be depended upon. In his summing up Lord Coleridge supported this view of the reports as confidential documents, and Browne considered that he would have supported the university in a refusal to produce them, had there been occasion for this. Finally a verdict was found for the headmaster.

On the edge of the examining world is a fringe, sometimes comic, sometimes eccentric, lunatic even, to which Mr J. A. Gregory, whom we have already met, really belongs. There are some very amusing examples in Keynes' Commonplace Book.[3] He received curiously addressed envelopes like 'Provost of Keynes, Syndicate Buildings, Cambridge'. He was the target of petitioners like the boy in Ceylon who wrote: 'So I beg you again as a matter of charity to have mercy and compassion upon me in order to release me from this fiery grief which burns my heart every now and then when I do remember the great difficulties that I have to undergo.' One private student who had failed four times complained that there must be 'some hideous undercurrent' which prevented him from passing and claimed that he was far better than any candidate who had

[1] This account is taken from a paper on the Kingsbridge case, written by Browne, in the Local Examinations Syndicate Minute Book.
[2] Local Exams. Synd., Minutes, 12 January 1882.
[3] See p. 168.

merely got through at his first attempt! Much more ingenuous is the letter of a youthful 'no. 4733':

Dear Mr Examiner,

I am sorry I have do such a bad paper but I never did know much Trigonometry. We are all rather excited to-day since all the others boys have gone home this morning while we have had to stop till now for the exam. So you will be able to understand under what conditions we are doing your exam. when you have learnt that we have been here 14 weeks on Monday at a stretch and that we will be in the train in a few hours. I don't suppose I must wait to write any more but wishing you a MERRY XMAS and PROSPEROUS NEW YEAR.

P.S. I am sending you a few blank sheets since I believe you are paid by weight.

One girl candidate wrote to ask if she could buy a certificate. 'Mother would gladly pay double the money to get it rather than me to sit and fail. So if you will state your own price, we will gladly pay it.' She may be forgiven; it is however more difficult to sympathize with the father who wrote to say that his daughter was heartbroken at her failure. Perhaps, the father thought, some mistake had been made and if such a mistake could be discovered, he would be ready in return to send the secretary and his wife for a trip to Paris!

PART III

THE PUBLIC CONTEXT
1855–1900

8

THE CIVIL SERVICE
EXAMINATIONS: TO 1870

In the concluding section of this study the consequences of the crucial decisions taken in the 1850s must be assessed. The first topic to be considered is the development of the Civil Service Examinations. The administrative reforms of the fifties had been launched into stormy waters. In India the new system had hardly begun when the Mutiny of 1857 broke out and the rule of the Company was brought to an end. In England the shock caused by the administrative failures of the Crimean War was serious. One expression of public criticism was the Administrative Reform Association. The new body proclaimed its intention of shutting 'all the back doors which lead to public employment' and 'throwing the public service open to all England'.[1] Events moved at very different speeds in India and at home. The creation in 1855 of the Civil Service Commission was a very partial victory for reforming principles in administration, and techniques of examination, in so far as they were applied at all, were applied in England to only a small degree, and at a low level of performance. In India the new system came into effect at once. Like the Chinese Imperial Service, the rulers of India were to be selected on the basis of their proficiency in the highest academic culture of their native land. Power and influence were to be gained by skill in purely literary tests, and practical achievement was expected to follow from intellectual skill.[2] A *corps d'élite* recruited by success in examinations ruled in China for over a thousand years. The rule of the British mandarins of Calcutta and Delhi was very brief in comparison, though they passed on many of their characteristics to the Indian administrators whom they trained.

British India was a conquered country and its administrative structures were comparatively simple. In the much more complex

[1] H. L. Beales, 'A Centenary Tribute to an Appeal for Modernization', *Essays on Reform, 1867; A Centenary Tribute*, ed. B. Crick (1967), p. 7.
[2] N. Morris, 'An Historian's view of Examinations', *Examinations and English Education*, ed. S. Wiseman (Manchester, 1961), pp. 40–2; A. V. Judges, 'The Evolution of Examinations', *The World Year Book of Education*, ed. J. A. Lauwerys and D. G. Scanlon (1969), p. 18.

and more closely articulated political world of England, the new traditions naturally took longer to establish themselves. Yet in both countries the problems caused by the creation of an examinations-based administrative group had common elements. The world in which the administrative reformers worked was one, as we have seen, which took social distinctions very seriously and which accepted personal clientage as one of the facts of life. The political and administrative expression of personal clientage was patronage. Here two quite different attitudes were possible. Lord Cromer, who created a modern administrative structure in Egypt, thought that those who had to exercise patronage were very happy to be relieved of duties in the exercise of which they were certain to incur a great deal of misrepresentation and abuse, and to receive very little gratitude.[1] Disraeli, on the other hand, valued the exercise of patronage, and was sceptical about tests of merit, because they provided no guarantee of the practical fitness of the man who had succeeded in them.[2]

The concept of suitability for which Disraeli was arguing was expressed by most of his contemporaries in terms of the existing class structure. It was very generally agreed that it was desirable to maintain class divisions in society and government. If this were an axiom of political life, it must follow that those who directed the administration should be men of a social status equal or superior to that of those with whom they were brought into contact. It was widely felt that the idea of the 'gentleman' needed to be brought up to date. In a more competitive world he clearly needed qualifications which had not been demanded of him in a more easy-going past. But, however much it might be modernized, the concept of gentility was a constant to which nearly all the Victorians paid tribute. It remained the gentleman's role to be a leader and inspirer of other men, even though the terms in which he operated might have been radically changed.

Here the idea of competition for administrative posts raised problems which caused difficulty to the men of the time. Would selection by literary tests continue to bring to the top men with a traditional claim to power? Tocqueville, observing English affairs with deep interest, was doubtful. When George Cornewall Lewis,

---

[1] Quoted in P. J. Hartog, *Examinations and their relation to Culture and Efficiency* (1918), p. 44.
[2] Blake, *Disraeli*, pp. 682–3.

who became chancellor of the exchequer in succession to Gladstone, in February 1855, asked for an analysis of the French system of Civil Service Examinations, Tocqueville warned him against the principle of examinations for the public service as incompatible with the English constitution.[1]

Gladstone, observing the same circumstances, drew exactly opposite conclusions. In January 1854 he had written to Russell:

I do not hesitate to say that one of the great recommendations of the change (to open competition) in my eyes would be its tendency to strengthen and multiply the ties between the higher classes and the possession of administrative power. As a member for Oxford I look forward eagerly to its operation. There, happily we are not without some lights of experience to throw upon this part of the subject. The objection which I always hear there from persons who wish to retain restrictions upon elections is this: 'If you leave them to examinations, Eton, Harrow, Rugby, and the other public schools will carry *everything*.' I have a strong impression that the aristocracy of this country are even superior in natural gifts, on the average, to the mass; but it is plain that with their acquired advantages their *insensible* education, irrespective of book-learning, they have an immense superiority. This applies in its degree to all those who may be called gentlemen by birth and training.[2]

There could be no clearer statement of the role which well-educated gentlemen might be expected to play in a reformed administrative order. Gladstone specifically refers in his remarks to the University of Oxford. A very similar motivation directed the efforts of Jowett and the Balliol circle to marry high academic achievements with service to the public and successful individual careers. The Civil Service Commissioners in their annual reports frequently provided, as we shall see, details of the schooling and the family background of successful candidates for the higher posts. The information which they gave substantiated Gladstone's case that good birth and favoured schooling produced success in the new administrative tests.

In England the strength and coherence of the traditional ruling class made it unlikely that they would cede their power to any new social groups. If the conditions of success were changed, the English gentleman was intelligent and adaptable enough to meet the new

---

[1] S. Drescher, *Tocqueville and England* (Cambridge, Mass., 1964), pp. 179–80.
[2] Quoted in E. Hughes, 'Civil Service Reform, 1853–5', *Public Administration* vol. XXXII, pp. 28–9.

conditions. In India circumstances were not necessarily the same. Indian service had always been well rewarded, but the separation from home and family, and the difficult working conditions had always meant that opportunities in India were more open than in England to men of modest station who were prepared to accept these disadvantages.

Macaulay, when he was at work on the new scheme of competition, wrote to his friend Ellis that he had been receiving 'the most delicious letters' about the new scheme. The best of them, he thought, was 'that of a clerk in a cornfactor's house at Limerick who begs that I "will send him a prospectus informing him in what he is capable of undergoing an examination for admission into above service"'.[1]

In fact, the Indian Empire stood in no danger of being infiltrated by cornfactors' clerks. The Civil Service Commissioners informed the India Office in 1875 that no information was available about the social standing of Haileybury students under the old system though they thought it unlikely that as nominees of a commercial body 'they were all of aristocratic patronage or connexion'. About men selected under open competition, however, information was available:

It is certain that of the 668 civilians sent to India between 1860 and 1874, as large a proportion as 78 per cent were the sons of parents belonging to the aristocracy, gentry, army, navy, Indian Civil Service, or one of the learned professions. The remaining 22 per cent would include the sons of merchants, bankers, farmers and tradesmen, the proportion from the last-mentioned class being 4 per cent of the entire number.

Of those who had occupied the top forty places in 1874, thirty had been at public schools, of whom fourteen had been at a university, while four of the remainder who had not been at a public school had been at a university or college.[2]

These statistics bring out the important point that the development of competitive examination in the public service was closely bound up with the growing success, in this same period, of the universities and the endowed schools. The decades from 1850 to

---

[1] Macaulay to Ellis, 23 January 1855 (Macaulay Papers, Trinity College, Cambridge).
[2] *Papers relating to the Selection and Training of Candidates for the Indian Civil Service*, PP 1876, LV, p. 311.

1880 were a period of steady reform at Oxford and Cambridge. The Clarendon Commission of 1861–4 investigated the nine older public schools and the Taunton Commission of 1864–8 the hundreds of endowed grammar schools. In the ensuing decades the older public schools went from strength to strength, and were joined by many new recruits like Thring's Uppingham and Benson's Wellington. Under the guidance of the endowed schools commissioners and the charity commissioners old grammar schools were re-invigorated and set on the road to new success. 'University extension' was a popular goal of reformers, for it was often pointed out that the university population of England was much smaller than that of countries like France and Germany. The University of London steadily broadened its work. By the seventies the development of provincial colleges like Owens' at Manchester was well under way. They were all originally under the tutelage of London, until the Victoria University, which was to develop later into the independent Universities of Manchester, Liverpool and Leeds, was chartered in 1880. A number of these colleges also had links with Oxford and Cambridge for they grew partly out of centres for extra-mural lecturing organized by those universities. Not only were there more universities; in all of them courses were offered in new subjects. To the traditional disciplines of classics and mathematics were added the natural sciences and engineering, law, history and modern languages. In all subjects examinations in honours were more and more rigidly assessed, and they grew in reputation as they provided an avenue to the new careers offered by an expanding society.

In the fifties and sixties the Indian Civil Service Examinations were the honours examinations of the public service. The broad outlines of the Macaulay committee scheme has already been sketched in an earlier chapter.[1] Macaulay's direct personal responsibility for the plan is made clear in his letters to his friend Ellis. The upper age limit of twenty-three which he succeeded in carrying through clearly made the Indian appointments very attractive to young graduates.[2] In April 1858 the India Board asked the Civil Service Commissioners to undertake the management of the examinations for that year, and the Government of India Act

---

[1] See pp. 25–6.
[2] Macaulay to Ellis, 23 January 1855, 9 January 1856.

of the same year put the examinations definitely under their supervision.[1] The mark scheme which the commissioners took over was that which had been suggested by Macaulay's committee. It covered a very wide range of studies to meet the circumstances of candidates who had been trained in several systems of higher education. Among the subjects covered were the classical Indian languages, partly because Macaulay had always intended that natives of India should have a chance of success in the competition. Able young Indians would thus be able to compete with their peers in England, and would gain their place, as Macaulay told the House of Commons, 'in the most honourable manner, and not as a mere eleemosynary donation'.[2] Some such Indian candidates did come forward from very early days, though their numbers were limited by the fact that the examination was held only in England and not in India as well.

The marks were distributed as follows:

English language, literature and history	1,500
The language, literature and history of Greece	750
The language, literature and history of Rome	750
The language, literature and history of France	375
The language, literature and history of Germany	375
The language, literature and history of Italy	375
Mathematics	1,000
Natural sciences (chemistry, electricity and magnetism, natural history, geology and mineralogy)	500
Moral sciences (mental, moral and political philosophy)	500
Sanskrit language and literature	375
Arabic language and literature	375
Total	6,875

Owing to the fact that candidates got no credit for the mere smattering of knowledge of a subject, the effective maximum mark was probably about half of this total. It can be seen that the marks fall into certain very large blocks. The large total given for the English subjects is surprising, since they did not form at that time a separate part of higher academic education. Proficiency in them would

---

[1] For the following details see C[ivil] S[ervice] C[ommissioners], *Fourth Report*, 1859, *PP* 1859, VIII, pp. 19ff.

[2] *Parl. Deb.* 3rd ser., vol. CXXVIII, 758.

clearly be very important to Indian candidates, who would learn English as a foreign language. The English total (1,500) is the same as the total for Latin and Greek and greater than that for mathematics (1,000). Two modern languages or Sanskrit and Arabic together are worth the same as either Greek or Latin separately (750), while the natural and the moral sciences score separately only two-thirds of that total.

About the final examination which was taken by the successful candidates after a period of probation there is less to say. It was professionally oriented and covered the subjects which would be needed in India; law, political economy, a vernacular Indian language, and the history of India.

In the examination of 1858, the first held by the Civil Service Commissioners, there were sixty-seven candidates, of whom twenty-one were selected, one of whom declined appointment. All the other twenty successful candidates passed the second examination which, under the peculiar circumstances of the time, in the aftermath of the Mutiny of 1857, was held only a few months after the first. Of the twenty-one selected all were university men. Six, including the first three in the order of merit, came from Trinity College, Dublin, nine from Oxford, four from Cambridge, and one each from London (King's College) and from Edinburgh. The professions of the fathers of those selected were as follows: clergymen, five; army officer, four; physicians, three; merchants, two; agent, trader, stockbroker, consul, professor, solicitor, Wesleyan minister, one each. Out of the 6,875 marks which were a maximum, the top candidate scored 2,908, and the twenty-first and last successful candidate, 1,621. The commissioners, looking back over their first experience of the India candidates, pointed out that the financial advantages of an Indian career were very great and the scheme of examination highly appropriate for a young man aiming at high university honours. The consequence must be, they thought, that many young men would be drawn away to India 'from the severe and uncertain competition of the bar, the moderate expectations of the Church, and still more from the laborious future which the various employments of a scholastic nature hold out'.[1]

In subsequent years the Indian regulations were changed from time to time. In 1859 the maximum age of entry for the first

[1] CSC, *Fourth Rep.* 1859, *PP* 1859, VIII, p. 39.

examination was reduced to twenty-two and in 1866 to twenty-one, since by that time successful candidates were required to spend two years' probation in this country, and it was thought important that they should not begin their careers in India at too late an age. No official course of study or formal requirements about residence were laid down for the probationers, who were simply required from 1864 to pass four half-yearly examinations before their departure for India.[1]

After ten years the new Indian system was establishing itself. In 1866 the secretary of state asked for a report on the efficiency of the new arrangements. The government of India in their reply pointed out that it was too early to give any conclusive judgment since all the 'competition-wallahs' were still in comparatively junior positions. Their tentative judgment was favourable. The new system excluded great inefficiency which was not always excluded under the old system and the new entrants were certainly more highly educated than the old.[2]

The history of public examinations seems to run a settled course. The first controversy is one of principle: should the idea be accepted at all? Once this has been settled controversy does not die away. It merely moves from ends to means. Men accept the fact, but they dispute about the methods by which the agreed principles are carried out. Examinations for the public service have always suffered from the peculiar difficulty, as Henry Latham, a shrewd critic of the seventies, pointed out, that they are completely separated from any regular course of teaching.[3] The Indian Examinations, because of their very wide range, were criticized very early on for encouraging a superficial knowledge of many subjects and for providing good opportunities for special preparation – less elegantly known as 'cramming'. In 1865 the commissioners reported that, in order to discourage desultory reading, a deduction was to be made from all marks of an amount representing a minimum level of competence.[4] In the following year the commissioners claimed that success was not gained in the Indian Exam-

[1] CSC, Tenth Rep., 1865, PP 1865, XVI, pp. 9–11; CSC Thirteenth Rep. 1868, PP 1867–8, XXII, p. 15.
[2] CSC, Thirteenth Rep. 1868, PP 1867–8, XXII, p. 18; Roy, The Civil Service in India, pp. 76–7.
[3] Latham, On the Action of Examinations considered as a means of Selection, pp. 40–1. Latham's book is fully discussed in ch. 11.
[4] CSC, Tenth Rep. 1865, PP 1865, XVI, pp. 11–12.

inations as the result of taking up a large number of subjects and by concentrating on those which were not taught at public schools and universities. In fact, they argued, classics, mathematics, English and French, the basic subjects of the public-school course, were those to which were allotted the highest total of marks. It was in these subjects too that the successful candidates obtained the highest proportion of the maximum marks. Of the whole aggregate of marks obtained by thirty-two successful candidates in the previous year, eighty-two per cent were due 'to the ordinary curriculum of a public school'.[1]

Whatever criticisms may have been voiced the Civil Service Commissioners had no doubt either of the success of the scheme or of the strong links which it had forged between the Indian Service and the public schools and universities. Their arguments are set out very clearly in their tenth report for 1865. After reviewing the arguments used by Macaulay's committee and explaining the method of examination adopted, the report goes on:

For the valuable prizes thus held out candidates of ability have presented themselves, not only from the great English universities and public schools, but from the Scottish and Irish Universities, from numerous schools and colleges scattered over the three kingdoms, and even from the most distant parts of the Empire: from the College of Benares and the University of Melbourne. Among others a Brahmin of high caste, though unacquainted, as might be expected, with the classical languages of Europe, passed such an examination in the classical languages of his own country, viz Sanskrit and Arabic, together with English and other subjects, that he obtained a place among the successful competitors, and is now a covenanted servant of the Crown.[2]

The whole number of persons who have been successful in these competitions during the ten years from 1855 to 1864 inclusive has been 458. Of these, 101 had been educated at Oxford, 80 at Cambridge; 37 at the University of London; 27 at that of Edinburgh; 76 at Trinity College Dublin; 58 at other universities, and 79 at various other institutions, or under private tutors.

It need hardly be pointed out how great a stimulus has been given to education in its widest sense by thus offering an opportunity of distinction to merit, both in institutions and individuals, which might otherwise have remained undeveloped or unacknowledged.[3]

---

[1] CSC, Eleventh Rep. 1866, PP 1866, XXV, p. 7.
[2] Satyendra Nath Tagore, Forty-Third in 1863.
[3] CSC, Tenth Rep. 1865, PP 1865, XVI, p. 6.

This lengthy quotation is important because it brings out the points which were so important to the administrative reformers. The vital connections between a rejuvenated public service and a developing system of higher education is clearly stressed. Of the total number of successful candidates rather less than half (181) were Oxford and Cambridge men. They were outnumbered by the products of universities in other parts of the kingdom (198) – Scotsmen, Irishmen, and alumni of the University of London, an institution still in its comparative youth. Macaulay's aim of offering a very wide range of opportunity to the well-educated certainly seemed to have been achieved. From this point of view, the success of an Indian candidate should be noted. As early as 1859 the commissioners had pointed out that the opening of Calcutta University (1857) had made it more likely that Indians would present themselves.[1] Another very important point to note is the considerable number of appointments made – an average in the ten years 1855–64 of forty-five per annum. The number of Indian appointments offered annually long remained far higher than the number of home appointments at a comparable level, even after the introduction in 1870 of genuine competition. By their sheer number the Indian posts long remained an important factor in the calculations of British parents and of their sons.

At home the world of the circumlocution office lingered long after the creation of the Civil Service Commission. The problems involved were, as has already been suggested, very much more complex. The question of political patronage was far more difficult in England than in India. For India only candidates for the most senior appointments were recruited in England itself. Once the principle of competition had been established it was comparatively simple to frame a scheme of recruitment closely related to university examinations. In the home country every type of appointment had to be considered from the permanent secretary to the postman. Charles Trevelyan had pointed out this problem to Gladstone before the Civil Service Commission had been set up.[2] Many of the posts would, he argued, be filled by young men of the middle class who had received a good English or commercial education. Above them would be the holders of the higher posts,

---

[1] CSC, Fourth Rep, 1859, PP 1859, VIII, pp. 41–2.
[2] 10 March 1854; see Hughes, 'Sir Charles Trevelyan and Civil Service Reform, 1853–5', English Historical Review, vol. LXIV (1949), pp. 217–18.

who would be Oxford or Cambridge men, and below them those who had received an education in 'national school second-rate English studies'.

Very broadly the posts in the Home Civil Service fell into three grades, though it was a long time before precise definitions of each grade were adopted. The three grades covered what would be called today the administrative and the executive classes, and the very large manual or non-professional group, like letter-carriers and tide-waiters. The reformers were anxious to spread the gospel of education and competition over the whole range of posts, but the opportunities offered them by the Order-in-Council of 21 May 1855 were extremely limited.

The Order duly laid down that all young men who were to be appointed to any situation in the Civil Service should, before they were admitted to probation, be examined by the Civil Service Commissioners and should receive from them a certificate of qualification. Such a certificate was to be granted only after the candidate had proved that he possessed 'the requisite knowledge and ability for the proper Discharge of his official Duties', and after proper enquiries had been made into age, health and character. Yet the position of the heads of departments in the service was safeguarded in such a way as to make the commissioners' certificate a very modest hurdle indeed. After the regulations which have already been explained the Order goes on:

The Rules applicable to each Department under each of the above Heads should be settled, with the Assistance of the Commissioners, according to the Discretion of the Chief Authorities of the Department, but, except that Candidates for admission to any of the Junior Situations in any Branch of the Civil Service will be required to obtain Certificates of Qualification as aforesaid, such Examining Board shall not make any alteration in respect to the Nomination or Appointment of Candidates by those who are or may be charged with the Duty of Nomination and Appointment.[1]

The certificate of qualification proved to be little more than a test in basic literacy, which indeed many candidates failed to pass. Until Gladstone's reforms of 1870 heads of departments had the power to decide whether their vacancies should be filled by simple nomination or by limited competition among nominated candidates.

[1] For the Order-in-Council, see *CSC, First Rep.* 1856, *PP* 1856, XXII, pp. 365–6.

The common departmental attitudes can be illustrated by two examples taken from the commissioners' reports. Mr Labouchere of the Colonial Office expressed his belief that 'a system of open competition, under which duties ... should be simply entrusted, without other guarantee, to the performance of the cleverest and most ambitious youths, would be at best of doubtful advantage for the purposes of this department'.[1] The postmaster-general, the Duke of Argyll, in asking the commissioners to examine for clerkships in his office was even more explicit:

His Grace would be glad, therefore, if the Commissioners would undertake to conduct these examinations, and to favour him with their opinion on the comparative merits of the candidates. At the same time ... it must be distinctly understood that he will not consider himself bound to be guided exclusively by that opinion, and that he reserves to himself the full power of ultimate decision.[2]

The standard demanded for certificates was not very high, either for the higher or for the lower posts. After they had made enquiries from the departments, the commissioners explained in their first report, that almost all of them had required 'good handwriting, correct spelling and some knowledge of arithmetic, usually including vulgar and decimal fractions'. Many departments had asked, in the higher situations, for précis-writing and English composition and sometimes for book-keeping. In addition there were to be examinations in general subjects, such as history, geography and a foreign language.[3] The Treasury required for a certificate of qualification for a clerkship, one of the most desirable of official posts, the following subjects: handwriting and orthography; arithmetic; the first three books of Euclid; the history of England; geography; a translation chosen among Latin, French, German and Italian; a précis or abstract.[4]

These examinations were, of course, qualifying not competitive. They aimed merely to set a standard below which candidates should not be allowed to fall. Even so it is clear that what was required was extremely elementary knowledge of a schoolboy kind. It might have been expected that tide-waiters and letter-carriers should be

[1] *CSC, First Rep.* 1856, *PP* 1856, XXII, p. 371.
[2] *CSC, Second Rep.* 1857, *PP* 1857, III, p. 81.
[3] *CSC, First Rep.* 1856, *PP* 1856, XXII, p. 368.
[4] *Ibid.* pp. 372–3. The requirements of the Home Office were very similar (*CSC, Second Rep.* 1857, *PP* 1857, III, p. 79).

required to do only very simple arithmetic and an easy passage of dictation.[1] If there had been a universal system of primary education, it would have been unnecessary for the commissioners to examine these people at all. Even for the higher class of appointment the arithmetic involved nothing more than vulgar and decimal fractions with 'nothing of a puzzling character'. In English composition a theme or essay was not required, but very few candidates showed facility in composing a letter or in writing a précis. In general the commissioners thought the standard of their papers was lower than that set by the Society of Arts and the Oxford and Cambridge Local Examinations.[2]

Where certificates were not granted the cause of the trouble did not lie in failure in the higher subjects. During the first eighteen months of the commission's existence (21 May 1855–31 December 1856) 2,686 candidates were examined, of whom 1,587 obtained certificates and 880 were rejected. Of this 880, 425 were rejected for spelling alone or for spelling with other subjects except arithmetic. 147 failed in arithmetic alone or in arithmetic with other subjects except spelling. 243 failed in spelling and arithmetic, while only 65 were rejected for deficiencies not involving spelling and arithmetic.[3] This experience was typical of what the commissioners found during the early years of their work.

They naturally asked themselves the reason for this state of affairs. They concluded that it did not arise from the state of education in the country as a whole, but rather from the defects associated with the traditional system of patronage. Covertly at first and more openly as the years went on, they attacked in their reports the hydra-headed monster of personal influence which had been the foe of so many reformers for so long. The danger in the case of the inferior appointments arose, they argued, from the recommendations of persons desirous 'not of supplying the public with a useful officer, but of making a competent provision for a friend'.[4] A candidate under the Order-in-Council had to learn, they claimed, that his position 'is not that of a person possessing a *prima facie* right to Government employment, subject to deprivation of that right upon cause shown; but is rather that of a person

[1] *CSC, Second Rep.* 1857, *PP* 1857, III, pp. 75–6.
[2] *Ibid.* pp. 76–8, *CSC, Sixth Rep.* 1861, *PP* 1861, XIX, p. 29, note.
[3] *CSC, Second Rep.* 1857, *PP* 1857, III, pp. 84–5.
[4] *CSC, First Rep.* 1856, *PP* 1856, XXII, p. 382.

whose whole title to such employment depends upon the qualification which he may be able positively to establish'.[1]

To the minds of the commissioners there was no doubt that such
qualifications were best established by competitive written examinations combined with securities about age, health and character.
The case for such examinations was hardest to make for the most
subordinate posts, where, it might be argued, nothing was required
except health and strength and personal dependability. Yet, even
in the case of the letter-carriers and tide-waiters, the commissioners
did not flinch. They denied that the tests which they used demanded
too high a standard. They affirmed that it was just as possible at this
level as at any other level to frame questions which would pick out
the most intelligent and the most industrious candidates.[2] Once
again the familiar educational argument was brought into play.
If people in this station of life knew that a sound education would
give their children a better chance of securing these posts, they
would be encouraged to obtain for them such an education. To
depend on this for entry to public employment instead of on personal
clientage of the old kind 'cannot fail to have a purifying effect on the
minds of the artizan class generally'.[3]

This moral argument implied a claim that the power of the state
should be used to achieve a new pattern of excellence in administration, legislation and education. In their sixth report the
commissioners printed some correspondence with the postmaster-
general whose decision to return to the traditional method of
appointing letter-carriers they regretted. Their secretary wrote as
follows:

But if, in the selection of candidates for the police, where physical
strength must be, even more than in the case of letter-carriers, the great
requisite, compared with which all others are of minor importance, it is
possible to insist on ability 'to read and write' – if it is reasonable to
interfere with the rights of private employers of labour in factories and
mines, by compulsory provisions, with regard to the education of young
persons whom they receive into their service – and, above all, if the large
amount of public money expended in teaching those whose duties in
after-life will in all probability be not less mechanical than those of
letter-carriers is rightly so expended – it is difficult to believe that the

---

[1] *CSC, Ninth Rep.* 1864, *PP* 1864, XXX, p. 25.
[2] *CSC, Sixth Rep.* 1861, *PP* 1861, XIX, p. 19.
[3] *CSC, Eighth Rep.* 1863, *PP* 1863, XX, p. 13.

power of writing from dictation, with moderate correctness, a short passage containing only words of common use, and of performing sums in addition and subtraction ... is one which it would be hazardous or unreasonable to expect in any class of public servants.[1]

As the commissioners gradually felt their way, their arguments gained in breadth and assurance. From the very beginning of their work they had conducted a certain number of examinations which were competitions among a certain number of nominated candidates. In their first report they claimed that those who succeeded in such competitions were normally men of higher attainments than those who came in on simple nomination.[2] Of course the level of such competitions depended on the numbers nominated and the standard of the competitors. In their report for 1857 the commissioners explained that a competition had been held in their own office for four situations, which had not been advertised but had been made widely known through various channels. The result both socially and educationally had been highly successful. Forty-four competitors had been examined of forty-six who offered, twenty-eight of them being the sons of professional men and independent gentlemen. Of the forty-six, twenty-five had been at universities and of the remaining twenty-one, sixteen had been at public schools, or well-known grammar schools. The general standard of the examination had been high and the commissioners used this example, and a similar examination the following year, to make the point that young men of ability were available and that, if free opportunities were afforded to them, they could be recruited for the public service.[3]

But limited competition was generally an unsatisfactory instrument of selection because in most cases very few candidates, and they often of a low educational standard, were nominated for the vacancies. As time went on the commissioners became more and more critical of such competitions which in their eyes were hardly competitions at all. The true pattern they believed was true open competition, and their claims seemed to be triumphantly vindicated by the offer on open competition of 8 Writerships in the office of the secretary of state for India in 1859. For these 8 posts 391

[1] CSC, Sixth Rep. 1861, PP 1861, XIX, p. 16.
[2] CSC, First Rep, 1856, PP 1856, XXII, p. 383.
[3] CSC, Second Rep. 1857, PP 1857, III, p. 89.

candidates came forward, of whom 339 actually sat the examination. Once again the social and educational level was satisfactory. Sons of professional men and gentlemen were well represented. There were not many university men but there was a strong public-school contingent including two Etonians and a Rugbeian. Once again the commissioners felt that they had proved their point. They concluded that the examinations had shown that there were plenty of young men with intelligence and industry available. They came in general from the professional and middle classes. There was no difficulty in conducting such a large examination and in preventing fraud and personation in it.[1]

By this time the waters were slowly beginning to move. In 1860 a Select Committee of the House of Commons on Civil Service Appointments reported in favour of extending open competition though they were not prepared to take the whole step at once. Broadly speaking their recommendations involved the strengthening of the system of limited competition. This indeed was suggested by the Civil Service Commissioners themselves as an intermediate stage towards full open competition.[2] In their report the Select Committee, of which both Northcote and Robert Lowe were members, argued that there had not been sufficient time for a fair judgment of the arrangements of 1855. It was, however, generally agreed that they had tended to exclude men who were intellectually unfit for the service.[3] The evidence, the committee thought, was in favour of open competition, and in departments like the Indian Civil Service it had already been introduced.

Yet to introduce it at once into England might lead to a dangerous reaction because of the disturbance of private interests, the breach of political patronage and the harm done to local interests. The immediate step therefore, as the commissioners had themselves argued, must be to improve the present system. A preliminary examination should be instituted to ensure that those who competed were 'educationally qualified to receive a certificate from the Commissioners'.[4] There should also be at least three such qualified candidates for a single vacancy and, in order to increase the range of

[1] *CSC, Fourth Rep.* 1859, *PP* 1859, VIII, pp. 42–9. The occupations of the parents and the schools of successful candidates are on pp. 46–7.
[2] *Report from the Select Committee on Civil Service Appointments, PP* 1860, IX, pp. 335–8 (paper by Ryan and Shaw-Lefevre).
[3] *Ibid.* pp. 10–11.
[4] *Ibid.* p. 14.

competition, several vacancies should be competed for at once. In the manual grades intellectual competition was not suited for mechanical duties. Health and moral character should be strictly investigated and a simple educational test be given. From time to time the India House experiment of 1859 in open competition should be repeated 'by which a further comparison between the limited and unlimited system may be instituted with a view to that ultimate extension of the area of competition, to which your Commission look forward as the legitimate result of the changes now recommended'.[1]

The report reaffirmed, to a large extent, the wisdom of the commissioners' policy, though to judge from their annual reports during the sixties progress in raising the level of the examinations was very slow. The plan of a preliminary test examination was adopted in 1861 by the Treasury for the clerkships under its control. The subjects of this examination as suggested by the commissioners included orthography, handwriting, arithmetic, English composition and in some cases book-keeping and Latin.[2] Subsequently the same examination was adopted by the War Office, the National Debt Office, the India Office and the Office of the Clerk of the Parliaments.[3] However, a number of offices made no use of the preliminary test with the result that many competitors were quite unqualified and limited competition remained in many cases a mere phantom test. The commissioners gave examples in almost every annual report, of which the following in 1865 is typical:

The number of *competitive examinations* has been 131, in which 784 candidates have competed for 251 places, making an average of 3·1 competitors for each vacancy. Out of these 784 candidates, 290 who contended for 98 situations had already passed a preliminary test examination; the remaining 494 competitors for 153 situations had undergone no previous test. Of this latter group 231 failed to show a qualifying knowledge of the prescribed subjects; so that in reality not more than 263 qualified candidates contended for 153 vacancies; or, on an average, 1·7 qualified competitors for each vacancy.[4]

It looks as if during the sixties the effective number of qualified competitors was not much more than one candidate for one

<hr />

[1] *Ibid.* p. 15.
[2] *CSC, Sixth Rep.* 1861, *PP* 1861, XIX, pp. 7–14.
[3] *CSC, Ninth Rep.* 1864, *PP* 1864, XXX, p. 21.
[4] *CSC, Tenth Rep.* 1865, *PP* 1865. XVI, p. 3.

vacancy. Where preliminary tests were held almost half those who took them failed. Sometimes, indeed, there were more vacancies than there were qualified candidates to fill them.[1] The total number of nominations was rising, partly because of the extension of the Order-in-Council to new classes of official, and partly because, under the provisions of the Superannuation Act of 1859, no one appointed after that date could receive a pension unless he had received the commissioners' certificate.[2] Though competitions had grown in number there were still a large number of nominees, many of whom failed to reach the commissioners' standard of competence. Thus the report for 1866 gives 831 nominees for superior posts, 313 of whom failed to obtain appointments, in almost all cases for deficiencies in 'knowledge and ability'.

The commissioners in their report for 1868 provided statistics which may serve as a useful summary of what had happened under the system of 1855. Between 1855 and 1868, 46,523 candidates had come before them, 28,596 of whom had gained certificates of qualification. Of this latter total 9,826 had been awarded for higher situations and 18,770 for lower. 9,461 candidates had been rejected as disqualified, 7,323 of whom were deficient in 'knowledge and ability'. Of this 7,323, 7,107 had failed in elementary and practical subjects and only 216 in scholastic subjects. To divide the 28,596 certificates granted in another way, 18,770 had been granted for inferior posts, and here competition had hardly been tried at all. The examinations had consisted merely of reading and writing and sometimes of reading alone. Of the 9,826 certificates for higher situations, 28 had been granted after open competition, 2,765 after limited competition, and 7,033 without competition at all.

The commissioners re-affirmed that, from the tiny number of cases where open competition had been used for the higher situations, it was clear that there was an ample supply of good candidates. Once again the report showed that the arrangements for limited competition suggested by the Select Committee of 1860 had proved illusory. In only 100 of 858 such competitions held since 1 January 1862 had the stated proportions of qualified candidates to vacancies (5 to 1 in the case of a single vacancy, 3 to 1 in the case of more than one vacancy) been maintained. As they had done year after year the commissioners reaffirmed that the best method of recruitment

---

[1] See CSC, Sixth Rep. 1861, PP 1861, XIX, pp. 14–15 for some statistics.
[2] CSC, Eighth Rep. 1863, PP 1863, XX, p. 7.

for the lower as well as for the higher posts was by open competition. Indeed, they took as an example of their claim, the humble task of the copyist, that Victorian precursor of the typewriter. If it were thought desirable to replace regular clerks by mere copyists, they argued, the best way to select the copyists would be by a competitive examination in handwriting alone. 'If the conditions of such examinations were duly made known and publicly advertised beforehand, we do not doubt that a class of copyists might be secured to the Civil Service whose average handwriting would be distinctly superior in quality to that of an equal number of persons appointed by simple nomination, or as the result of a limited competition.'[1] To the commissioners the principle of open competition admitted of no limitations. It was capable of adaptation to all circumstances.

[1] *CSC, Thirteenth Rep.* 1868, *PP* 1867–8, XXII, pp. 4–13. The quotation is on p. 13.

9

THE CIVIL SERVICE
EXAMINATIONS: AFTER 1870

Open competition was finally introduced by Gladstone in an Order-in-Council of 4 June 1870. The prime minister had been urged to take this step by his chancellor of the exchequer, Robert Lowe. Both of them were, of course, distinguished Oxford men, who had been concerned with the original reforms of the fifties. The victory of the reformers in 1870 was a triumph for the Civil Service Commissioners and for those who thought like them, but it marked merely a stage in a long story. It was one thing to adopt a principle. It was quite another to forecast how that principle would work out, for the development of the examinations was bound to be deeply influenced by the way in which the Civil Service itself developed. Two Royal Commissions, the Playfair Commission of 1874 and the Ridley Commission of 1886, were set up to study its organization and to recommend improvements. Under the old order there had hardly been a single service at all, but rather a congeries of departments with little definition of the different grades of responsibility in each office. These problems are deep-rooted and intractable in all governmental structures. The North-cote–Trevelyan report had tried to deal with some of them. They have endured into the twentieth century to be the subject of the Fulton report of 1968. Indeed, as the sphere of government becomes wider, the structure of administration becomes more complex. This study is not a history of the Civil Service and no attempt will be made to examine these issues more fully here. But they have a profound influence on recruitment. As the structure of government changes, so different demands are made of those who come to serve it.

The Order-in-Council of 4 June 1870 repeated the general arrangements of the order of 1855 with the crucial addition that, in the case of all departments mentioned in an attached schedule, appointments were to be made 'by means of competitive examinations, according to regulations to be from time to time framed by the said Civil Service Commissioners, and approved by the Commissioners of Her Majesty's Treasury, open to all persons (of the requisite age, health, character and other qualifications prescribed in the said regulations) who may be desirous of attending the same'.[1]

The regulations for open competition did not cover the wide range of inferior posts, such as office-keepers and messengers, which continued as before to be subject to a qualifying examination only.[2] Nor, at the other end of the scale, did it cover clerkships in the Foreign Office or first appointments in the Diplomatic Service, where candidates entered by limited competition on the nomination of the Secretary of State.[3] By the time of the Ridley Commission it was clear that the standard of these posts was high and that able young men were nominated. The argument for preserving this relic of the older system was the requirement of personal suitability which we have met before. Only a young man whose antecedents and character were thoroughly known could be regarded as 'a fit and proper person to be entrusted with the affairs, often delicate and confidential, of the British Foreign Office'.[4]

With these exceptions the remaining posts which were open to competition were organized into two schemes of examination. Scheme I corresponded to the examination for the Indian Civil Service. The age limits were from eighteen to twenty-four and it was planned to appoint highly educated candidates. The mark scheme was in fact very similar to the Indian Civil Service scheme worked out by Macaulay's committee, though more weight was given to mathematics and to natural sciences, and both political economy and jurisprudence were included. Scheme II covered the entry of clerks at a lower level. The age limits were from sixteen to twenty, and the examination covered handwriting, ortho- graphy, arithmetic, copying MSS, indexing or docketing, digesting returns into summaries, English composition, geography, English history and book-keeping.[5] Scheme II covered very broadly what the men of the time called a middle-class or a commercial education though its educational demands were somewhat moderate. For

[1] *CSC, Fifteenth Rep.* 1870, *PP* 1870, XIX, p. 8.
[2] *CSC, Seventeenth Rep.* 1872, *PP* 1872, XIX, p. 16.
[3] Limited competition for Foreign Office clerks came into force after December 1857, and for the Diplomatic Service in 1880 (*CSC, Twenty-Ninth Rep.* 1885, *PP* 1884–5, XXI, p. 578).
[4] *Royal Commission appointed to Inquire into the Civil Establishments. Fourth Report, PP* 1890, XXVII, p. 9.
[5] For the regulations, see *CSC, Sixteenth Rep.* 1871, Appendix I, *PP* 1871, XVII, pp. 7–18.

instance, it did not include a foreign language, or anything of mathematics more complex than arithmetic. Thus the range of subjects was much narrower than that covered by the Local Examinations. In both schemes candidates had to pass a preliminary examination.

The plan of organization which lay behind the whole scheme was as follows: in each office there should be a small number of superior officers selected under scheme I. The great bulk of the work of the office would be done by subordinate clerks selected under scheme II, with the assistance, for the purely mechanical part of their duties, of writers who were not on the permanent establishment. In fact, things did not work out as harmoniously as that. It was a matter of policy to reduce the numbers of clerks of the first class as much as possible, but there were wide variations in the numbers of clerks of the first and the second classes employed in the different offices. In addition coherent planning was made much more difficult by the considerable number of clerks who survived from the old order. Until they retired, there was nothing that could be done about the posts which they filled. Problems of departmentalism were made worse by the fact that there were no common salary scales between departments.

The commissioners' ideal for the first-class clerkships remained the public-school and university man who would bring to the public service the highest type of knowledge and ability which the best education could bring out. What they hoped to achieve is set out in their Report for 1877 where they described a competition which had brought forward a very strong field, partly because of the offer of two clerkships in the Colonial Office 'exceeding in value any which up to that time had been competed for under this scheme'.[1] 61 candidates finally competed, of whom 11 were selected, most of them being public school and university men. The education of the successful candidates and the offices chosen by them were as follows:

1	Winchester	Balliol	Colonies
2	Winchester	New College	Colonies
3	Winchester	New College	G.P.O. (Secretary's Office)
4	—	Corpus, Oxford	India Office

[1] *CSC, Twenty-First Rep.* 1877, *PP* 1877, XXVIII, pp. iv–v.

5	Eton	Trinity, Cambridge	India Office
6	Harrow	Balliol	Declined
7	Harrow	Pembroke, Oxford	Civil Service Commission
8		Privately educated	G.P.O. (Secretary's Office)
9	—	Corpus, Oxford	G.P.O. (Secretary's Office)
10	—	Trinity College, Dublin	Record Office, England
11	Haileybury	Trinity, Cambridge	Record Office, England

This was, from the standpoint of the day, an impressive list. Yet if the first-class clerkships be thought of alongside the Indian Civil Service appointments, as another door opened for young men of ability and good education, it must be emphasized that during the last quarter of the nineteenth century, the Home Civil Service provided comparatively few openings for such men. In their report for 1895 the commissioners gave the total number of first-class clerkships filled by open competition since 1870 as 232, which is an average of roughly 10 per year.[1] This was very substantially less than the number of Indian appointments. To take some figures at random, there were 38 Indian appointments in 1874,[2] forty in 1883[3] and thirty-two in 1891.[4] It is difficult to make absolute comparisons because the age limits for the Indian appointments were changed on several occasions, but the broad statement that the Indian Service continued to offer many more opportunities to well-educated young men than the Home Service is certainly true.

The second-class clerkships open to young men in their late teens tell a different story. There were a considerable number of them, and they attracted a large and growing number of competitors. In that sense they became an important professional objective for men who had been educated at the commercial or middle-class level. In the first examinations under scheme II 95 appointments were offered. 738 candidates came forward, of whom 374 actually competed, having passed the preliminary examination.[5] In the

---

[1] CSC, Thirty-Ninth Rep. 1895, PP 1895, XXVI, pp. 234–5.
[2] CSC, Nineteenth Rep. 1875, PP 1875, XXII, p. 6.
[3] CSC, Twenty-Eighth Rep. 1884, PP 1884, XXI, p. 293.
[4] CSC, Thirty-Sixth Rep. 1892, PP 1892, XXVII, p. 300.
[5] CSC, Seventeenth Rep. 1872, PP 1872, XIX, p. 7.

mid-seventies the proportion of competitors to vacancies was about 3 to 1.[1]

By that time the structure of the Civil Service had been considerably affected by the report of the Playfair Commission of 1874, which had been established as a result of the problems of organization which have already been mentioned. The commission recommended the establishment of a higher and of a lower division with salaries in the range respectively of £100–400 and of £80–200 and further promotion dependent on merit. The great difference between the types of work to be done could be met only by establishing two distinct and separate grades. It was envisaged that if this policy were followed the numbers of higher-division clerks would be curtailed and more lower-division clerks would be appointed.[2] Nothing was done to create a uniform higher-division structure, but by an Order-in-Council of 12 February 1876 a lower division of two classes, men and boys, was set up. Each was to be recruited by open competition, in the first case among candidates between the ages of seventeen and twenty and in the second of boys between the ages of fifteen and seventeen.[3]

During the ensuing decade the lower-division examinations proved more and more popular among young men of varying social backgrounds. In 1884 the proportion of competitors to vacancies had risen as high as eleven to one, and the commissioners noted that the number of competitors seemed to have no close relationship to the number of posts offered for competition.[4] In the following year the commissioners made some interesting reflections about the competitions at this level.

There does not yet appear to be any diminution in the attractiveness of these appointments for the general public. Thus, whereas the number of competitors in 1876 was 370, it rose in 1879 to 1,269, and in 1885 to 2,075, the proportion being 10·3 candidates to each vacancy. In this connection it is noteworthy that a very large proportion of the candidates who succeed in the examinations are drawn from a much wider social area than that from which the service was recruited before the days of open competition. The statistics given in the appendix, relating to the 221 clerks appointed in the year 1885, show that as many as 95 received their education in National, British, Wesleyan or Board Schools; while,

---

[1] *CSC, Twenty-Eighth Rep.* 1884, *PP* 1884, XXI, p. 289.
[2] *Civil Service Inquiry Commission, First Report, PP* 1875, XXIII, pp. 8–23.
[3] *CSC, Twentieth Rep.* 1876, *PP* 1876, XXII, pp. 3–4.
[4] *CSC, Twenty-Ninth Rep.* 1885, *PP* 1884–5, XXI, p. 580.

of the residue, only about a dozen were educated at schools of so high a class as that to which Dulwich College, and the City of London School belong. Out of 173 who had been in any occupation, 92 had been employed as Boy Clerks or Temporary Copyists; 28 had been pupil-teachers or assistants in schools. Not fewer than 135 had been in employment yielding less than 1 l. per week and of these 52 were earning less than 15s. a week, and 22 less than 10s. a week. The occupations of the parents are, it will be seen, in harmony with these facts. To young lads, with such antecedents, permanent situations carrying salaries of 80 l. to 95 l. rising to 200 l. or 250 l., and a prospect of 350 l., besides pension, must needs be very alluring, as being much beyond what they could reasonably hope to obtain in any career otherwise open to them.[1]

The social role of competitive examination was twofold. At the higher levels it provided the upper classes with a reinforcement to their traditional power because they enjoyed the advantages of the best education. By encouraging all classes to obtain a better educa-tion for their children because a good education was the road to monetary reward, it also opened doors which were closed before. The point has already been made in the case of H. G. Wells and the examinations of the Science and Art Department.[2] The examina-tions for the middle and lower reaches of the Civil Service reinforce it. These examinations certainly created a wider opportunity. Their educational effects were, as we shall see later, much criticized. The result of putting large numbers of candidates in for a compara-tively simple examination on a few subjects was to lead to cramming and mark-grubbing.

Both the good and bad results of the Civil Service Examinations are seen very clearly in the entry to the Post Office. The posts of junior clerk, newspaper-sorter and telegraph-messenger were not included under the relevant schedule of the Order-in-Council of 1870, but they were examined from the beginning of the new system at the wish of the postmaster-general, and large numbers of candidates came forward.[3] Much of this type of work was suitable for women, and the Post Office inherited some women clerks when it took over the telegraph system in 1870. In 1881 the postmaster-general determined to throw open to competition the posts of female clerk and of female and male telegraph-learners. The first competi-tion for female clerks in the London offices took place in September

[1] CSC. Thirtieth Rep. 1886, PP 1886, XX, p. 93.
[2] See p. 8.
[3] CSC, Seventeenth Rep. 1872, PP 1872, XIX, pp. 9–10.

of that year. The candidates took a preliminary examination followed by a test in arithmetic, spelling, English composition, geography, and English history.[1]

At a time when opportunities of employment for women were few, these Post Office appointments soon attracted a very large number of candidates. In 1883 331 candidates were examined for 60 female clerkships in the General Post Office after 377 other candidates had failed to pass the preliminary examination. 1,682 girls were also examined for 160 appointments in the telegraph school.[2] In 1898 3,812 females competed for 479 appointments and 1,986 males for 682 appointments in the Post Office.[3] As in the case of the lower-division clerkships very keen competition on a limited syllabus led to tremendous concentration on winning marks. The very success of these competitions was bound to encourage special preparation among those who took them, as indeed was the case throughout the whole range of Civil Service posts.

This keen rivalry for lower-division clerkships and Post Office appointments reflected not only the attractions of the Civil Service as a secure career, but also the steady development of secondary education in the country. The grammar schools had been improved. Many of the school boards had created higher-grade schools. Not only were lower-middle-class parents more conscious of the importance of a good education for their children. Such an education was becoming much easier to obtain than it had been in 1850.

Alongside the improvement of secondary education at the middle and lower levels had gone the even more striking development of the public schools. Some of the abler products of these schools found their way into the public service through the examinations for India and for first-class clerkships at home, but these were always a distinguished minority. In terms of sheer numbers it was the army examinations which entered into the calculations of parents of the professional and upper classes. The opening of commissions in the army to open competition marked an important extension of employment to young men of good education whose families lacked influence of the traditional kind.

The Civil Service Commissioners were asked in February 1870 by Edward Cardwell, secretary of state for war, to conduct the

[1] *CSC, Twenty-Sixth Rep.* 1882, *PP* 1882, XXII, p. 10.
[2] *CSC, Twenty-Eighth Rep.* 1884, *PP* 1884, XXI, p. 291.
[3] *CSC, Forty-Third Rep.* 1899, *PP* 1899, XIX, p. 134.

entrance examinations for the Royal Military Academy, Woolwich and the Royal Military College, Sandhurst. This policy had been recommended by the Royal Commission on military education of 1868, which had been anxious to base the competition on a liberal education of the kind obtainable in the public schools.[1] In 1870 the abolition of the purchase of commissions marked another important step in the same direction. The commissioners inherited a competitive examination for entry to Woolwich, and they created a competitive examination for youths between the ages of seventeen and twenty who were candidates for first appointments in the cavalry and infantry.[2] After 1 December 1876 candidates for these appointments had to pass through a course at Sandhurst. In order to gain entry they were required to pass a preliminary examination, and an examination in not less than two nor more than four among the subjects: mathematics; English composition, literature and history; Latin; Greek; French; German; experimental sciences; geography and geology; freehand drawing.[3]

Very large numbers took the Sandhurst preliminary examination, though many of the candidates failed it. This initial hurdle was abolished in 1894 because it was not effective; candidates could pass it in sections and were allowed unlimited attempts.[4] The number competing for places at Sandhurst remained very large. In 1893 there were 979 candidates for 202 appointments.[5] At Woolwich many aspirants failed to reach the necessary standard in mathematics and the number finally emerging from the examination was not usually much greater than the number of vacancies. Those who had planned the army examinations had been anxious to relate them closely to the curriculum of the public schools. In one sense they had been successful, but in another they had failed. They certainly recruited public-school boys into the army in large numbers, but they often received special preparation outside their normal school courses. The commissioners' report for 1889 gives the number of Woolwich and Sandhurst candidates as about 1,200 per year. Of these about two-thirds came from public schools, and about half that number entered after special preparation. This was more common for Sandhurst than for Woolwich, where the

[1] CSC, Fifteenth Rep. 1870, PP 1870, XIX, p. 15.
[2] CSC, Seventeenth Rep. 1872, PP 1872, XIX, p. 22.
[3] CSC, Twenty-First Rep. 1877, PP 1877, XXVIII, pp. 591–3.
[4] CSC, Thirty-Eighth Rep. 1894, PP 1894, XXVII, p. 110.
[5] CSC, Thirty-Ninth Rep. 1895, PP 1895, XXVI, p. 241.

standard was higher but the boys were more intellectually promis-ing.[1] In 1893, of 198 successful candidates for infantry and cavalry cadetships, only 72 came straight from school or from home tuition. Of 100 successful Woolwich candidates 59 came direct from school.[2] The demands of the army examinations encouraged the public schools to create their army classes and their modern sides. In that sense they created the world of *Stalky and Co.*, yet in another they encouraged the profitable labours of the crammer, that distinctive Victorian product. In one way they stimulated the schools, yet in another the very keen competition for all these openings in government service encouraged special agencies to prepare those who wished to do well. The very success of competi-tion weakened the direct connection between government service and the schools and universities of the country which the admini-strative reformers had been so keen to achieve.

Much the same is true of the Indian Examinations after the maximum age had been reduced to twenty-one in 1866. This made it very difficult for candidates to attend a university, while they were clearly too old to remain at school. Into the gap marched the crammer, and many people felt that the ties between the service and universities and schools were being loosened. In 1874 84·2% of the successful Indian candidates had been specially prepared, and the average time spent on this preparation was fifteen to sixteen months. Between 1870 and 1874 only 44 out of 186 successful competitors had entered without special preparation, and of this 44, 35 were university men.[3] By the early seventies the situation was causing disquiet. Many people argued that the way to success lay through a smattering of many subjects rather than a solid knowledge of a few. Problems had also arisen about the probationary period of two years which the successful candidates passed working on their own in London. These young men lacked in consequence, it was argued, the *esprit de corps* and the social education which characterized the products of old Haileybury, and which they might have gained in a university. Particular emphasis was laid on this drawback since, after arrival in India, there was little which the young civilian could do to remedy it. For the early years of his service at least he was

[1] CSC, *Thirty-Third Rep.* 1889, *PP* 1889, XXVIII, p. 180.
[2] CSC, *Thirty-Eighth Rep.* 1894, *PP* 1894, XXVIII, p. 109.
[3] *Papers relating to the Selection and Training of Candidates for the Indian Civil Service*, *PP* 1876, LV, pp. 316, 318.

likely to be thrown very much on his own resources in places remote from European companionship.

When Lord Salisbury became secretary of state for India in the Conservative government of 1874 he quickly set about collecting opinions about the system of recruitment. The Civil Service Commissioners themselves defended the existing system. Special preparation was, they thought, the result of the anxiety of parents that their children should succeed. It was not the same as mere cramming, and they pointed out that candidates presented by the most successful of the private tutors had done better in classics and mathematics than the university candidates. Nor did they accept the argument that success came from a mere smattering of many things, and they pointed out that a wide range of subjects had to be offered if a really wide choice were to be given to all the candidates. They did not consider that the civilians on probation should be brought into collegiate residence. Since they had to spend a lot of their time in legal studies, there were important advantages for them in living in London.

The commissioners also discussed the argument that the calibre of men offering for Indian Service was not sufficiently high. They pointed out that circumstances had changed very much since 1855 because of the wide extension of opportunities for able young men at home. Their remarks form an interesting commentary on the position of graduate employment at the time:

The monopoly of openness which these examinations for a time enjoyed has long ceased. The number of fellowships now annually thrown open to competition at Oxford and Cambridge is said to fall little short of the number of well qualified candidates, and for many of them celibacy is no longer a condition. Looking beyond these there has been, in the scholastic field alone, a vast increase in the number of employments to which a good university degree is a direct passport, such as professorships in universities, tutorships and lectureships at colleges, schoolmasterships, inspectorships and examinerships in the Department of Education; while there has grown up a great and ever-increasing demand for men of high education to fill posts of importance in other spheres, including those which are connected with the press.[1]

Though these remarks suggest a widening of graduate employment during the previous twenty years, the universities were still determined to get the Indian appointments more closely into their

[1] *Ibid.* pp. 288–99. The quotation is on p. 296.

own sphere. Not everyone agreed, however, how this might best be done. Dean Liddell of Christ Church, Oxford, as chairman of a committee set up by the Hebdomadal Council, wrote to Salisbury in November 1874, proposing that candidates should be selected for India at eighteen or nineteen, and should then be allowed to take a degree, either in one of the existing schools or in a new final school in Indian subjects. Jowett, on the other hand, wished to retain the existing age limits of seventeen to twenty-one with an extension to twenty-two in some cases. In his view the candidates ought to be brought to a university, and he thought that the best colleges at Oxford and Cambridge would be very prepared to receive them. Though they would be able to reside only for two years, arrangements could probably be made for them to take a degree. The advantages of such a university course would not be limited to the degree itself. The civilians would benefit tremendously from what Jowett characteristically described as 'the more solid advantages of society and increased knowledge of the world'.[1]

Though Liddell and Jowett differed about the age limit, they were in entire agreement about the social advantages of a university course. The opinion of senior Indian civilians was similarly divided about the age limits, though most of them thought that the candidates should receive a communal education, and the university was the natural place for this. Salisbury's final decision came down in favour of the age limits seventeen to nineteen.[2] It was desirable, the official despatch argued, that the candidates should receive 'the ordinary education of English gentlemen', of which a university course formed an essential part. Under the circumstances of the candidates only the early age of entry could secure this advantage to them. If they were to be selected at a later age, they were bound to devote themselves to special preparation for the examination, and a university course might not be the best way of doing this. If the selection had been made at an early age, the successful candidates could benefit from what a university had to give without the worry of future competitive tests. Those who were unsuccessful, since they knew by the age of nineteen what their fate was to be, would not be impeded in their search for other professional openings. To make it advantageous for probationers to

---

[1] For Liddell's and Jowett's views, see *ibid.* pp. 283–4, 285–8.
[2] His dispatch of 24 February 1876 is in *CSC, Twentieth Rep.* 1876, *PP* 1876, XXII, pp. 6–9.

pursue their further study at a university, it was provided that they should receive an allowance of £150 per annum if they passed their probation 'at some university ... at which moral responsibility for the conduct of the students is undertaken, and rules of discipline are enforced'.

These regulations put a premium on residence at Oxford and Cambridge as against London or the Scottish universities. Much was done at the ancient universities to arrange for tuition for the probationers, and Balliol was particularly active. From 1879 onwards more than half the selected candidates were in residence there for the two years of their probation. Though the college authorities had been so active in working the scheme, Jowett himself was not satisfied with it. In 1882 he wrote to the secretary of state for India, pointing out that the number of candidates had fallen sharply and that the probationers were much too young and inexperienced. He suggested that the age limits be raised to eighteen to twenty and the period of probation raised to three years.[1]

The changes were not popular with many people in India for much the same reasons. Native Indian opinion disliked the system because it put further difficulties in the way of Indian candidates, and the nationalist voice was beginning in the eighties to make itself heard. The Indian National Congress at its first session asked for a maximum age of twenty-three and for simultaneous examinations in England and in India.[2] The Indian association of Calcutta not only stressed the difficulties of the Indian candidates, but quoted the testimony of Mr Wren, the most successful of the coaches, that the pressure of the examination was too heavy for boys of seventeen and eighteen. Official opinion in India leant in the same direction. In 1884 the government of India expressed itself in favour of a higher age, and in 1886–7 the Indian Public Service Commission under Sir Charles Aitchison recommended a return to the age limits nineteen to twenty-three so that the general education of students should be completed before selection.[3]

The commissioners themselves once again favoured the status quo, as they had done in 1874–5. In 1885, after seven examinations

[1] E. Abbott and L. Campbell, *Life and Letters of Benjamin Jowett* (1897), vol. II, p. 348.

[2] R. J. Moore, *Liberalism and Indian Politics, 1872–1922* (1966), p. 59.

[3] Roy, *The Civil Service in India*, pp. 83–6.

had been held under the system of 1876, they concluded that the proportion of competitors to vacancies had not varied very much under the lower and the higher age limits. Nor had there been any changes in the social background of the candidates. More successful candidates had come from the public schools without special preparation under the new system, though this higher total only amounted to 80 out of 220 candidates between 1878–84. As might have been expected, very few candidates were coming forward from the English and Irish universities. 5 per cent were still coming from the Scottish universities, presumably because they had a lower age of entry to their courses.[1]

The secretary of state for India finally decided in 1890 to make the age limits twenty-one to twenty-three and to reduce the period of probation to one year. Once again the familiar argument came forward that the present system was not thought to attract candidates 'trained in the best and highest form of English education'. It was also argued that the lower age limits did not enable natives of India to compete on equal terms, though the Indian government was against holding the examinations concurrently in India and in England. The commissioners, in expressing their views, were doubtful about the changes. They re-affirmed their belief in the system of examinations which had endured since 1855, and merely suggested certain modifications which would take account of recent developments in university studies. Thus they suggested extending the scope of history as a subject because of the attention given to it in universities, and adding law and jurisprudence because Final Honours Schools in these disciplines had been created.[2]

The new regulations came into effect in 1892, and they were to endure. With a minor change to twenty-two to twenty-four in 1906, this general pattern remained throughout British rule in the case of candidates examined in London.[3] So the decision finally favoured an advanced general education before selection for Indian service on the lines of Macaulay's original scheme. In the first examination under the regulations of 1892, thirty-two competitors were successful. Of these seventeen had completed a full university course and came in without other special preparation. Ten had followed a university course of some length with other

[1] CSC, Twenty Ninth Rep, 1885, PP 1884–5, XXI, pp. 584–6.
[2] CSC, Thirty-Fourth Rep. 1890, PP 1890, XXVI, pp. 198–216.
[3] Roy, The Civil Service in India, p. 87.

special preparation, while five had special preparation exclusively.[1] By this time more native Indian candidates were coming forward. In the competition of 1896 the first place was occupied by A. C. Chatterjee of Calcutta University and King's College, Cambridge (second class in history). On the same list A. K. Cama of Bombay University and St John's College, Cambridge (twenty-first wrangler) was thirteenth.[2]

After 1892 the pattern of entry to the Indian and the Home Services was so similar that to create a common examination was a natural step. In the Home Service another Royal Commission had, as we shall see, been set up in 1886. Since it was believed that the service was over-staffed, no competitions for first-class and lower-division clerkships were held for several years. When these were resumed for class 1 vacancies, it was decided in 1894 that they would in future be held jointly with the Indian competitions. The Civil Service Commissioners, in suggesting that this step be taken, pointed out that the class 1 competitions had brought forward very few candidates because they were held so infrequently.[3] It was natural to hope that a common competition would bring forward the maximum number of good entrants.[4]

The first competition for the Indian Civil and for class 1 of the Home Service, held at the same time and on the same papers, took place in August 1895. The highest candidates who chose the Indian Service were numbers four, six and seven on the total list. The lowest ranking man to receive a Home appointment was number fourteen and he would have taken seventeenth place among the sixty-six successful candidates. Three candidates who were successful for both services preferred to go to India, but, the commissioners remarked, 'in the course of obtaining the final choices of the candidates it was found that several of those but little lower down on the list would have preferred Home appointments'.[5]

It is worth noting the commissioners' view, expressed at this time, that the new system was likely to obtain for the Home Service 'candidates equal to the best of those who proceed to India'. The point is put that way round, and Home Service given the second place. The Indian Examinations had during the previous forty

[1] CSC, Thirty-Seventh Rep. 1893, PP 1893–4, XXV, p. 258.
[2] CSC, Forty-First Rep. 1897, PP 1897, XXIV, pp. 143–4.
[3] CSC, Thirty-Ninth Rep. 1895, PP 1895, XXVI, pp. 234, 248–54.
[4] CSC, Thirty-Fifth Rep. 1891, PP 1890–1, XXVI, p. 117.
[5] CSC, Fortieth Rep. 1896, PP 1896, XXV, p. 139.

years built up a strong position. Year by year a considerable number of posts had been offered. There had been changes in the age of entry, but no breaks in the sequence of appointments. The class I posts at home certainly attracted good candidates. The commissioners published the schools and university records of the eleven men who were successful in the last separate Home competition in January 1895. All of them were public-school men with Oxford or Cambridge degrees in the first or second class.[1] But the total number of posts offered had been very small, and India offered greater prospects of advancement to an ambitious young man. The sheer disparity in the number of entries to the two services continued to be very marked. In 1898 there were 224 candidates for the Home, Indian and Eastern appointments. 65 posts were offered in India, 23 in the east and 20 at home.[2]

At the end of the eighties another Royal Commission had considered the organization of the Home Service. There was a general feeling that the departments were overstaffed, and in particular that the boundary between the work of the higher and of the lower divisions had not been properly drawn. In its second report the Ridley Commission of 1886 declared that the suggestions of the Playfair Commission of 1874 on this subject had not been carried out. The great difficulty in making the change had been the survival of many clerks from the old establishments. As a result of this highly paid men were in many cases doing low level tasks. Many of the lower-division clerks were dissatisfied with their pay and prospects, and the commissioners considered that the abler among them should have the right of promotion to the higher posts. If the clerks of this division were given more responsible work, it would be possible to reduce the number of higher-division clerks, though there would always remain the need for a small body of men in the public service 'of the same standard of liberal education as those who now adopt the open professions'.[3] As part of the reorganization proposed, there should be much more centralized control of the whole service, and many more transfers between departments.

The Ridley Commission wished, in the case of the higher-

[1] CSC, Thirty-Ninth Rep. 1895, PP 1895, XXVI, p. 236.
[2] CSC, Forty-Third Rep. 1899, PP 1899, XIX, p. 128.
[3] Royal Commission appointed to Inquire into the Civil Establishments. Second Report, 1888, PP 1888, XXVII, pp. ix–xiii.

division clerkships, to make the service as attractive as possible to the best university men, and suggested that the subjects for examination 'should be grouped in some such manner as they are in the Final Schools at the Universities'.[1] The lower-division clerks were, they thought, men of excellent quality. Indeed the competition for these posts had been so severe that the able men who had been successful tended to be dissatisfied with the work which they were doing. The commission was not, however, in favour of raising the level of the examination 'as it appears now to afford a sufficient test of a good commercial education'.[2]

The organization of the service concerns us in this study only indirectly. Once again the Ridley Commission had repeated the constant aspiration that the higher division clerks should be men of high academic standing. Much of their attention had been concentrated, not on these people, but on the lower division (rechristened the second division in 1890). Here the keenness of the competition had led to very widespread cramming among the candidates, and much is said about this in the commission's evidence. Cramming, said Sir G. W. Dasent, one of the Civil Service Commissioners, was rampant, and some boys who had studied with crammers had been incapacitated for intellectual work afterwards.[3] Mr Cleghorn, pressed to answer the question whether the class of candidates was improving, concluded that they were more thoroughly prepared rather than better educated.[4] This problem of special preparation had, as we have seen, been a constant difficulty in all the competitive examinations for the public service, but it was clearly at its worst in the case of the lower-division clerkships.

Since syllabuses were limited and competition was very keen, there was often little differentiation between the candidates. The Civil Service Commissioners themselves considered the problem in their report for 1889.

The effect of examining a great number of highly trained candidates in subjects requiring a somewhat restricted range of intelligence is deserving of notice. The candidates are obliged to devote much time to putting a high degree of polish upon a rather low though useful order of accomplishment. The consequence is that as their performance in the

---

[1] *Ibid.* p. xvii.   [2] *Ibid.* p. xiv.
[3] *Ibid.* Minutes of Evidence, p. 179: 15207, 15228–9.
[4] *Ibid.* p. 121: 13629–33.

examination often reaches a high degree of excellence, while the appointments for which they compete are few in number, it becomes a matter of
extreme difficulty to distinguish with exact precision the relative merits
of the last of the successful and the first of the unsuccessful candidates.
For example, in the last 'female sorters' competition for 30 appointments there was a difference of only thirty marks between the first
candidate and the 31st., or actually one mark per place.[1]

An admirable analysis of the problem, but the commissioners
were less certain what to do about it. Dasent, when examined by
the Ridley Commission, thought that no alteration in schemes of
examination would make any difference,[2] and the Civil Service
Commissioners argued that the lower-division examinations did not
affect education in the schools. As in some other cases which we
have studied, their attitude seems to have been that an existing
situation could not be improved. By the nineties the schools were
becoming much more vocal in matters of this sort, and many
headmasters demanded that something should be done. Indeed criticism of the Civil Service Examinations formed an
important part of a widening assault on the whole examination
structure which was being mounted during the last decade of the
century.

This attack will be much more fully discussed in chapter 11.
Here it is sufficient to point out that, during the nineties, the
Incorporated Association of Headmasters were very critical of the
examinations for boy clerkships and second-division clerkships.
The association's case centred round the point which the commissioners themselves had made in their report for 1889. Since
the subjects for examination were so limited, parents were encouraged to take their boys away from school and send them to
crammers where they would receive intensive preparation in a
narrow field. The headmasters argued, indeed, that intelligent
boys who had followed a wider curriculum at school were actually
put at a disadvantage in comparison with boys of inferior ability
who had limited themselves to the prescribed subjects.[3] In the
course of correspondence with the commissioners the headmasters

---

[1] *CSC, Thirty-Third Rep.* 1889, *PP* 1889, XXVIII, p. 174.
[2] *Royal Commission of Inquiry into the Civil Establishments. Second Report,*
Minutes of Evidence, p. 180: 15267.
[3] The correspondence is in *The Report of the Committee of the Headmasters'
Association, 1892,* pp. 32–5.

quoted the following extract from a paper circulating among future candidates for the service:

We must now conclude with a few words of advice to the parents and and guardians of boys who are destined to enter this service. Do not keep the boy at school too long, for it is only throwing away good money to no purpose. After he has reached the age of 13, whatever knowledge he may subsequently acquire at school, is usually of little or no assistance to him in passing this examination; nay, it is in some cases positively detrimental to his chance of success. Seek out a good firm of Civil Service tutors in whom you may have thorough confidence, and send him, if possible, to the oral class; when this is not possible, let him join the Correspondence Class of such an institution as the ... He will thus be early initiated in to the mysteries of the Civil Service examinations, and when he reaches the age of 15, will be able to pass successfully – possibly at the head of the list, without any apparent effort.

Such a situation was far removed from the ideals of the reformers of the fifties. The commissioners had shown every anxiety to relate the first-class examinations to the curricula of the universities and the army examinations to those of the public schools. Clearly the middle-class secondary schools had gone much further in the range of education which they were offering than the commissioners appreciated. What the headmasters wanted was that their pupils should get an advantage from their general education in a wide range of subjects. A few years later the commissioners informed them that changes on these lines were being considered.[1] Their report for 1897 records the addition of French and German as alternative subjects for candidates for women clerkships in the General Post Office.[2] After 1900 the examination for second-division clerkships was to include (a) Latin, or French, or German; (b) elementary mathematics; (c) inorganic chemistry, with elements of physics. The number of subjects to be offered was also limited. Similar alterations were made in the examinations for boy copyists.[3] These changes illustrate how much secondary education had developed during the last third of the century. The commissioners had long been sensitive to the opinion of the universities and the public schools. The appearance of the heads of secondary schools as an organized group foreshadowed many of the social and educational changes which were to come in the new century.

[1] *Report of the Council of the Headmasters' Association*, 1896, p. 42.
[2] *CSC, Forty-First Rep.* 1897, *PP* 1897, XXIV, p. 147.
[3] *CSC, Forty-Third Rep.* 1899, *PP* 1899, XIX, pp. 133-4.

As that century began Britain was faced with many problems of social organization. The system of open competition for entry to government service had fully established itself, and no one wished to give it up. It was agreed that it provided better-educated and more efficient public servants than patronage had done. Yet the very success of competition had raised, as we have seen in the case of the lower-division clerkships, all kinds of other problems. The commissioners tended not to look beyond the system which it was their duty to work. Sir G. W. Dasent was asked by the Ridley Commission whether he saw any harm in encouraging so many people to qualify themselves for clerkships where there were so many candidates for every vacancy. His answer was that this question was none of his business. To consider what became of those who failed was 'what I should call sentimental; it is their own concern. I do not think it probably detracts anything from the strength of the nation. I should think it was rather a good thing to be educated.'[1] The sting of Dasent's remark comes in the tail. He is assuming that to train a boy to pass a highly competitive examination set on a narrow syllabus is the same thing as giving that boy a good education. By the eighteen-nineties this assumption was being more and more widely questioned.

[1] *Royal Commission of Inquiry into the Civil Establishments. Second Report*, Minutes of Evidence, p. 182: 15304–5.

10

SCHOOL EXAMINATIONS – FROM TAUNTON TO BRYCE

The last chapter ended with the question how far education and preparation for examinations were the same thing. The question had beset the Locals ever since their foundation. They had brought forward able young men, and their defenders used this as one of the main arguments in favour of the system. The critics, who were vocal from the very first, were less happy, especially in the early days when it was very uncommon to enter whole classes. Had the achievements of the few, they asked, been purchased at the expense of the large majority of boys who did not take the examinations at all?[1] Did the examinations reach only 'the few picked boys of a few picked schools'?[2] No one believed that examinations could be abolished altogether. What many of the critics wanted was some sort of general inspection and examination of schools such as had been suggested at Cambridge in 1857.[3] This would ensure that the whole school was systematically tested in its ordinary work, it would prevent cramming, and it would discourage concentration of effort on the few promising boys who were likely to do the school the most credit in an external examination. Since efficient school-management always means good teachers, the advocates of school inspection and examination very often wanted to combine them with the training and registration of teachers.[4] Some argued like E. R. Humphreys in a paper to the Social Science Association that this work could be undertaken only by the government. The studies and teaching of endowed schools and of private schools, if they wished, should be in the hands of a government board of examiners. These would not interfere with the powers of trustees over property and appointments, but they would popularize the

---

[1] J. G. Fitch, 'The Proposed Royal Commission of Inquiry into Middle-Class Education', *Transactions of Social Science Association, 1864*, p. 392.

[2] F. V. Thornton, *The Education of the Middle Classes in England* (1862), p. 28.

[3] See p. 84.

[4] Report of Syndicate on an examination for schoolmasters 1869, CUA University Papers, October 1868–December 1869, no. 84.

best methods and the newest textbooks and raise the status and efficiency of the whole teaching profession.[1] The problem was ultimately one of control. If a scheme of government examination had been introduced, this would have involved state control of secondary schools. The idea put forward by E. R. Humphreys and by many others was bound to come into conflict with the strongly individualist traditions of English secondary education. Had it been put into practice, as seemed very likely about 1870, it might have brought a state system of secondary education forward by a whole generation. The plans for government examination and inspection achieved practical importance when they were adopted in the report of the Schools Inquiry Commission, commonly called the Taunton Commission, in 1868. This report advocated a centralized system of state control over secondary schools. The scheme was never put into effect. That it was suggested at all, and strongly supported by many people, shows that some mid-Victorians were ready to consider sweeping measures of state supervision where the situation appeared to demand them. The commission carefully reviewed the work of the Locals, and its detailed criticisms will be considered later; broadly it considered that the Locals system could not be applied to the whole country. The commission recommended the creation of both a central authority and of provincial authorities. In each area there was to be a district commissioner, a government servant who should be responsible for inspecting endowed secondary schools and for presiding over the annual schools examinations, which they regarded as the pivot of all their recommendations. These examinations were to be regarded not as competitive but as a fair test of average work. One-third of a school should be examined at one time and the examiners were to be chiefly masters engaged in teaching. The body responsible for this work might have been either the state or the universities, but in order to bring together the largest amount of available skill, the commission recommended the creation of a council of examinations, partly representing the Crown and partly the Universities of Oxford, Cambridge and London. Its duties were to be both to examine schools and to examine and certificate schoolmasters. Finally it was suggested

---

[1] E. R. Humphreys, 'Examination of Endowed Schools', *Transactions of Social Science Association, 1857*, pp. 136–7.

that private schools might be admitted to the same privileges if they were registered with the provincial authority.[1]

If these recommendations had ever come into force, the whole pattern of public examining would have been transformed and a system created on the same lines as that which already existed in Prussia, the educational Mecca of the day. Matthew Arnold, always deeply influenced by German practice, was putting forward a similar plan for a 'High Council of Education' at the same time.[2] The Oxford report of 1868 pointed out that, so far as junior candidates were concerned, the commission's proposals would supersede the action of the universities and the Delegacy did not propose to take any steps until Parliament's intentions were known.[3] The commissioners' proposals on school endowments were passed into law by the Endowed Schools Act of 1869, but part II of the original Bill, embracing the clauses on inspection and examination, were not proceeded with because of pressure of business. These clauses provided that every endowed school should be open for examination and that no one might teach in an endowed school unless duly registered. An educational council of twelve members should be set up, six representing the Universities of Oxford, Cambridge and London and six nominated by the Crown, though of the second six three were eventually to be elected by the registered teachers. The council's primary duties were firstly to examine teachers and to keep a register. They were to examine endowed schools not more than once a year, though they might not examine in religious knowledge and they could adopt any existing system conducted by persons of whom they approved. Finally they were to keep a register of private schools and to examine scholars in such schools. Provisions were made for the necessary payments for registration and examination, though the latter were not to exceed a fixed sum per head.[4]

Many public school headmasters were extremely apprehensive of the results of the Endowed Schools Act. It was indeed these feelings of apprehension which created the Headmasters' Conference at whose very first meeting 'The Endowed Schools Bill No. 2' appeared on the agenda.[5] Thring of Uppingham, one of

[1] *SIC*, vol. I, pp. 619–22, 648–51, 652–3.
[2] *Schools and Universities on the Continent* (1868), p. 283.
[3] *Del. Local Exams., Eleventh Annual Report* (1868), p. 9.
[4] For the text of Part II of the Bill, see *Educational Times*, XXII, pp. 128–30.
[5] G. R. Parkin, *Life and Letters of Edward Thring* (1898), vol. I, p. 206.

the moving spirits behind the conference, thoroughly disapproved of the Bill's proposals. He thought that, so far as university men were concerned the proposal to examine them before appointing them was absurd. In the case of the Government Examination it would be very difficult to find men with the rank and knowledge to do the work. The result would only be, he wrote to a correspondent, that 'in a given number of years the inspection becomes either a farce or a tyranny'.[1]

In some circles, however, the government proposals were warmly welcomed. A conference of teachers summoned by the College of Preceptors to discuss the report of the Taunton Commission in January 1869 pointed out the confusion caused by the many existing examining bodies and was anxious for the creation of some sort of central board to be operated in conjunction with local agencies.[2] The Social Science Association too was warmly in favour of the proposals. It urged in a memorial to the Lord President of the Council that a register of private schools was urgently needed and that even a voluntary examination of teachers would greatly help the public in discriminating between the efficient and the non-efficient. As for the educational council, it was necessary to prevent the recurrence of the very abuses which the Endowed Schools Act of 1869 had been passed to correct.[3] At a meeting in November 1871 the association adopted a resolution urging the adoption of school examinations and of the attestation of schoolmasters according to the Bill of 1869.[4] In the discussion the chairman (Lyon Playfair) again stressed the importance of school examinations and cited the example of Prussia where the rule was that 'the examination must be of such a character as a scholar of fair ability and proper intelligence might, towards the end of his school course, come up to with a quiet mind and without painful effort'.[5] The example of the Prussian leaving certificate was to recur constantly for the following generation, as we shall see. Playfair in the same speech explained that he had seen W. E. Forster and that there was hope the government might take the matter up in the session after next. By the spring of 1872 the government had decided to take

[1] Parkin, *Life of Thring*, vol. I, pp. 172–4.
[2] *Educational Times*, vol. XXI, pp. 279–80.
[3] *Sessional Proceedings of the National Association for the Promotion of Social Science, 1870–1*, pp. 270–1. The date of this is probably March 1871.
[4] *Sessional Proceedings, 1871–2*, pp. 23–30.
[5] *Sessional Proceedings, 1871–2*, p. 29.

no further steps because Parliament was disinclined to grant money for middle-class education and because it wanted to see whether the School Boards could be utilized for that purpose.[1] In fact the abortive Bill of 1869 never saw the light of day again and remained buried in the well-filled graveyard of forgotten legislative measures. Yet the ideas which the Bill expressed were too deeply rooted to be completely abandoned and some of them were to be adapted by the public schools themselves for their own purposes.

In 1870 the Headmasters' Conference meeting at Sherborne discussed the question of leaving examinations and the committee was instructed to confer with Oxford and Cambridge about a possible scheme.[2] At Cambridge a syndicate was appointed in March 1871 after Ridding of Winchester, the chairman of the Headmasters' Conference, had been in touch with the vice-chancellor. The report of the Syndicate reviewed the headmasters' requests. They had asked that the universities should examine all first-grade schools 'as schools, in their own work'; that boys should be examined individually according to a standard considered suitable, (a) for those under nineteen years and (b) for those under sixteen years; and that the higher of these certificates should be accepted in place of the Matriculation Examination or part of the Previous Examination. For the certificates candidates were to be examined both in languages and in mathematical and scientific subjects. The Syndicate considered that to undertake this work would be merely to extend to the highest-grade schools work which was already being done for schools of a different grade, and that there was a great demand for 'a more systematic and authoritative inspection of endowed schools than is afforded by the school examinations as now conducted'. Consequently they recommended the acceptance by the university of the headmasters' proposals, the expenses of the examinations being borne by the schools themselves, and they further suggested that steps be taken to reach an agreement on standards with other universities.[3]

This report was accepted by the Senate, as was a further report setting out a definite scheme for a syndicate with power to conduct the inspection and examination of schools and to confer with the

[1] *Educational Times*, vol. XXV, p. 35.
[2] Lady Laura Ridding, *George Ridding, Schoolmaster and Bishop* (1908), p. 113.
[3] *Camb. Univ. Rep.* (1871–2), pp. 27–9.

delegacies of other universities.[1] The headmasters had been especially anxious that Oxford and Cambridge should work together and in 1873 they jointly created the 'Oxford and Cambridge Schools Examination Board' which held its first Certificate Examination in 1874. On 7 May 1874 the Cambridge Senate passed a Grace providing that the Board's certificates in the appropriate subjects should confer exemption from the Previous Examination. There was a good deal of opposition to this when the report was discussed and G. F. Browne made a speech complaining that this decision was unfair to the Locals; however the Grace passed easily by sixty-two votes to fifteen.[2] Similar steps were taken at Oxford and the Oxford and Cambridge Board began its work. It dealt primarily with the first-grade or public schools. To illustrate the scale of its work, thirty years later in 1903 it examined 100 boys' schools and 92 girls' schools; in July 1903 there were 2,140 candidates for the Higher Certificate Examination and 1,131 for the Lower.[3]

The creation of the Oxford and Cambridge Board caused some controversy at the time, and the questions at issue are of considerable interest for our purposes. The connection between the new examination and the proposals of the Endowed Schools Bill, Part 2 is very clear. A paper prepared for the Local Examinations Syndicate in the early days of the negotiations in 1871 quoted Ridding as saying 'that it appeared nearly certain that Government would introduce a Bill next session for controlling the first-grade schools throughout the country, and that the committee would greatly prefer committing the work of Examination to Examiners appointed by the Universities, rather than to Examiners appointed by the Government'.[4] Among those who joined in the controversy were Henry Latham of Trinity Hall, a very experienced Cambridge tutor, and Edward Bowen of Harrow, probably the best-known public-school assistant master of the day.[5] Latham, whose views will be considered in the next chapter, was against multifarious

[1] *Camb. Univ. Rep.* (Easter term, 1873), pp. 15, 28, 32.

[2] *Ibid.* (1873–4), pp. 319, 332–4, 381.

[3] CUA Guard Book 59.1, no. 2. *Annual Report of Highest Grade Schools Examination Syndicate*, 1 December 1903.

[4] CUA University Papers, 1867–1883, no. 372.

[5] Henry Latham, *On the Propositions made by the Head Masters of Schools to the University of Cambridge* (Cambridge, 1871); Edward Bowen, *The Proposed Control of the Public Schools by the Universities*, reprinted in W. E. Bowen, *Edward Bowen: A Memoir* (1902), pp. 316–27. For Latham's important book on examinations, see pp. 272–7.

examination in many subjects which would, he thought, throw boys into the hands of private tutors. The examination should be framed to fit the course of teaching, and there should be a system of Leaving Examinations conducted by commissioners under the Endowed Schools Act. Bowen argued that the headmasters' proposals would cramp freedom of teaching and that the universities already devoted quite enough of their attention to examining. If the work was to be done at all, it would be much better done by the government. A council of education should be set up; University Entrance and Scholarship Examinations regulated so as not to interfere with school studies; the age of university students should be lowered and the curriculum enlarged.

Ridding replied both to Latham and to Bowen, very much on the lines which might have been expected.[1] He argued that the universities were doing a great deal of school examining anyway by private arrangements and that there was everything to be said for regularizing this. If there were to be examinations at all, boys ought to know something of modern languages and natural science as well as of Latin and Greek and such broadly planned courses ought to be the natural means of entry to the university instead of pushing specialized university work down into the schools. In this way the university syllabus would be based upon a properly integrated school curriculum. The core of Ridding's argument really centred round the proposition that the universities should act as 'Independent Heads of National Education'. Their examinations were likely to be more flexible and less subject to the whims of cranks or bureaucrats than anything controlled by the government. Moreover the government would have to use a staff of permanent examiners, and there were strong arguments against such a body. The proposals of the headmasters, Ridding argued, were in accordance with the demands which were being made on the schools; professional bodies were likely to accept the new examination for their qualifications, and it would comply with the requirements of Part II of the Endowed Schools Bill. The proposed system would, he told Bowen, preserve the schools from 'the centralized uniformity, or the arbitrary caprice, of a Government Department'.

[1] *A Letter to the Rev. Henry Latham, M.A. Trinity Hall, Cambridge, In reply to his Observations* (1871); *A Letter to Edward Bowen, M.A., In reply to a Pamphlet* (1872).

As we have already seen the government took no further action on the Endowed Schools Bill, and the educational picture was made even more confused by the creation of a new examining body whose certificates conveyed the valuable privilege of exemption from Responsions and the Previous Examination. English education has usually developed on lines of status, and a new layer had been inserted between the Universities and the Locals, which had always primarily been concerned with schools of the second grade. The Social Science Association, always alert to mark new educational developments, welcomed the new scheme. E. C. Hawkins pointed out that the Locals were not very well fitted for highest-grade schools where the boys had reached a higher standard in classics; moreover they examined only picked boys whereas schools ought to be examined as a whole.[1] E. A. Abbott, headmaster of the City of London School, repeated much the same arguments as those used by Ridding, demonstrating the great advantage to the schools of the university connection. The system of a university board was far preferable to examination by a minister of education, and it was much better to act privately than to wait for the government. So far as practical arrangements went, the senior boys would be examined by university examiners, the junior boys by their own class-masters with occasional revision by the external examiners.[2]

The creation of the Oxford and Cambridge Board was bound to have an effect on the fortunes of the Locals which had been doing very similar work for nearly twenty years. In particular it raised the question of division of effort and set many people wondering whether greater harmony could not be secured between so many different agencies. There were naturally many different opinions about the effectiveness of the Locals in their existing form. One hostile critic was Dorothea Beale of Cheltenham who thought that the set-books and subjects were not always well arranged and that there was a danger of neglecting the dull pupil. Consequently she urged that girls' schools should adopt the newly devised system.[3]

[1] E. C. Hawkins, 'The Scheme under Consideration for establishing Examinations of Public Schools to be conducted by Members of the University', *Transactions of Social Science Association, 1872*, pp. 307–9.

[2] Edwin A. Abbott, 'On the Proposed Examination of First Grade Schools by the Universities', *Sessional Proceedings of the National Association for the Promotion of Social Science, 1872–3*, pp. 33–49.

[3] 'University Examinations for Women' *Transactions of Social Science Association, 1874*, pp. 478–83.

On the other hand one active local centre, the Sussex Board of Examinations, petitioned in January 1872 against the proposals made for the first-grade schools. They argued that the term was an inexact one and that it was difficult to see any real distinction between the proposed examination and the work already done by the Locals. Any system of examination ought to be national not sectional and the proper course to take was to modify the Locals so as to include the highest-grade schools within their sphere. Bearing in mind the great emphasis laid at the time on the success of the Locals in bringing forward promising boys, it is not surprising that the Sussex Board emphasized that 'three Senior Wranglers and one Senior Classic have already been introduced to the University of Cambridge through the Local Examinations'.[1]

In February 1874 the Cambridge Syndicate considered an approach from a group of schools including Hurstpierpoint, Framlingham, Whitgift and the Devon County School. Their headmasters, impressed by the success of the universities in agreeing on a common examination for the first-grade schools, urged that the Locals too should be amalgamated or at the very least co-ordinated under a common board so that the schools might avoid the many difficulties created by the large number of different examinations. They also suggested that the Preliminary might be separated off as an examination for younger boys for which there was a real need.[2] The same group organized a conference in London in July 1874 which advocated a union between the Locals and the new Oxford and Cambridge Board. They also suggested that candidates who passed in certain subjects should be admitted to the university without a Matriculation Examination and urged that it would be a great advantage if the government would accept the University Certificates in place of some of the Civil Service Examinations.[3] In fact neither the Delegacy nor the Syndicate were prepared to contemplate union and each considered that there were definite advantages in the independence of the two systems. They pointed out that the Oxford and Cambridge Board did not classify its candidates in order of merit, 'a special and valuable part of the system which is adopted in the Local Examinations', and

[1] CUA University Papers, 1867–1883, no. 439.
[2] Local Exams. Synd., Minutes, 24 February 1874.
[3] Minutes, 24 October 1874.

they did not consider it to be their province to urge the government to accept university certificates in lieu of its own examinations.[1] Barclay Phillips of Brighton, who had been one of the leaders of the amalgamation plan, prophesied in 1875 that the new Schools' Examination would brand the Locals as inferior and in time destroy them entirely,[2] but this prophecy of doom remained unfulfilled, and the different bodies went their own ways. As in 1860 the forces against co-ordination were far too strong. The only direct result for the Locals of the establishment of the new board was the extension to their Senior Certificates of the right of exemption from the Previous Examination and Responsions. A committee of the Delegacy reported in December 1875 on the requirements which would ensure that candidates in Latin, Greek and mathematics reached a standard equivalent to that of the Joint Board Certificate; in that year eight candidates would have reached such a standard and three more have fallen only slightly below it.[3] The Statute allowing exemption from Responsions on the Senior Local Certificate passed Convocation on 13 February 1877.[4] At Cambridge the matter had been under discussion at much the same time as at Oxford and parallel Graces passed the Senate on 19 April 1877.[5]

These changes gave the Senior Certificates of the Oxford and Cambridge Locals an enhanced value as the means of partly fulfilling the requirements for a degree. Apart from this important step, the creation of the Oxford and Cambridge Board seems to have affected the workings of the Locals very little. They had never been concerned with the public schools which had generally made their own private arrangements for the examination of their pupils. The establishment of the Oxford and Cambridge Board, however, like the foundation of the Headmasters' Conference, is an important landmark in the development of the modern public schools as a coherent group, made up essentially of three elements – the ancient collegiate foundations like Eton, the one-time grammar schools like Rugby, and the new schools like Marlborough. It was natural

[1] The letters of Edwardes, the Oxford Secretary and of Browne, the Cambridge Secretary to the committee, dated 24 November and 12 December 1874, are printed in a paper enclosed in the Cambridge Minute Book.

[2] 'Proposed Amalgamation of University Local and other Examinations', *Transactions of Social Science Association, 1875*, pp. 462–3.

[3] Del. Local Exams., Minutes, 4 December 1875.

[4] Del. Local Exams., Minute Book (1877), note.

[5] *Camb. Univ. Rep.* (1876–7), pp. 292–3, 338.

that, as they achieved cohesion as a group, they should want their independent examining arrangements, free from any fear of interference by government and unimpeded by other schools inferior to themselves. The Oxford and Cambridge Board, like the Headmasters' Conference, marks one of the stages on the road of the public school towards educational supremacy in mid-Victorian England.

The public schools had successfully provided themselves with an examination system free from the control of the state. This system was to some extent a reflection of their desire, for both educational and social reasons, to keep themselves separate from other schools, yet the scheme of examining which they adopted owed much to the plans for government control which were going the rounds of political and educational discussion in 1870. The public-school headmasters had successfully stolen the thunder of their foes.

By the seventies it was widely recognized that the state alone could deal with the enormous problem of primary education, but the middle classes still believed that they could look after themselves. At the level of the public-school group they were probably right; lower down the scale the proposition was far from certain. Since central control was excluded examination became the only measuring rod. A German observer pointed out one very curious feature of the English scene. Alongside this deeply felt fear of state interference and bureaucracy went a readiness to submit to a system of examinations over which the schools had no control:

From time to time something like an alarum bell sounds throughout the country: come and be examined! And they come, boys and girls, young and old, having crammed into themselves as much knowledge as they could. How they have acquired what they know is never asked, nor are they shown what is the best method; and yet what work could after all be more worthy of a university than to point this out? Results! results! this is characteristic of England, and best explains the present high value set upon examinations in schools and universities.[1]

The tone of these remarks is very similar to Matthew Arnold's attacks on the Philistinism of his countrymen. Yet examinations were never accepted uncritically, as this quotation suggests. The

---

[1] L. Wiese, *German Letters on English Education: Written during an Educational Tour in 1876* (English trans., 1877) p.151.

comments made on the Locals in the report and evidence of the Taunton Commission are, for instance, extremely searching and comprehensive. There was a great deal of praise which need not be considered here because it followed the lines which have already been reviewed. Some of the criticism has also been touched on, like the frequent complaint that the examinations forced the teacher to concentrate on the ablest boys and to neglect the others. Many of the statistical facts and inferences are interesting. Liveing, the professor of chemistry at Cambridge, analysed the schools which sent the Syndicate candidates. 45 grammar schools had sent approximately 180 boys, 38 proprietary schools about 220 boys and 105 private schools about 420 boys. Of the failures the grammar schools had the lowest proportion, the private schools the highest.[1] Professor Rawlinson, one of the Oxford delegates, also thought that in the examinations the endowed grammar schools had been the most successful.[2] Rawlinson's colleague, Professor Bartholomew Price, also considered that there was a certain difference of emphasis between the examinations of the two universities. Oxford had aimed at a complete course leading to business or commerce, Cambridge had rather led up to the idea that the boys would be prepared for a university examination.[3] Curiously enough the *Educational Times* had made the same comment a couple of years before,[4] though there is no means of further substantiating it. In their views of the future the two Oxford delegates disagreed. Rawlinson thought that the system could not be extended to cover more than 3,000 candidates; Price thought there was no limit.[5]

Some of the most valuable information was contained in the reports by the assistant commissioners on the areas which they had visited. The position of the Local Examinations naturally varied from district to district. In most areas they had been comparatively little taken up by the schools, but the assistant commissioners, though often critical of the examinations in detail, generally believed that they had done much good and that they would do more as they became more widely known. In London the examinations had been practically ignored by the grammar schools and, although some

[1] *SIC*, vol. IV, pp. 26–27: 233, 236.
[2] *SIC*, vol. IV, p. 64: 591.
[3] *SIC*, vol. IV, p. 81: 730.
[4] *Educational Times*, vol. XVI, p. 6.
[5] *SIC*, vol. IV, pp. 71–2: 636, 638.

private schools used them, they had altogether very little influence.[1] In the West Riding the more important schools did not use them and the smaller schools could not reach the level of the Junior Examination,[2] while in Lancashire only the wealthier middle class and its schools had been affected.[3] T. H. Green, who visited Staffordshire and Warwickshire, found that a number of the leading grammar schools had sent in candidates,[4] though King Edward's, Birmingham had largely stood aside.[5] Green picked out Brewood in Staffordshire as a successful grammar school which combined effective preparation for the Locals with good training for the universities. Several boys had gone to Cambridge where they had done very well. On an average about twelve juniors and two or three seniors were sent every year to the Cambridge Locals examination at Wolverhampton. The school was stronger in mathematics than in classics and had done particularly well in the Locals in English subjects, though this was rather the result of effective teaching than because a great deal of time was spent on them.[6] From the schoolmaster's point of view, Green thought, the Locals had increased the time which the better boys gave to their education by at least a year.[7] In his area they had not had much effect on the private schools.[8]

One point made by several of the assistant commissioners was that parents had little understanding of the purpose of the examinations and disliked paying a fee for entry. As D. R. Fearon wrote about London, 'they care nothing for the benefit which a boy gains from undergoing a public examination; and being made to pay a fee for a pluck they consider as an addition of insult to injury'.[9] The report of the Commission emphasizes that the examinations were expensive. Oxford charged an entrance fee of twenty shillings for juniors and thirty shillings for seniors. Cambridge charged twenty shillings a head for all candidates. On top of this there was

[1] *SIC*, vol. VII (D. R. Fearon, general report on the Metropolitan District) pp. 319–20, 337–8.
[2] *SIC*, vol. IX (J. G. Fitch, general report on the West Riding of the County of York), p. 210.
[3] *SIC*, vol. IX (J. Bryce, general report on the County of Lancaster), p. 541.
[4] *SIC*, vol. VIII (T. H. Green, special report on Birmingham Free School and general report on the Counties of Stafford and Warwick), p. 175.
[5] See p. 87.
[6] *SIC*, vol. VIII, pp. 178–9.
[7] *SIC*, vol. VIII, pp. 179–80.
[8] *Ibid.* p. 199.
[9] *SIC*, vol. VII, p. 378.

a fee to be paid to the local centre, and, unless a boy happened to live in the town where the examination was held, there were expenses of board and lodging for a week or so while the papers were being written.[1] The total cost was in fact too great for the people who patronized many of the schools which the Locals were designed to benefit. A further serious drawback was that the Locals lacked prestige. Some illustrations of this have already been given,[2] and these are confirmed by the verdict of two French observers. They considered that the certificates lacked the cachet of true university degrees. The state did not demand them; business men were not interested in them and preferred to depend on testimonials of good character. Consequently the progress of the Local Examinations was slow.[3]

Two closely related criticisms were very commonly made; the first was that the examinations tended to lead to concentration on a few able boys and the second that the standard was too high and that this led to cramming and overstrain. Some witnesses denied that these were serious dangers,[4] but the assistant commissioners certainly produced some very damning examples. T. H. Green commented that he often found boys reading a book which was too hard for them because one or two members of the class would have to take it in the Local Examination. Similarly lower forms would be prematurely attempting Euclid or 'English analysis' in order to get the small minority who were likely to take the examination into training.[5] James Bryce in Lancashire thought that there was a real danger of overstrain, especially in the case of the fourteen- and fifteen-year-olds, and believed that if the examination for juniors were retained, it ought to be for a pass standard and not for honours.[6]

His description of one private school which he visited deserves quotation, though it is rather long, to show how a schoolmaster could achieve success if he set out on certain lines:

It was [Bryce wrote] and had always been comparatively small, the pupils not exceeding forty, and appeared to be conducted with a special view to

---

[1] *SIC*, vol. I, pp. 332–3.   [2] See pp. 87–8.

[3] J. Demogeot and H. Montucci, *De l'Enseignement secondaire en Angleterre et en Ecosse: Rapport adressé à son exc. M. Le Ministre de l'Instruction Publique* (Paris, 1868), pp. 300–1.

[4] E.g. Joseph Payne, the historian of the College of Preceptors, *SIC*, vol. IV, pp. 664–5: 6889–90.

[5] *SIC*, vol. VIII, p. 176.   [6] *SIC*, vol. IX, pp. 772–6.

the University local examinations. Fully understanding that the examination art is an art by itself, needing special cultivation, the headmaster held written examinations weekly, taking each week some three subjects, and every fourth week all the subjects which were being prepared. Classes were formed several months beforehand of boys going in for the Oxford or Cambridge examinations, as the case might be, and all subjects which it was not intended to offer this were dropped. Thus, at the time of my visit no Latin was being learnt, 'for boys', said the master, 'cannot do Latin at the same time with mathematics and the English subjects. When the next Oxford or Cambridge local examination is past, these boys or some of them, will be set to work at Latin, and perhaps French, so as to pass in those subjects the time after.' Feeling a little curious to see what were the results of so peculiar a system, I examined one class minutely on some of the subjects in which they had last been trained. The training proved to be no sham; the boys knew a great deal about many things; in English history, for instance, it was difficult to puzzle them; but they had been not taught, but crammed. They answered hurriedly, not stopping to think what the question meant, but pouring out stores of information which they did not understand. Every reply witnessed to large knowledge, but then it was not a reply to the question put. Their minds, to use a familiar illustration, were like a full sack of corn, which if you press it down at one point, rises and runs over at some other. It was noticeable that they usually answered in the words of their text-book; and that while knowing English history minutely, they were wholly ignorant of the course of events in other European countries. In English grammar and analysis, as it is called, they did not, as I had first expected, answer by rote, but seemed to have mastered the principles sufficiently to take any ordinary sentence to pieces, and describe correctly the relation of its parts. Something in their manner showed that this was a forced capacity, the result not perhaps of cramming, but of overteaching, and that it did not witness to any natural and healthy growth. But such as it was, the capacity was there. These boys looked jaded and overworked, and the whole aspect of the school was one of discomfort. The assistant masters were numerous in proportion to the numbers of the pupils, and seemed to be employed manipulating them in small classes, with a view to individual preparation. They were very inferior people; no others would have taken such salaries. Of the headmaster it is better to say nothing since I have nothing good to say.[1]

Bryce's description might fit certain schools today; it certainly shows the lengths to which dominance by examination could go.

[1] *SIC*, vol. IX, pp. 558–9. For comments made by schoolmasters to the commissioners, see A. Creak, *SIC*, vol. V, p. 198: 10870; C. N. Hankin, *SIC*, vol. IV, pp. 464–5: 4678; F. W. Walker, *SIC*, vol. V, p. 219: 11064–5.

The commissioners, in their report, argued that the examinations would be really effective only if about one-third of the pupils in a school could be tested.[1] In later years, as we have seen, their aims came close to fulfilment when it became more and more common for schools to send in whole classes. In the mid-sixties, however, this was not yet an objective which could be generally achieved. At that time the great criticism levelled at the Locals by the report and evidence of the Taunton Commission was that, though they were doing useful work, the scale was much too small, and they were influencing only a small proportion of the teachers and pupils who needed stimulus and encouragement.

During the seventies and eighties there was much general controversy about examinations which will be reviewed in the final chapter. The practical problem of control remained the same as at the time of the Taunton Commission. Were the existing examining bodies to go on with their work, a policy which avoided uniformity or regimentation, or should there be some sort of central council charged with responsibility for examining and probably conducting a leaving examination at the end of the school course on the lines of the German *Abiturientenexamen*? The latter policy was in general advocated by the *Journal of Education*, founded under that title in 1879, which was highly critical of the Locals and thought that, though they had once been in advance of the schools, they had subsequently fallen behind them and grown stereotyped. Their examiners had no real experience of the schools they examined and the whole responsibility ought, as in Germany, to be in the hands of the schoolmasters themselves with the supervision of an external inspector to keep up standards and the ultimate control of a state educational council. 'Whatever the objection to outside examinations', wrote a contributor in December 1899, 'there can be no doubt that there is in the teaching world at present a strong feeling in favour of the adoption of a uniform leaving certificate granted by the State or other recognised authority, the possession of which shall be to the public trustworthy evidence that the pupil has passed through his school course successfully.'[2]

On the other side the old fear of centralized authority was still strong. A good example of this comes from the *Educational Times* of October 1878. The article in question described with approval

---

[1] *SIC*, vol. I, p. 333.
[2] *Journal of Education*, vol. XXI, p. 791 (December 1899).

a Bill which Lyon Playfair intended to introduce into Parliament proposing the registration of teachers in secondary and higher education. It then went on to deal with the 'compulsory Examination and Inspection of Middle Class Schools', quoting opinions from *The Times* and other journals. All the views quoted were against any such project. It was argued that the Endowed Schools Act of 1869 had already effected very great improvements and that an inspection of secondary schools would be incomparably more complex to arrange than the existing state inspection of elementary schools. Moreover since the state provided no money for secondary education, it had no claim to interfere. The best course was to leave the matter to the discretion of parents. Moreover the field had largely been covered by the university examining bodies who were already doing efficiently what was needed. A passage quoted from the *Spectator* drew the conclusion that the best middle-class schools were already seeking inspection by the universities and that very soon parents would be unwilling to send their children to schools which could not produce evidence that their methods were efficient.[1] The assumption behind all these articles is that the middle-class parent is in a completely different position from the working-class parent. The latter needs the tutelary authority of the state to ensure that his children receive at least the minimum of education. The middle-class paterfamilias can stand on his own feet. Examining machinery exists in the hands of the universities who enjoy the confidence of the upper and middle classes; it is therefore the responsibility of the parent and of the school to make whatever arrangements seem best according to their independent judgment of the situation. This attitude was intensely deep-rooted; it worked in favour of what may be called educational voluntaryism and of leaving things as they were. A free choice between the existing examining bodies worked well enough and had been tested by experience. Moreover, as Oscar Browning told the Social Science Association, an elaborate system of inspection might well turn out to be a sham, and it would be an intensely difficult task to create a really good system of examination on a national scale.[2] It seemed better to accept what was already known and tested.

[1] *Educational Times*, vol. XXXI, pp. 253–6.
[2] In the discussion of a paper by S. F. Hiron, 'The Compulsory Examination and Inspection of Secondary Schools, with suggestions for the avoidance of the evils of an excessive centralization', *Transactions of the Social Science Association, 1884*, pp. 485–6.

9

By the end of the century a new factor had to be reckoned with in the determination of policy. This was the increasing self-confidence and self-assertiveness of the schools. They were much more ready than they had been to put forward criticisms and suggestions, and the examining bodies showed themselves more receptive to their views. Quite a new note was struck by the Delegacy in 1898, when in appointing assistants to the revising examiner in mathematics, it was decided that 'whenever it is possible the three examiners so appointed be persons who have had experience as teachers in schools'.[1] One or two headmasters, in corresponding with the Delegacy, suggested reasons for the greater popularity of Cambridge in comparison with Oxford. One mentioned the view, held by some people, that the Cambridge results always agreed with the school's own examinations, but that the Oxford results rarely did so.[2] Another thought that Cambridge arranged its classification more attractively and was more generous in giving honours.[3] The problems of many small grammar schools are brought out in a letter from a headmaster who complained of the difficulties he encountered in preparing, single-handed, all the Cambridge subjects together with work for other examinations.[4]

The most effective criticism, of course, was that of the teachers' organizations, the most active of them being the Incorporated Association of Headmasters, founded in 1890, which seems to have enjoyed particularly close relations with the Cambridge Syndicate.[5] The new Association appointed a sub-committee on examinations in December 1891, and after the general meeting of the Association in the ensuing January, certain suggestions were sent to the Syndicate. In modern languages preference might be given in the junior syllabus to the works of modern writers, and a wider selection of set-books, 'not necessarily confined to the publications of the Pitt Press', was desirable. Changes were proposed both in the

[1] Del. Local Exams., Minutes, 2 June, 1898.

[2] Owen Owen of Oswestry High School, 16 January 1886 (Del. Local Exams., Minute Book).

[3] Frederic McDowell of Camberwell Grammar School, 3 June 1886 (Del. Local Exams., Minute Book).

[4] Thomas Allan of Alleyne's Grammar School, Uttoxeter to Browne, 21 March 1888 (CUA Guard Book 57.2, no. 126).

[5] Other examples in the Syndicate Minutes of memorials from professional associations are from the Association of Principals of Private Schools (25 October, 2 November 1882), Liverpool branch of the Private Schools Association (27 April 1898).

science syllabus and in the examination time-table. The suggestions about modern languages set-books and about the time-table were favourably received, though the proposals about the natural sciences were not accepted.[1] In 1893 the Syndicate agreed to requests from the Association that in the junior examination the test in reading should be given up and that English history should be divided into three periods. One of these periods should be set each year and the special period should be abolished.[2] There is no point in going through all the suggestions made year by year by the Association to the universities, to the Civil Service Commissioners and to the Science and Art Department. It should be noted however that the new syllabuses for juniors in elementary experimental science, adopted by both Oxford and Cambridge and considered by them to be very successful, were based on proposals made by the IAHM.[3] Of their other recommendations some were successful, some were not. What is important is not whether a particular idea found favour, but the fact that a representative body of head-masters was bringing regular pressure to bear on all the examining bodies in a way which had not happened before.

The papers set in the Locals also came in for much criticism in the educational press. The perpetual question whether examina-tions led to overwork and overstrain continued to be aired at regular intervals. In January 1889 the Syndicate considered a correspondence in *The Times* about the number of hours during which Locals candidates might be under examination. 'The letters which have been published', wrote the *Educational Times*, 'seem to imply that it is no unusual thing for a boy or girl under 15 years of age to have to undergo the immense strain of nine or ten hours of examination in a day, beginning at 9.30 a.m. and ending at 9 p.m.'[4] In order to get to the bottom of the problem the Syndicate decided to send round a series of questions to local secretaries, enquiring about cases of strain which they had witnessed at their own centres. After these answers had been received and considered, Browne wrote

[1] Local Exams. Synd., Minutes, 11 May, 12 November 1892, 6 May 1893. *Incorporated Association of Headmasters, Reports* 1891–8, report of the committee ... for 1891, pp. 1–2; report of the committee ... for 1892, p. 31. (These reports are kept at the offices of the IAHM, 29 Gordon Square, London, W.C.1, and I have seen them through the kindness of the secretary of the association.)
[2] Local Exams. Synd., Minutes, 4 November 1893; *IAHM Reports*, report of the committee ... for 1893, p. 12.
[3] *IAHM Reports*, report of the council for 1896, pp. 7–8; see also p. 160.
[4] *Educational Times*, vol. XLII, p. 73 (February 1889).

a letter to *The Times* in March in which he affirmed, both that cases of serious strain were uncommon and that when they did occur, they were often primarily due to the unwisdom of parents and teachers in pressing candidates too hard. If proper care was taken, Browne argued, for instance by not overworking candidates during the period of preparation, there was no real danger of harm.[1] The *Educational Times* of the next month considered that too much play had been made with exceptional cases by the critics. The schedules of the Oxford Junior Locals showed that the average hours worked at the London centre during the six days of examination were $3\frac{3}{8}$ per day and a little more at Liverpool and Birmingham. The worst case on the College of Preceptors list had worked $5\frac{3}{4}$ hours per day.[2]

Later in the same year the Syndicate had a direct brush with the *Journal of Education*, a periodical which, as we have seen, was highly critical of the Locals. The editor, Mr Storr, had reflected unfavourably in his number for August 1889 on the standard of Latin accepted in the Senior Locals, using as his example the paper of a girl candidate who had in fact failed both in Latin and in the whole examination. After enquiries had been made it was discovered that Storr had obtained the script because the invigilator had made a copy of it and had shown it to him. The invigilator later apologized to the Syndicate and a retractation appeared in the October *Journal of Education*. The Syndicate further decided that a letter should be written to the editor which he should be required to publish, and, although he demurred at printing it in the required place in the paper, he finally did so in the November number.[3]

This incident was merely an episode in a constant line of criticism carried on by the *Journal* over a number of years. It disliked the competitive aspect inherent in the Locals system; 'it is a dubious gain', Storr had written in 1882, 'to have opened a National Derby for Prizes and Scholarships to the Middle Class in imitation of the University Goodwood for the Upper Ten'.[4] The examiners were said to be out of touch with the schools and the form of the papers to be such as to encourage cramming and memory-work. In two

---

[1] *The Times*, 22 March 1889.
[2] *Educational Times*, vol. XLII, p. 181 (April 1889).
[3] Local Exams. Synd., Minutes, 12 October, 23 November 1889. The details are contained in a printed paper inserted in the Minute Book. See also *Journal of Education*, vol. XI, pp. 550–1 (1 November 1889).
[4] *Ibid.* vol. IV, p. 386 (1 December 1882).

perceptive articles published in 1887 the author pointed out that an able boy who took the Junior Examination early in his school career was crammed over and over again with English subjects and religious knowledge because that was the easiest way to pick up marks.[1] Almost everything in the syllabus was voluntary so that boys were entered for the minimum number of subjects and there was no assurance that a co-ordinated scheme of work was being provided.[2] If this claim was correct, however, it was not very consistent with the oft repeated statement that the examination time-table was overcrowded and too great a strain for juniors.[3] Particular scorn was reserved for the Preliminary Examination; this was certainly a profitable venture, but it was hardly consistent with the dignity of the ancient universities to conduct 'a private Tripos for children of thirteen and under'.[4]

By the time the preliminary examinations had been set up the whole pattern of English secondary education had become so complex that some definite action by the state was clearly necessary. At Oxford and Cambridge the Locals and the Joint Board were at work. Many schools sent in candidates for London Matriculation. In addition, as scientific subjects became more and more important, many schools entered their pupils for the examinations of the Science and Art Department; indeed the grants which the department paid for success in its examinations were one of the cornerstones of school finance. New authorities were beginning to share the work of secondary education. Under the Technical Instruction Act of 1889 County Councils became authorities for technical education; they were actively concerned too with the award of scholarships from elementary schools. The School Boards too were infiltrating into secondary education through the higher-grade schools. As all these bodies developed their activities, the confusion grew greater from year to year. A speaker at the Oxford conference of 1893 on secondary education described one headmaster in a manufacturing town, who had to run two time-tables,[5]

[1] *Ibid.* vol. IX, pp. 185–7, 218–20 (1 April, 1 May 1887).

[2] *Ibid.* vol. XXI, pp. 361–3 (1 June 1899).

[3] *Journal of Education*, vol. XIII, p. 13 (1 January 1891); vol. XV, p. 12 (1 January 1893).

[4] *Ibid.* vol. XVII, p. 708 (1 December 1895).

[5] *Report of a Conference on Secondary Education in England convened by the vice-chancellor of the University of Oxford and held in the Examination Schools, Oxford, 10 and 11 October 1893*, p. 44. The speaker was E. F. M. MacCarthy, headmaster of King Edward's, Five Ways, Birmingham.

9*

one from January to March, having as its object 'to keep general subjects steadily moving, but to *press forward the Science and Art side*'; the other from June to December, in which the object is 'to keep the Science and Art side slowly moving, and to *press on the General work*'. By these methods my friend, who has a perfect genius for organization, succeeds in passing a good proportion of his upper boys for the Cambridge Locals in December, in earning considerable grants for Art and for Science from the Science and Art Department Examination in May, and besides, good grants from the County Councils for technical work.

On such a scheme of work, however, a headmaster needed the abilities of a juggler rather than those of an administrator or an educationalist!

In October 1893 the vice-chancellor of Oxford convened a conference to discuss the whole subject of secondary education. Many of the speakers at this conference stressed that far too little was known about the whole matter and that what was needed was a full enquiry by a Royal Commission.[1] Convocation followed this up in November 1893 with a memorial to the prime minister asking that such a commission should be appointed before any legislation on the subject was passed,[2] and the Oxford initiative was generally believed to have had considerable influence in the appointment in March 1894 of a Royal Commission on Secondary Education under the chairmanship of James Bryce.[3] The report of the Bryce Commission, issued in 1895, recommended the establishment of a central authority under a minister who would have charge of both primary and secondary education and whose responsibilities would cover both the Science and the Art Department and the Charity Commission (in so far as educational endowments were concerned). Quite quickly the log jam which had blocked English secondary education for a generation began to break up. In 1899 the Board of Education was created. In 1902 the Balfour Education Act instituted a system of state secondary schools which were rapidly developed by the genius of Sir Robert Morant. With the new century a new period of education begins. The Bryce Com-

[1] E.g. Dean Gregory of St. Paul's: 'I am delighted to find that men of all schools and opinions seem to require a Royal Commission to inquire into questions of this kind as an essential condition of future success', *Report of Oxford Conference on Secondary Education*, p. 171.

[2] *Ibid.* pp. 231–2.

[3] J. N. Keynes, the Cambridge Secretary, said in a discussion on 26 November 1896 that 'it was believed that great weight has been attached to this Memorial from Oxford', *Camb. Univ. Rep.* (1896–7), p. 297.

mission marks a real watershed and the comments made in the Report and in the Minutes of Evidence provide a very useful conclusion to the survey of School Examinations in the later nineteenth century which has been attempted here.[1] The Report showed that educational opinion was still divided about examinations on the lines fixed thirty years previously.[2] The Commission's recommendations were conservative. They favoured the activity of the universities in secondary education and considered that it was desirable for them to be in close contact with the schools.[3] They suggested that the existing examinations should continue under the general control of the proposed central office since it would be very difficult to create any uniform authority. The central office should arrange to make the various certificates interchangeable and might make them available as leaving certificates at different levels. The inspection, as opposed to the examination of secondary schools, should be carried out by the local authorities at their own expense.[4]

The evidence and memoranda which the commission received were voluminous, and much of it repeated criticisms and suggestions which have already been made. The philosopher Henry Sidgwick made a lengthy and able defence of the Locals, though he frankly pointed out several of their drawbacks, like the danger that the Syndicate and the examiners might not have sufficient practical experience of schoolwork.[5] This problem was much in people's minds in the nineties; for instance at the Oxford Conference of 1893 Sidgwick's brother Arthur had emphasized the great value of the teacher's advice in questions of examination and inspection.[6] J. N. Keynes, the Cambridge secretary, put much emphasis in his evidence on the overseas work of the Syndicate and on its work in awarding scholarships both overseas and at home.[7] His figures for the schools from which the Cambridge candidates of 1893 came are also interesting. Private schools are still very prominently

[1] *Royal Commission on Secondary Education, Report, Minutes of Evidence, Memoranda etc.* (9 vols.) *PP* 1895, XLIII–XLIX. This is hereafter referred to as *Bryce Comm.* with the appropriate volume and page.
[2] *Bryce Comm.* vol. I, pp. 161–3.
[3] *Ibid.* p. 248.
[4] *Ibid.* pp. 304–7.
[5] *Ibid.* vol. V (Memoranda and Answers to Questions), pp. 243–6.
[6] *Report of Oxford Conference on Secondary Education*, p. 143.
[7] *Bryce Comm.* vol. V, pp. 270–1.

represented, and the few higher-grade elementary schools show the increasing range of the work undertaken by the School Boards. The boys came from 205 endowed schools, 61 other public schools, 9 higher-grade elementary schools and 338 private schools; the number of schools sending in girls under the same heading was 54; 100; 8; and 720.[1] An old weakness which reappears is the small number of candidates per school. F. E. Kitchener pointed out that in the populous Lancashire hundreds of Salford and West Derby in the years 1893–4 only 28 boys' schools and 28 girls' schools had passed 5 candidates and upwards in the Locals, the Preceptors and the Joint Board Examinations taken together.[2]

Many witnesses greatly preferred the Joint Board system to that of the Locals.[3] They liked the fact that it examined whole classes and not individual boys, that it operated on a pass rather than an honours standard, and that the examination left the school a wide freedom to pursue its own methods and range of studies. The chief objection cited was that the Joint Board system was expensive. The Board's two secretaries, E. J. Gross and P. E. Matheson, made considerable claims for it. They stated that the Board had advanced the study of Greek and Latin by requiring unprepared translations, that it had extended the teaching of modern languages, and promoted thorough methods in mathematics.[4] The Board's success, Gross claimed, had been due to the close collaboration between the Universities of Oxford and Cambridge and to the frank relations which it had always maintained with headmasters.[5] Some independent witnesses like the Cambridge classical scholar Henry Jackson also spoke well of the Board's examinations,[6] but others were less well satisfied. G. W. Prothero of King's, one of the pioneer Cambridge history tutors, thought that the examinations tended to discourage initiative and to produce a level of mediocrity below what the best boys might otherwise have attained. He admitted, however, that they had probably helped the smaller schools.[7] His colleague at King's, Oscar Browning, the creator of the Cam-

---

[1] *Bryce Comm.* vol. V, pp. 274–5.
[2] *Bryce Comm.* vol. VI, p. 239.
[3] E.g. F. Storr (chief master of modern subjects, Merchant Taylor's), *Bryce Comm.* vol. III (Minutes of Evidence), p. 124: 7421.
[4] *Bryce Comm.* vol. V, pp. 280–1.
[5] *Ibid.* p. 188.
[6] *Ibid.* p. 172.
[7] *Ibid.* p. 219.

bridge Training College for Men, was a more trenchant critic. He thought that the certificates of the Board had come to acquire an honours character instead of a merely pass character. Consequently the schools had tended to push large numbers of boys through them by cramming methods, and the standard of the education in the first-grade schools had been degraded in consequence. He claimed that the German leaving certificate was a much better plan because every pupil going to university had to pass it, because there were no set-books, and because the examination was conducted at each school mainly by the teachers themselves so that the idea of competition was not introduced.[1]

The idea of a general leaving examination on these lines was strongly favoured by many of those who gave evidence. It was recognized that it would have to be planned to allow for wide diversities; one witness, for instance, thought that there might be two grades, a lower level and a higher admitting to the professions and the universities.[2] Lord Reay put much more emphasis on inspection and on teaching than on examination, and he was very clear that these were the responsibility of the state not of the universities.[3] Much interesting information about a state examination already in full working order was contained in the evidence of Henry Craik, Secretary of the Scottish Education Department, about the Scottish Leaving Certificate which had first been held in 1888. There were three grades, lower, higher and honours, and a certificate might be obtained in a single subject. Candidates were admitted only from schools which had been inspected by the Education Department and whose curriculum had been approved. Craik made the point in his evidence that without the inspection of schools the Scottish system would be incomplete. He considered that the scheme could be applied in a larger country like England, though the inspection would naturally be more difficult to carry out.[4] In any organization of a state-controlled leaving examination, the inspection was really the crux of the matter. J. N. Keynes had pointed out in his evidence that the German *Abitur* was effective only where the state controlled the curriculum and satisfied itself of the efficiency of the schools. It was difficult to see how the

---

[1] *Bryce Comm.* vol. v, p. 139.
[2] *Bryce Comm.* vol. iii, p. 130: 7494 (F. Storr).
[3] *Bryce Comm.* vol. iv (Minutes of Evidence), pp. 290–7: 15159–62.
[4] *Bryce Comm.* vol. iv, pp. 181: 14236 ff.

system could work in England where neither of these conditions applied.[1]

The advocates of a general leaving examination did not always want to put it into the hands of the state; many of them preferred to make use of the universities. This contrast in attitudes comes out interestingly in the evidence of the heads of the three constituent colleges of the Victoria University, Ward of Manchester, Rendall of Liverpool and Bodington of Leeds. Ward thought that the universities should harmonize their examinations as far as possible, but that ultimately there should be a state examination.[2] Rendall and Bodington laid more weight on the co-operation between schools and universities:

What weighed with me in the judgment that I gave [Rendall commented] was partly the fact that a State examination would mean displacing or supplanting a large amount of existing created university action which I feel is very healthy on both sides. I think that for the schools and the universities it is equally important; for this reason, that really the school examination work in various forms is the one direct contact between the universities and the schools.[3]

This partnership between schools and universities to which Principal Rendall referred had put down very deep roots during the previous forty years. The veteran Frederick Temple, now Bishop of London, told the commission, with all the authority of one of the pioneers of 1857, that the provincial authorities might inspect but that examination should be in the hands of the universities, since this was the most thorough and most impartial method which could be devised. The governors of schools would define the school course and the universities would then examine the boys to see if they had been taught in accordance with it.[4] This was the relationship which many of the witnesses before the commission wished to preserve, and the existence of this tradition made the development of a uniform state system of examinations in England very unlikely. The traditionalists were keenly aware of the dangers arising from a giant common examination. J. G. Fitch, a veteran of great experience, also pointed out the dangers of an over-rigid system of

[1] *Bryce Comm.* vol. v, p. 273.
[2] *Bryce Comm.* vol. iv, p. 228: 14619.
[3] *Bryce Comm.* vol. iv, p. 229: 14627.
[4] *Bryce Comm.* vol. ii, p. 386: 4015 ff.

inspection which might be even more perilous to the independence and originality of the teacher than any examination could be.[1] The commissioners in their report decided to support the existing examining bodies. They took on the whole the traditionalist point of view which seems to have been dominant in the evidence before them. On this subject, in fact, the recommendations of the Bryce Commission was far less radical than those of the Taunton Commission thirty years earlier. In the intervening decades the examining bodies had dug their roots very much more deeply into the educational sub-soil. Though they were ready subjects for criticism, they had grown too strong to be easily swept aside and for all their faults they had the advantage of familiarity. Although both the Delegacy and the Syndicate had plenty of critics to face, they were entitled to feel at the end of the century, which coincided almost exactly with their fortieth birthdays, that their achievements had not been inconsiderable. They had helped to raise the general standard of secondary education in the country, to bring together the universities and the schools, to make teachers aware of their responsibilities. The three men, Brereton, Acland and Temple, who were really in their different ways the founders, were alive when the Oxford Delegacy completed its first forty years.[2] Out of their ideas and plans, the talks with Fortescue at Castle Hill, the trial scheme at Exeter, the discussions at Oxford in the early summer of 1857, had grown institutions so deep-rooted that they have adapted themselves to all the changes of the twentieth century. It has always been clear that they are far from perfect, but it has been easier to find fault with them than to replace them.

The Bryce Commission had come at a crucial moment of change, and radical recommendations about examining methods would certainly have had a great effect. No such recommendations were made, though many other educational reforms were suggested. In the ensuing decades the education of England was to come closely under state control. The concept of elementary education was first broadened and then rendered obsolescent by the success of the new local authority secondary schools, and by new pressures to treat the lower standards of the public day school as a primary stage on the way to secondary education. This development once more created a demand for scholarship examinations. After the First

World War the universities were more and more brought under the influence of the University Grants Committee. Yet public examining, with all its crucial implications for entry into the universities and professions, remained basically in private hands as it had been during the nineteenth century. In this respect England is unique among European countries. We think of it sometimes as the land of independent schools; it might also be remembered as the land of independent examining bodies. These bodies have certainly come into very much closer relationship with the state system, but they are not directly responsible to the state. The acceptance by the Bryce Commission of the university examining bodies has never been reversed with the result that the Victorian system of school examinations has survived in its essentials into the middle of the twentieth century.

11

CRITICS AND CRITICISM

If the review of the Locals which was attempted in the last chapter is extended to a more general critique of examinations, it is natural to begin with the universities, since both the Civil Service and the schools had very close links with them. The school examinations had by 1900 been controlled by the universities for over forty years. The Civil Service was anxious to acquire for its higher posts men who had won distinction in university tests. By 1900 the universities, Oxford and Cambridge in particular, the public administration and the secondary schools formed a whole of closely interrelated parts, each of which sharply reacted to changes in the others. The point was clearly made at Cambridge in the nineties when the university sent a memorial to government asking for legislation on secondary education. Some opposition to this course was expressed on the ground that secondary education was not the university's business. The Council of the Senate urged on the contrary that: 'Whatever tends to increase or diminish the efficiency of the work in Secondary Schools is certain to react favourably or unfavourably, as the case may be, upon the universities themselves. It therefore seems fitting that the university should not hesitate to take action with the object of doing what lies in its power to promote such efficiency.'[1]

Just as the secondary schools had improved after the reports of the Taunton and Clarendon Commissions and standards had risen in the Civil Service during the same period, so Oxford and Cambridge had made great strides. New studies had been developed. Physical Science, Mark Pattison wrote, had worked 'a revolution in the scope and functions of Oxford life far greater than has been effected by two successive Commissions'.[2] Numbers had grown, old restraints had been loosened, and new spheres of work such as extra-mural lecturing developed. Closer links had been forged with the worlds of politics and administration which looked more

[1] *Camb. Univ. Rep.* (1896–7), p. 235.
[2] *Memoirs*, p. 305.

and more to the universities to provide them with young men of talent and trained ability.

If one man may be identified with a movement which involved a whole generation, that man would be Benjamin Jowett of Balliol. He had developed a new and deeper conception of the work of the college tutor. His links with the administrative reformers of the fifties have already been brought out in the first part of this book. He was deeply interested in strengthening the links between Oxford and the Indian Civil Service. It is a mistake, as Sir Geoffrey Faber has pointed out, to regard him as a kind of super-crammer for the public service,[1] but the connection which he created between that service and Balliol was to a great extent deliberate. He believed that scholars and teachers should play an active part in the world and in society. He was anxious to launch able young men where he could; he believed in success and spoke of his 'general prejudice against all persons who do not succeed in the world'. Such success was valuable to him rather as the reward of hard work and perseverance than in the vulgar sense of place and profit, but he did mark out a direction which was closely followed both in his own college and in Oxford generally.

The university to Jowett was an institution with severely practical aims. The student was to be offered the best and most stimulating teaching and social atmosphere. It was then his task to carry what he had learned out to the service of the wider world. Jowett was often condemned as a tuft-hunter and a snob who sought the rich and the successful. The charge is unfair. He had long been interested in bringing up poor boys to Oxford. He took an active part in the extension of university education to the great cities. His own influence lay primarily in Oxford – in his own college and in other colleges through old Balliol men. Similar ideas of the role of the universities in public service affected leading men at Cambridge like John Seeley, the founder of the modern Cambridge history school. It would be a mistake, however, to think of the university spirit as confined to the banks of the Isis and the Cam. In more modern forms it spread to new sectors of the national life, first through the University of London and later through the provincial

---

[1] G. Faber, *Jowett. A Portrait with background* (1957), p. 358. See also J. P. C. Roach, 'Victorian Universities and the National Intelligentsia', *Victorian Studies*, vol. II, 2 (December 1959).

colleges which were themselves to become independent universities in the twentieth century. The University of London, chartered in 1836, was a pioneer in many directions. Its degrees were, from the beginning, free from any religious test. Under the Charter of 1858 degrees were opened to students whether or not they had studied at affiliated institutions. The standards of the degrees were demanding, but they were in future to be open, as a contemporary wrote, to 'self-denying solitary students, who have laid siege to knowledge in the midst of hardship and privation'.[1] In 1860 the first examinations for the new degree of Bachelor of Science were held. The supplemental charter of 1878 opened the degrees of the university to women, the first British university to take such a step.

Unquestionably London University was a major force in broadening the sphere within which universities operated, and in that sense widening opportunities for young men and women. During the first thirty or forty years of the life of the new university the wider opportunities offered to Dissenters and to Catholics, both excluded from the ancient universities, were of particular importance. William Smith, of the *Dictionary of Greek and Roman Antiquities*, gave evidence to the Taunton Commission that the University of London had improved the teaching of many middle-class schools and of the Catholic and Dissenting Colleges. Standards had risen at the Jesuit College of Stonyhurst because of the London Examinations, and the Dissenting Colleges had been impelled, in order to prepare their students for them successfully, to spend much more money on their tutorial staffs.[2] Walter Bagehot and R. H. Hutton of the *Spectator* are examples of men from Dissenting backgrounds who were able to study for degrees at London, which would not have been available to them at Oxford and Cambridge. Mark Rutherford emphasized something which was happening in chapels all over the land when he made the new minister of Tanner's Lane 'a student fresh from college, who had taken an M.A. degree at the University of London'.[3]

A broader religious background might often mean a broader social background too, since the Established Church was so closely

[1] P. Dunsheath and M. Miller, *Convocation in the University of London: The First hundred years* (1958), p. 150.

[2] *SIC*, vol. IV, p. 112: 970–2.

[3] Mark Rutherford, *The Revolution in Tanner's Lane* (5th edn., n.d.), p. 386.

linked with the dominant groups in society. There was a widespread demand in the sixties and seventies for 'university extension', because it was felt that England's university population was so low in comparison with that of countries like France and Prussia. London was already an example of what could be done, and something similar was needed in the great provincial centres. The pioneer institution here was Owens' College, Manchester, opened in 1851, the ancestor of the modern University of Manchester. Similar colleges followed during the next thirty years at Leeds, Sheffield, Liverpool, Birmingham, Newcastle and Bristol, all of which were in their time to develop into the modern civic universities. Owens' College had a hard struggle and for some years success seemed very doubtful, but it gradually established its position until in 1880 it became one of the constituent colleges of the new Victoria University. Until the provincial colleges gained their independent university charters, their students studied for London Degrees. London University is not only an institution of capital importance in itself. It was also the nursing mother of many other universities both at home and overseas, which grew to maturity under the guidance of the standards which it had already established. The last of the English provincial university colleges did not in fact gain their independence from London until after the Second World War.

Money was short, and the industrial districts became convinced only slowly of the value of their own institutions of higher education. There is nothing glamorous or arresting in the story of the growth of the civic universities, which was slow, troubled and often uncertain. Yet London and the provincial colleges were doing a work of immense importance between the middle of the nineteenth century and the outbreak of the First World War. They had broadened the basis of the whole educated class and brought opportunities of learning and culture into regions and social groups which would never otherwise have known these things. It was a remarkable achievement, and one to which the historians have paid little tribute.

The early life of the great physicist, J. J. Thomson, illustrates the kind of new opportunity which was becoming available to hundreds of young men. Thomson was born in Manchester in 1856. He went to a private day-school and was to be apprenticed as an engineer. The firm for which he was designed could not take him and a friend of his father's advised that he should be sent to Owens' College while he was waiting. This accident, wrote Thomson in his auto-biography: 'which I regard as the most critical event in my life and which determined my career, could not have happened in any English provincial town except Manchester, for there was no other which had anything corresponding to Owens' College'.[1] In fact Thomson never became an engineer because his father died at the end of his second year and his mother could not afford the large premium which was then generally demanded for apprenticeship. He stayed on at the college, having won some small scholarships and eventually won a minor scholarship to Trinity College, Cambridge. 'I think', Thomson wrote, 'few can have owed more to scholarships than I do, for without them I could not have stayed at Owens or gone to Trinity.'[2]

Educational opportunities were broadened only slowly in the late nineteenth century, but the creation of the provincial colleges was certainly one major factor in enabling men from wider social groups to gain a higher education.

London University also acquired a strong influence on the schools through its Matriculation Examination, which developed into an important qualification in its own right, quite apart from its role as one stage on the way to the first degree. During the latter part of the century several schemes were put forward for a Schools Examination Board of the University of London on lines similar to those of Oxford and Cambridge, but nothing was done until 1902.[3] Quite informally, however, the Matriculation Examination had established itself as a kind of secondary-school leaving certificate. The university itself in a petition to Parliament of 1869 on the Secondary Schools Bill commented that Matriculation 'marks the termination of the literary and scientific education received by large numbers of schoolboys'.[4] In 1858 there had been 299 candidates for matriculation.[5] By 1890 the examination was attracting 3,000 candidates a year.[6] It was a difficult test and the qualification it gave was highly valued. A French observer of the period described it as the highest and most complete test of the education given in English secondary

[1] J. J. Thomson, *Recollections and Reflections* (1936), p. 2.
[2] *Ibid.* p. 31.
[3] Dunsheath and Miller, *Convocation in the University of London*, pp. 49–50.
[4] University of London Library: *Minutes of Committees, 1867–1880*, p. 47.
[5] *University of London, The Historical Record, 1836–1912* (1912), p. 13.
[6] *Journal of Education*, vol. XIII (n.s., 1891), p. 78.

schools, and one which opened up a whole host of careers.[1] As an examination it was a good deal criticized. There were said to be too many compulsory subjects, and the pass standard fluctuated considerably from time to time.[2] Of its high prestige there was no doubt, and of course its difficulty limited the numbers of those who could attempt it. Philip Magnus, the pioneer of technical education, wrote in 1883 that very few boys could take it without special preparation. Many schools which were able to enter twenty or thirty boys for the Local Examinations were unable to send up more than two or three for London Matriculation.[3]

The Matriculation Examination epitomized many of the problems inherent in the whole secondary-school situation at the end of the century. Because there was no generally accepted leaving examination, the Matriculation test had been put to a use for which it was never intended and which it did not fit very well. Because it had no organic relationship with the work of the schools, it pressed upon them as an outside force, something for which special preparation was needed. Something has already been said in the previous chapter about the confusion of examinations and of authorities in the nineties.[4] The schools were lost in a situation in which teaching and assessment had very little connection with one another.

The University of London suffered acutely from the same difficulties. Colleges like University and King's had existed from the beginning but the university itself was a purely examining body which took no share in the teaching of its own students. The standard of its examinations was very high, and the university had done, as we have seen, a great deal for the development of higher education both at home and abroad. Yet the same criticisms could be levelled against it as were levied against the Civil Service Commissioners and the authorities controlling the University Locals. Since it controlled an examining structure without any direct link with the teaching of the students who took its tests, its very existence encouraged the crammer and discouraged genuine education.

---

[1] M. Leclerc, *L'Education des classes moyennes et dirigéantes en Angleterre* (1894), p. 324.

[2] *Journal of Education*, vol. XIII (n.s., 1891), p. 13, vol. XVIII (n.s., 1896), p. 358.

[3] *Ibid.* vol. V (n.s., 1883), p. 58.

[4] See p. 249.

Professor Karl Pearson wrote in a letter published in December 1884:

London does not possess any University at all ... To term the body which examines at Burlington House a university is a perversion of language to which no charter or Act of Parliament can give real sanction. A University is essentially a teaching and a learning body, and its function of examination is purely secondary – a practically convenient, but by no means necessary, method of graduating its members ... The Science and Arts Examinations of the so-called London University are a check rather than an incentive to genuine teaching.[1]

After years of controversy the University of London Act (1898) established a genuine teaching university. Into its development we have no need to go here, but the long debate about the relationship between the examining and the teaching functions in London expressed in an extreme form a problem which had to be faced by all the universities of Britain in the age of reform which followed the fifties. Open competition for scholarships and fellowships and the primacy of examination tests had formed a major part of the programme of the Oxford and Cambridge reformers. Certainly the changes made under their banner had brought about great improvements. Before very long men began to be conscious of the dangers and to ask whether the reign of free competition and open examination imperilled the whole existence of the university as a place of higher learning. J. H. Newman had foreseen the dilemma in his Dublin addresses on university education (1852) before the movement of university reform had really got under way:

I protest to you, gentlemen, that if I had to choose between a so-called university which dispensed with residence and tutorial superintendence and gave its degrees to any person who passed an examination in a wide range of subjects, and a university which had no professors or examinations at all, but merely brought a number of young men together for three or four years, and then sent them away, as the University of Oxford is said to have done some sixty years since, if I were asked which of these two methods was the better discipline of the intellect – mind I do not say which is morally the better, for compulsory study must be a good, and idleness an intolerable mischief – but if I must determine which of the two courses was the most successful in training, moulding, enlarging the mind; which sent out men the more fitted for their secular duties;

[1] Quoted in Dunsheath and Miller, *Convocation in the University of London*, p. 69.

which produced better public men – men of the world, men whose names would descend to posterity – I have no hesitation in giving the preference to that university which did nothing, over that which exacted of its members an acquaintance with every science under the sun. And, paradox as this may seem, still, if results be the test of systems, the influence of the public schools and colleges of England, in the course of the last century at least, will bear out one side of the contrast as I have drawn it.[1]

Certainly Newman's words strongly condemned the type of university which had developed in London. They could be used as a criticism of many aspects of reformed Oxford, and they were so used by the most acute critic of Oxford in the Jowett era, Mark Pattison, Rector of Lincoln College.[2] Jowett was not a crammer for the public service, as I have already said, and it would be a mistake to draw too sharp a contrast between Pattison, as the devotee of high culture and the deepest intellectual development of the individual, and Jowett, as the efficient teacher entirely devoted to examination successes and public honours. But there is something in that exaggerated contrast. Pattison was certainly one of the first and one of the most powerful of the voices which spoke out against the dominance of examinations and the production by the universities of shallow young sophists, which in his view, followed from this dominance. He wrote in his *Memoirs*.

Our young men are not trained; they are only filled with propositions, of which they have never learned the inductive basis. From showy lectures, from manuals, from attractive periodicals, the youth is put in possession of ready-made opinions on every conceivable subject; a crude mass of matter, which he is taught to regard as real knowledge. Swollen with this puffy and unwholesome diet, he goes forth into the world regarding himself, like the infant in the nursery, as the centre of all things, the measure of the universe.[3]

As a young fellow of Lincoln, Pattison had been a follower of Newman and nearly followed him to Rome in 1845. He then took up the cause of university reform. In his evidence to the Royal

[1] J. H. Newman, *The Idea of a University, Defined and Illustrated* (new edn., 1898), p. 145.
[2] Pattison quotes them in *Suggestions on Academical Organisation with especial reference to Oxford* (1868), p. 248. For a modern study of Pattison, see John Sparrow, *Mark Pattison and the Idea of a University* (1967).
[3] Pattison, *Memoirs*, pp. 240–1.

Commission of 1850 he defended the traditional Oxford tutorial system against the ideal of professional teaching which many of the reformers favoured. Gradually his views changed. He suffered a very severe personal disillusionment when he failed to be elected to the Rectorship of his College in 1851. Years of withdrawal and of intense study followed. As he pondered he came to the conclusion that the tutorial system could not produce the results for which he had originally hoped. No college tutor could thoroughly master all that he had to teach or conquer the higher ranges of science. Pattison's attention, like that of Matthew Arnold and many others of his generation, was turned to Germany. There, it appeared to them, *Wissenschaft* reigned in the Universities. Oxford was merely a higher school turning out young men who had been crammed with superficial information. It was the German professors and students who had devoted themselves to the true culture of the mind. They had a freedom to teach and to learn which was not known in the limiting conditions of England. They had come nearer than anyone else to the true goal of the university which was 'not to enlarge the sciences, or to heap up libraries ... but to maintain through successive generations an order of minds, in each of the great departments of human enquiry, cultivated to the utmost point which their powers admit of'.[1]

This quotation is taken from *Suggestions on Academical Organisation with especial reference to Oxford*, published in 1868, in which Pattison elaborated his own programme of university reform. The whole course of change in the universities and schools during the previous twenty years had gone against his presuppositions. As he saw it, open competition and the increased stress on examination had produced cramming, and the dominance of shallow half-understood ideas. He made his point of view clear when he was examined by the Taunton Commission about the education of girls. Examinations certainly had advantages but the point soon came when the evils outweighed them. The Local Examinations had done excellent work but they were coming to control the work of the schools with bad effects. In the universities the evils of the examining system were increasing as the system itself grew more perfect. In the Indian Civil Service Examinations the crammers had beaten the examiners at their own game.[2]

[1] Pattison, *Suggestions on Academical Organisation*, p. 227.
[2] *SIC*, vol. v, pp. 951–2: 17869–72.

Suggestions on Academical Organisation is, of course, a study of the universities exclusively, though Pattison clearly believed that the same evils affected the schools and the public service as well. The case which he made in his book demanded nothing less than the complete reorganization of the University of Oxford. As he saw it, the university and the colleges concentrated entirely on the studies for the first degree. In the new pattern which he suggested the emphasis was to change from teaching to higher study and research. College endowments should be redistributed and devoted to the maintenance of the faculties of theology, law, medicine, classics, philology and language, historical and moral sciences, mathematical and physical sciences. Through the studies of these faculties there would come into existence what Oxford did not possess, 'a professional class of learned and scientific men.'[1] In this way the colleges would be restored to their original purpose. They had not originally been intended for elementary education but for the maintenance of men engaged in higher studies who were freed, through the existence of college endowments, from the necessity to earn their living by teaching. The colleges would cease to be boarding schools for youths of good family. They would in the new order become the centres through which Oxford might become a true national centre of learning and culture of a kind which England did not possess.

Within this academic structure the students' course of study would be radically changed. The pass degree would be abolished. Men would be allowed to come up without becoming members of a college. The university would attract many students who would be able to enjoy the attractions of a great centre of learning for the mere cost of board and lodging. Their general education would be continued until Moderations at the end of the first year. After this they would pursue a specialized course of study in one of the faculties. They might, if they wished, be examined for a degree, but examination would play a comparatively minor part in the whole structure. Professors would study and teach and students would learn primarily for the love of learning. They would be engaged in a common enterprise of the mind which would break away from the sectarian spirit which had dominated English higher education ever since the Reformation. The days of individual effort were drawing to a close. Great as its achievements had been,

[1] *Suggestions*, p. 169.

the problems of society were too great to be solved in that way: 'The conviction must ere long reach us that our knowledge is defective, and that such is the length of art and the shortness of life, that knowledge can only be made available for public purposes by concert and organisation.'[1]

Pattison was in many ways a very far-seeing man, and John Sparrow in his recent study makes the point that many of his ideas appeared to have had no result because they were too far in advance of their time.[2] His general ideas of university reform are not of primary concern to us from the point of view of this book, but they do contain ideas and criticisms which are of importance for the debate on examinations which was to grow in strength during the seventies and eighties.

Pattison commented in the *Memoirs* that the great achievement of the Oxford Executive Commission of 1854 had been to sweep away the closed fellowships. Like many of his contemporaries he was very doubtful whether open competition had really broadened the scope of the university by bringing there students who would not otherwise have been able to matriculate. He argued in the *Suggestions* that open scholarships had not provided opportunities for poor young men. Scholarships had continued to be awarded to men of much the same class as those who had gained them before. The point he is making is that which has several times been made in this book. Open competition gave a premium to those who had obtained the best, or in other words the most expensive, preliminary education. After all, Gladstone had defended it on the grounds that it would tend 'to strengthen and multiply the ties between the higher classes and the possession of administrative power'.[3] Nothing which had been done since 1854 had really closed the gap which cut off the universities from large sections of the community, including a great part of the wealthy and influential classes.[4] Nor had open scholarships produced a healthy effect on those who had won them. They had certainly stimulated the competitors but rather through quick and superficial knowledge than through solidly based scholarship. The same was true of the open fellowhips. There were too many of them and they were of too great a

---

[1] *Ibid.* p. 329.
[2] Sparrow, *Mark Pattison and the Idea of a University*, p. 135.
[3] See p. 193.
[4] *Suggestions*, p. 102.

value. The result was to create an artificial demand for a certain type of accomplishment, which stood a long way from real culture. In Pattison's mind the great danger threatening the university was that it should be regarded as a kind of higher school whose duty was discharged by turning out young men who had learned what it was fashionable to know. As the power of the middle class grew it was likely that they would measure the achievement of the universities by the possession of whatever helped towards success in life. Their aim would be to make Oxford even more successful as a school than it had already made itself:

> We should have a varied staff of masters, under whom every sort of accomplishment might be acquired in little time, or at little cost, and youth prepared to pass unnumbered competitive examinations in any subject. The hive would be purified; the drones would be driven out. The danger on which the *Times* dwells, that we are getting to know too much, and to do too little, would be abated. Every one would be doing a day's work, and receiving a salary in proportion.[1]

Pattison was arguing that the university had set on foot a great race for qualification and preferment. Great care was taken to see that the conditions under which each student competed were equal. There was less interest in the nature of the course and very little concern for the ultimate goal. The race had become exalted in itself, as if racing were something which met human needs and desires.

This type of criticism – against competition as a self-sufficient and self-justifying system–became very common during the 1870s. The subject was examined by the Social Science Association, whose proceedings are a good guide to the preoccupations of the progressive opinion of the time. Joseph Payne, the historian of the College of Preceptors, told the association in 1873 that, though examinations were to some extent desirable, 'he could not help thinking that many persons were going examination mad at the present moment. They were going down a precipice at the most violent rate, and would be dashed to pieces unless they could regulate the movement and pace they were going at.'[2] During the same year the Scottish educationalist, T. M. G. Meiklejohn, read the association a paper on the effects of competitive examination upon education in which he

---

[1] *Suggestions*, p. 138.
[2] *Transactions of the Social Science Association, 1873*, p. 331.

emphasized the evils of cramming and suggested the inspection of secondary schools by a central board. Among those who took part in the discussion on this occasion were Pattison himself and Lord Houghton, who criticized the effect of competition on the Civil Service.[1]

The type of criticism which appeared in the seventies may be divided into several heads. There had always been a current of resistance to the competitive examinations in the Home and Indian Civil Services. Disraeli has already been quoted.[2] A good deal of this criticism was rhetorical rather than reasoned, like that of the author of a pamphlet of 1872 which said: 'competition as at present conducted, is an unqualified curse – in the case of the Indian Civil Service, potential, it may be, rather than actual – to the public services, to its victims, whether successful or unsuccessful, and to national education and the national character, intellectual and moral'.[3] The Civil Service Examinations were particularly open to criticism because they were not connected with any system of teaching and they were the happy hunting grounds for the crammer. This was, as we have seen, one of the reasons why Lord Salisbury reduced the age limits for the Indian Civil Service to seventeen to nineteen for 1879 and subsequent years in order to encourage applicants straight from the public schools.[4] But the crammers were too efficient to be dislodged. The most successful of them, Messrs Wren and Gurney, passed 427 of their pupils into the Indian Civil Service out of 827 candidates admitted during the years 1870–92, and twelve times gained the top place.[5]

The idea of a very wide range of subjects had, of course, been basic to the Civil Service Reformers of the fifties. One of the complaints made against the Indian Civil Service Examination had always been that it was too easy to pick up marks in a multiplicity of papers. By the early seventies writers were beginning to discuss the suitability of different subjects for competitive examination. There was a widespread opinion that the newer subjects like natural science or history were less suited for this type of test than classics or mathematics, because they depended much more on the sheer

---

[1] *Ibid.* pp. 347–61.
[2] See pp. 30, 192.
[3] George C. M. Birdwood, *On Competition and the Indian Civil Service* (1872), p. 14.
[4] See pp. 218–20.
[5] Leclerc, *Les Professions et la société en Angleterre*, p. 128.

10

accumulation of knowledge through the memory than on the exercise of skills which brought into play what has been learned. Here the Cambridge mathematician, Isaac Todhunter, re-stated an argument which, in relation to university studies, certainly went as far back as William Whewell.[1] Like Pattison, Todhunter thought that too many prizes were being offered to students. The result was to make them neglect any study which did not promise an immediate pecuniary return. Consequently, if a new subject was to be brought forward, the only way of giving it prominence was to put it into the examination scheme. The new subject might well be adapted for private study or for the lecture-room, yet not at all well adapted for public examination. Todhunter argued that the traditional subjects, mathematics in particular, lent themselves to a very accurate comparison of results. In addition they required the student to give evidence of his own skill: for instance, in solving a mathematical problem or in writing a Greek prose. They were in that sense constructional as the sciences or history were not because they depended almost entirely on the mere use of memory. Even the practical side of science was of limited value because it cannot give to the schoolboy or the undergraduate the stimulus which it gave to the original discoverer. As Todhunter shrewdly pointed out:

The lecture rooms of professors of experimental philosophy must be devoted chiefly to the mechanical repetition of familar processes; the spectators are told what they may expect to see, and accordingly they see it with more or less clearness of conviction. The result of the whole performance may be that certain facts are impressed on the belief or on the memory, but it is difficult to secure any cultivation of the power of experimenting, or any mode of testing the existence of such a power.[2]

By the time Todhunter wrote, more and more sophisticated questions were being asked about the whole examining process, culminating in this period in the fundamental papers of F. Y. Edgeworth around 1890, which raised the whole study onto a new plane. Writers in the many reviews which published articles on examinations were working, in a rule of thumb way, towards stating the same problems. A. H. Sayce wrote in the *Fortnightly* in 1875 on the weakness of the examination system in the universities.

[1] I. Todhunter, *The Conflict of Studies and other Essays on Subjects connected with Education* (1873).
[2] *Ibid.* p. 19.

The same kind of evils were being produced at Oxford and Cambridge as existed in the Indian Civil Service Examinations. The achievement of a high class meant nothing more than the possession of certain abilities for examination purposes. It was often admitted at Oxford that a first-class man was inferior to a second-class man, while it was a fluke whether or not the best man got the fellowship. Sayce at least suggested, though he did not precisely state, that the system penalized independent thought and originality of character.[1] A. R. Grant, writing a few years later in the *Nineteenth Century*, carried the argument a stage further. Adding up the marks, he thought, tells you nothing more than that you have added up the marks, because the decisions are highly subjective and different examiners would draw up different orders. All that an examination could do was to test knowledge. It provided few means of eliciting originality or appraising mental capacity. It could not test the balance of mental powers or assess soundness of judgment. Grant's own suggestion for improving the situation was to introduce general qualifying examinations followed by competition 'in some exercise which tests power and originality as well as readiness'.[2]

The fact is that in 1880, as today, it was comparatively easy to frame tests for young men and young women which assess readiness. It is very much more difficult to frame tests which assess power and originality. There were those who tried to give a balanced view and to show what good as well as what evil had been done by the system of open competition since its introduction. Among them was Alfred Barry, principal of King's College, London, who, as headmaster of Leeds Grammar School, had been one of the supporters of the Locals scheme of 1857. He argued that, although the examining system certainly had faults, the proper course was to work for improvement rather than to reject the whole idea. Examining, Barry pointed out, is really an inherent part of teaching and the two should not be divorced. The separation between the two in the case of London Degrees was the chief reason why those degrees were not as highly esteemed as they should be. In the field of public appointments, he argued that more could be done to defeat the

[1] A. H. Sayce, 'Results of the Examination System at the Universities', *Fortnightly Review*, vol. XVII (n.s., 1875), pp. 835–46.

[2] A. R. Grant, 'Evils of Competitive Examinations', *Nineteenth Century*, vol. VIII (November 1880). The quotation is on p. 723.

crammer and that more use should be made of probation and of evidence of previous study. In some parts of the public service, for instance, in the army examinations, more credit should be given for physical vigour and prowess. Whatever their faults, the Civil Service Examinations were better than some sort of 'spoils system' which was the only alternative. If examinations come to an end, there was 'the risk of the dominion, either of official clique or political jobbery'.[1] So far as schools were concerned, the inspection and examination of a whole school had great value, and examinations did help parents to assess the efficiency of schools.

The plan of examining and inspecting schools was very much in the air at the time when Barry was writing because of the establishment in 1874 of the Oxford and Cambridge Schools Examination Board. Among those who contributed to the debate caused by the creation of this new body was Henry Latham of Trinity Hall, Cambridge.[2] In 1877 his work *On the Action of Examinations considered as a Means of Selection* appeared. It is a book of very real importance which summed up the whole debate in a magisterial way. Indeed, with Edgeworth's later articles it is the most important contribution to the literature of examinations in the latter part of the century. Latham spent the whole of his working career at Trinity Hall as tutor and later as master and his argument works very much within the traditional limits of Cambridge scholarship. Like his fellow Cantabrigian, Todhunter, he was strongly in favour of examining in subjects which demanded the exercise of a skill by the examinee rather than the mere repetition of information learned from a book. Like Pattison he used university history to support his points. The Trivium and Quadrivium, the ancient bases of university study, had value, Latham, argued, because they resulted in acquirements which could be put into practice: 'They did not merely furnish the student with the knowledge of physical facts or of what other men had said or done, but they undertook to equip him and train him to perform certain functions or operations, which required skill.'[3] The influence of the Mathematical Tripos, with its strong emphasis on problem-solving, is very obvious in the thought of both Latham and Todhunter.

---

[1] A. Barry 'The Good and Evil of Examination', *Nineteenth Century*, vol. III (1878), pp. 647–66. The quotation is on p. 662. See also Barry's *Educational prospects in England: A Lecture delivered at King's College, London* (1874).

[2] See p. 234.

[3] Latham, *Action of Examinations*, p. 85.

In general Latham wrote as a supporter, but a somewhat critical supporter, of the system of examinations. In sharp contrast to Pattison, or to Matthew Arnold, he accepted the mercenary competitive spirit of his age, and argued that the conventional values of the Englishmen of the day must not be rejected but must be used for educational purposes. 'The spirit of contest goes all through life', he argued,[1] and he clearly thought that this was something which the teacher must not reject but must make use of. He argued like a free-trade economist of his time that the value of competition is shown by the stimulus which it gives to the market. The reward was not something which was enjoyed only by the successful competitors. Because there were prizes to be won, sixth forms were larger than they would otherwise have been. The existence of prizes helped to produce a class of cultivated persons who raised the tone of English social life. Latham maintained: 'These advantages result from the prizes of learning, just as the improvement in the breed of cattle is effected by the money subscribed as prizes in the shows.'[2]

The book shows that he was well aware of educational developments in Europe. In discussing college fellowships and scholarships he made much use of German examples and he used foreign parallels to point out some of the difficulties in the English situation. In Germany all those who had passed through a course of secondary education had been trained in much the same way. The teacher was left wide freedom, while sufficient uniformity was maintained through the guidance of government officials. In France pupil and teacher alike worked to a minutely detailed official programme. In England alone was there no uniform system of any kind. This absence of uniformity was dear to the English, but it led them into considerable difficulties.[3]

Latham was far more sympathetic towards examinations which were closely linked with systematic teaching than to those like the Civil Service Examinations which had no such connection. Where examinations help a student by marking out portions of the course and giving an objective to aim at, many of the objections to their use disappear. Where they are external to the teaching and studies in which the pupil has been engaged, there are more serious difficulties.

[1] *Ibid.* p. 501.
[2] *Ibid.* p. 72.
[3] *Ibid.* pp. 64, 389, 421–2.

Such examinations crush spontaneity. They tend to over-stimulate with unfortunate results. Latham quoted the case of those who had been his college pupils, and who had just failed to get an appointment and who were therefore not likely to be very different in their general character from those who had just succeeded: 'I have found very generally indeed, that those who had gone through a series of such trials, had the same kind of mental defect. They were usually, for a long time, incapable of giving their minds steadily to any subject requiring close attention.'[1]

Clearly he feared that the Indian Civil Service Examinations encouraged the production of showy ideas on large subjects, as he shows in his discussion of the essay paper: 'A form of opening much in vogue in such cases, I am told, is the following: "This is one of these apophthegms which are regarded as truisms, until upon close investigation they are found to be falsehoods"; but pupils are cautioned against using the exact form of words, lest the similarity of their phraseology should strike the examiner.'[2]

The system of special preparation used for these examinations seemed to him to have educational disadvantages, and to be both wasteful and expensive because it diverted energies into many channels which ought to have been concentrated on the main course of school and college education. So far as higher education was concerned, he suggested that all candidates for higher government appointments should be required to pass a university examination after several terms of study, rather like Moderations at Oxford. Only those who had done well in such an examination should be allowed to compete for government appointments.[3] This idea of an intermediate university examination would have combined purely academic studies with subsequent selection for public service. It would also have been rather similar to Pattison's idea of Moderations as a general examination before specialized studies began. It is worth remembering too that academic opinion of the time was very interested in getting the preparation of Indian Civil Service candidates more closely under university control.[4]

One reason why Latham was lukewarm about the use of examinations as a means of selection for government employment was

---

[1] Latham, *Action of Examinations*, p. 48.
[2] *Ibid.* pp. 268–9.
[3] *Ibid.* p. 423.
[4] See p. 220.

because he appreciated that the accuracy which could be obtained by such means was distinctly limited. The best and the worst were not very difficult to pick out, but the closer we approach towards the mean the less the difference between the candidates and the more meaningless the decision where the dividing line was to fall. Latham put the matter like this: 'When many candidates are selected out of a great body, as in the Examinations for the Indian Civil Service and the Army, we go down so far that this plateau is reached; and there is, in fact, no difference worth considering between the last ten who are accepted and the first ten who are rejected.'[1]

Since no examination is necessarily correct in its assessment, its verdict needs to be accepted with caution. A man who has done well in an examination is likely to be an effective person but a man who has done badly is not necessarily and for that reason an ineffective one.

Latham's book is interesting because it is the most sophisticated assessment of the subject which had at that time appeared. An experienced college tutor writing twenty years after the system of competition had been introduced was in a good position to approach the subject in a more balanced and critical way than either the supporters or the opponents, who were writing when competitive examination was something very new. Naturally Latham's thinking contains echoes of earlier debates. Like Macaulay and Gladstone, he made a good deal of the moral argument – that conscientious devotion to a course of study elicits moral strengths and qualities of thoroughness and application which are a permanent possession. The struggle of the examination is a prelude to the struggle of real life:

it requires teachableness, concentration, and above all, the power of 'enduring hardness', of working when one would rather not work, and setting one's self to master thoroughly what may be distasteful. I believe myself that *one great effort* in the way of a heavy examination is a very valuable piece of mental discipline; it calls out the courage and the resources that there are in a man, and merely to have made this effort conscientiously, and have done his best, gives a moral elevation to the character, even if he fail in winning any very marked success.[2]

---

[1] *Action of Examinations*, p. 322.
[2] *Ibid.* pp. 35–6.

This was a very conventional argument of the time. Where Latham was much more original was in his analytical approach to the question: 'What does an examination set out to test?' It may be used, he says, to detect either knowledge or ability. The latter of these is the more important, and it had three main constituents. The first of these is memory, which may be portative – the mere reproduction of what has been learned – or analytical, where the mind holds together impressions selected from a mass of information. Portative memory has its use, but what is really important is the ability to sift and to analyse what has been learned and to make it a permanent possession. The second constituent of ability is imagination, though this needs to be closely controlled by the will, if it is not to peter out merely into brilliant talk and shallow generalization. The third constituent is reasoning power. All these – memory, imagination, reasoning power – add up to what he describes as 'energy of mind'.[1]

In practical terms the examiner has to discover firstly how much the candidate has learned, and in particular whether he has simply amassed facts or has learned how to grasp principles. Secondly he must find out whether the knowledge acquired will be valuable in the position which is being aimed at or will be valuable as a personal possession. Finally he needs to assess the permanence of the knowledge acquired. Things are better remembered if they arise from certain principles and if the mind is not disturbed by having to grasp too many different topics at once. In terms of the curriculum, as I have already shown, Latham was a strong defender of classics and mathematics, because proficiency in these subjects was expressed in practical exercises by the student. He was very dubious of the value of the newer subjects. English literature often meant merely 'the reproduction of footnotes and manuals'.[2] Proficiency in modern languages revealed nothing about the way in which a man has learned the language or about his real ability. He argued, therefore, that in the Indian Civil Service Examinations modern languages should be set only in qualifying tests.[3]

The book is long and full of interest. What is remarkable is the broad sweep of discussion which covers so many aspects of a complex subject. What Latham was attempting was to get away from

---

[1] *Action of Examinations*, p. 300.
[2] *Ibid.* p. 363.
[3] *Ibid.* pp. 374–9.

the rhetoric and the polemics into which discussions of this subject all too easily fell, towards a genuine analysis of the problem. His book might be called a first attempt at a psychology of examinations at a time when experimental psychology hardly existed. He was working towards the real problems of reliability and of accuracy which F. Y. Edgeworth was to tackle with far more sophisticated techniques a decade later. Essentially Latham is assuming that the competitive system has come to stay. What has to be done, therefore, is to discriminate and to refine, to ensure as far as possible that the means which are used achieve the results which are being aimed at. By the standards of a more statistical age, Latham's effort may not appear to go very far, but it is nevertheless a piece of real pioneer study. There was no other work of the day, in England, at least, which covered the subject with such finality and authority. Indeed, much of what Latham says in it is still of value in the consideration of current problems.

The controversy about examinations quietened down in the early eighties, but it flared up again towards the end of the decade. In March 1887 the College of Preceptors were discussing 'Competitive Examinations – the arguments pro and con: a review of the position'.[1] A year later a major review of the whole subject began again with the publication in the *Nineteenth Century* of a protest against examinations signed by some 400 persons. Many of these were people of distinction like the theologian B. F. Westcott, the positivist Frederic Harrison, Tom Hughes, Charlotte M. Yonge, and a strong group of academics – H. Nettleship, E. B. Tylor, E. A. Freeman, Mandell Creighton, J. A. Froude, and F. W. Maitland.[2] The discussion continued in later numbers of the periodical and the arguments were collected together in a symposium entitled *The Sacrifice of Education to Examination: Letters from All Sorts and Conditions of Men* (1889). This was edited by Auberon Herbert, an advanced Radical and an ardent individualist, who had been for some years a Liberal M.P. The protest of November 1888 claimed that examinations produced a danger of physical overstrain, especially for women and girls. They checked independence and free development in teaching, and quenched the love of knowledge for its own sake. Moreover they wasted valuable

[1] *Educational Times*, vol. XL (n.s., 1887), pp. 159–63.
[2] 'The Sacrifice of Education to Examination', *Nineteenth Century*, vol. XXIV (November 1888).

educational resources by locking them up in the award of prizes and scholarships. The protesters further outlined a campaign of action. The Queen should be petitioned to set up a Royal Commission to consider official appointments by examination. The universities and examining boards should be asked to look into the way in which their own examinations operated. Headmasters should be asked to enquire into the influences of examinations and to make suggestions for any substitutes which might replace them. A committee should be set up to enquire into the methods of appointment used by corporations and industrial firms.[1]

Most of the arguments used by both the protesters and by those who defended examination were familiar enough, and there would be little point in discussing in detail what has already been discussed in this chapter. Frederic Harrison's rhetoric is characteristic enough of much of the protest:

A man going through the full school, college and professional career now passed from ten to twenty of these examinations, at intervals perhaps of six months or a year. From the age of ten till twenty-five he is for ever in the presence of the mighty Mill. The Mill is to him money, success, honour, and bread and butter for life. Distinctions and prizes mean money and honour. Success in examinations means distinctions and prizes. And whatever does not mean success in examinations is not education.[2]

The defenders of the system generally made the point that, although improvements are possible, there is no real replacement for the system either in education or in public appointments. 'The competitive system with all its many imperfections,' wrote one defender, 'is merely the educational manifestation of the democratic movement in general.'[3] Political change, Lord Derby pointed out, would make nomination for public appointments even more of an abuse than in former times; 'with our democratic franchise, it would mean jobbery as unscrupulous as that which prevails in the United States. I am sure you would not support that.'[4]

However, certain new arguments did come forward in the debate which are of interest. One of these is the question of physical over-

[1] *Nineteenth Century*, vol. xxiv, pp. 636–7.
[2] *Ibid.* p. 650.
[3] *Ibid.* p. 926.
[4] Herbert (ed.), *The Sacrifice of Education to Examination* p. 21.

strain, and a much greater emphasis on the proper relationship between academic education and the laws of health. Latham had discussed briefly the dangers of overstrain, which he did not regard as a serious problem.[1] Indeed he did not place much emphasis on the question at all. Overstrain was particularly feared in the case of girls,[2] because it was argued that their physical and mental abilities were more easily damaged than those of young men. As more and more girls were being educated to a higher level, this problem naturally assumed greater importance. This may help to explain the concern about their children's health expressed by a number of parents in *The Sacrifice of Education to Examination*. Another possibility which arose from the same line of thought was to test physical qualities themselves. In this field Francis Galton put forward a scheme for a battery of physical tests which could be completed in fifteen minutes at no great cost and under the control of a person who need not be very highly skilled.[3]

The most important feature of the controversy follows from Auberon Herbert's strong personal commitment to voluntaryism and dislike of centralized control. Examination was, of course, extensively used as part of the state educational system. Much of the development of science teaching in the schools and in technical education depended entirely on the grants made through the examinations of the Science and Art Department. The elementary schools were dominated by the requirements of the Revised Code between 1862 and 1890. When Herbert's symposium appeared the Revised Code system was on its last legs. It had been condemned by the Minority Report of the Cross Commission (1888) and it was to be given up in stages after 1890.

The unpopularity of the annual examinations by Her Majesty's Inspectors may well have contributed to the distrust of examinations as an educational instrument which characterized many of those who joined in the protest. Herbert's symposium contains a good

[1] Latham, *Action of Examinations*, pp. 502–3.

[2] 'What may be the dangers of educational overwork for both sexes, with special reference to the higher classes of girls' schools, and the effects of competitive examinations', *Transactions of Social Science Association, 1880*, pp. 420–54.

[3] *Nineteenth Century*, vol. xxv, pp. 303–8. Galton had discussed the possibility of measuring intellectual abilities by simple laboratory tests in *Enquiries into Human Faculty and its Development* (1883), see Montgomery, *Examinations*, p. 109.

many criticisms of the system of elementary school grants of which the following is typical:

It is customary at the periodical meetings of Teachers' associations – in connection with the N[ational] U[nion of] E[lementary] T[eachers] – to spend part of the time on 'Wrinkles'. This term is synonymous with 'Tips', and the object in discussing this question is to be able to be prepared for the crochets and idiosyncrasies of HM Inspectors and their assistants. Consequently, boys are taught in such a manner that attention is not paid to their real training and education (as would be done by giving good object and science lessons), but they become mere automatic machines, into the slits (so as to speak) of which the Inspectors drop their favourite ideas embodied into questions, and out roll the answers. And yet I venture to think that the elementary teachers are not to blame, considering the present system of payment by results.[1]

By 1890 state control of elementary education in Britain had progressed a long way. In secondary and higher education very much less had been done. However the first government grants to universities and university colleges go back to the eighties, and in secondary education the Endowed Schools Bill, Part II of 1869 had sketched a very complete system of examination and inspection, though this had not passed into law.[2] By the nineties the difficulties of the whole situation were to lead to the Bryce Commission, followed by the acts of 1899 and 1902, which created an articulated system up to university level. Auberon Herbert feared the extension of central control, and it was primarily for this reason that he attacked examinations. No doubt the arguments about overstrain and crowded teaching programmes were perfectly genuine. The root issue in his mind was that examinations, which represented a common standard to which all had to conform, were a tool of centralization. They increased the power of those who were in control of them. They reinforced an established order of things, and made it much more difficult for innovations to take place. 'No remedy for existing evils', Herbert wrote, 'is to be expected by substituting some of these forms of centralisation for others, but only by allowing the utmost freedom for new wants and new forms of thought to express themselves in new systems and to compete with the old.'[3]

[1] W. Butler, in *The Sacrifice of Education*, pp. 39–40.
[2] See p. 231.
[3] *Sacrifice of Education*, p. 191.

Here Herbert was speaking as a free trade economist attacking the existence of monopoly. English life had changed very much between 1850 and 1890, and it is interesting to see how competitive examination had changed its role over a period of forty years. Originally it had been a reforming slogan to set people free from patronage and traditional interest, and to make sure that the best men came to the top. Now competition, instead of being a means of breaking up the traditional order, had been in one sense captured by that order, and had become the instrument of collectivist and centralizing power. It is worth noting that Herbert broadened his attack on examinations into an appeal for educational voluntaryism. He demanded the abolition of the Education Department and the conduct of elementary schools by local voluntary organizations.[1]

This fear of centralization was, of course, shared by supporters of examinations like J. L. Brereton[2] as well as by opponents like Auberon Herbert. Historically, as we have seen, examinations had gained much of their authority in English education from the fact that they appeared to be an alternative to a fully state-directed plan of teaching and inspection. Over and over again in this study we have come across the contrast between the English position and the position in countries like France and Germany, where the state was supreme in education. By 1890 the need for the English state machinery to take a greater share was becoming more and more apparent to many intelligent observers. One of those who contributed to Herbert's symposium was Samuel Dill, High Master of Manchester Grammar School (1877–87), who argued that the problem of examination could be dealt with only by setting up a central authority for secondary education. Such a step would not increase monotony and uniformity. It would actually release greater freedom if the central department were well run and if the teachers were able people, because it would give them more chance to do their work in their own way 'with confidence, freedom and individuality'.[3]

Dill's arguments both look back towards Matthew Arnold and forward to Robert Morant and the reforms of the early twentieth century. By the nineties the argument about examinations was merging into the much more fundamental debate about the

[1] *Ibid.* pp. 192–7.
[2] See p. 54.
[3] *Sacrifice of Education*, p. 126.

organization and structure of secondary education, in which the greatest landmark is the Act of 1902. The Bryce Commission had taken, as we saw in the last chapter, a generally favourable view of the existing examining bodies.[1] The *Nineteenth Century* protest of 1888–9 led no further than a debate in the House of Lords in February 1890. Lord Wemyss put forward the views of the protesters and asked for a Royal Commission to be set up. The Lord President (Lord Cranbrook) defended the existing system of examinations, and was supported by the Liberal statesman Lord Granville, by Lord Kimberley a former secretary of state for India, and by Lord Fortescue, who as a younger man had been one of the Devonshire pioneers of the fifties.[2] Though the protest had no result, the questions which it had raised were still being argued in the reviews,[3] and in 1903 a committee of the British Association produced a report on the influence of examinations, based on a series of questions to university teachers and to headmasters.[4]

The replies which the committee collected reflected some of the new developments of the day. There was a strong demand that examiners should confer much more systematically with teachers, an attitude reflecting the much more confident and critical tone among the schools which has already been noted.[5] There was widespread criticism of lack of co-ordination and a strong sense of the need for unity and simplification among examinations. This foreshadowed the report of the Consultative Committee of 1911 and the establishment of the School and Higher Certificate Examinations. Finally there was general agreement that examinations were necessary in some form, and that in recent years they had improved. By the end of the century it was quite clear that alike in the universities, in the schools and in the civil service public examinations had come to stay because no acceptable alternative

[1] See p. 255.
[2] *Parl. Deb.*, 3rd ser., vol. CCCXLI, 1445–83. For Fortescue (Lord Ebrington), see p. 65.
[3] See H. H. Almond, 'Competitive Examinations for Woolwich and Sandhurst', *Fortnightly Review*, vol. LXV (n.s., 1899), pp. 85–99; R. F. C. Clarke, 'The Examination System: its Use and Abuse', *The Month*, vol. XCIV, pp. 16–33 (1899); Sir Oliver Lodge, 'The Emancipation of the Teacher', *National Review*, vol. XL, pp. 417–29 (1902–3).
[4] 'Interim Report of the Committee on Influence of Examinations', *Report of the Seventy-Third Meeting of the British Association for the Advancement of Science held at Southport in September 1903* (1904), pp. 434–55.
[5] See pp. 148, 246.

was available. The problem, once that had been generally conceded, was to ensure that they worked as fairly and effectively as possible. Scholars and administrators are still working on these problems in the last third of the twentieth century, and no one would claim that a finally satisfactory solution has been achieved. Very important work on the statistics of examinations was done as early as 1888–90 by F. Y. Edgeworth of the University of Oxford. Much of his argument is too technical and detailed for reproduction here, but the general conclusion of his papers was to outline the limits within which examination results might be expected to vary.[1] He argued that the means of calculating the accuracy of examinations lay in 'that part of the Calculus of Probabilities which is known as the Theory of Errors'.[2] Error was likely to occur only within certain limits. Thus, if a number of competent critics marked a piece of Latin prose, the full marks for which was 30, there would be some one mark, say 20, which was assigned most frequently, and which might therefore be regarded as the true value of the prose. Most examination results depend on an aggregate of marks. Whatever the probable error might be in individual cases, the proportionate error of an aggregate was ten times less than that to which each item was liable because of the compensation between individual errors.

Despite this tendency for errors to cancel out, Edgeworth showed that a normal examination result, which consisted of an aggregate of a number of papers, would vary according to the examiners employed. A number of reasons were given for this. There is a point beyond which an examiner cannot define degrees of merit, a point which Edgeworth called 'a "minimum sensible" in our perceptions of excellence'.[3] In addition examiners have their own personal idiosyncrasies, and they may fail to preserve a constant scale in their marking. As an example he took the papers in mechanics of one year and of the year preceding. If it were assumed that the real average of both sets of papers was 150, 'yet in the sortition of examiners it is as

[1] F. Y. Edgeworth, 'The Statistics of Examinations', *Journal of the Royal Statistical Society*, vol. LI (1888), pp. 599–635; 'The Element of Chance in Competitive Examinations', *ibid*, vol. LIII (1890), pp. 460–75, 644–63. These are summarized in P. J. Hartog, *Examinations and their Relation to Culture and Efficiency* (1918), Appendix E. I have used Hartog's summary here. Edgeworth wrote popular accounts of his work in *Journal of Education*, 'The Statistics of Examinations', vol. X (n.s., 1888), pp. 469–70: 'The Uncertainty of Examinations', vol. XII (n.s., 1890), pp. 95–6, 203, 469.

[2] *Journal of Education*, X, p. 469.

[3] *Ibid*. p. 469.

likely as not that the average may be pushed up to 156 or down to 144; and it is possible that it may deviate much further from the ideal mean.'[1] Edgeworth concluded that, if the marks from a number of papers were added together, the aggregate was liable to an error of two or three per cent, which meant that in many cases the award of distinction or of honours was accidental. In the Civil Service Examinations, for example, 'important differences in the position and income of the candidates are made to turn upon differences in the aggregates of marks which, according to the reasoning of this paper, must be regarded as largely if not altogether accidental'.[2]

These arguments led Edgeworth to the view that the arrangement of honours lists in order of merit should be withdrawn where the distinctions did not correspond with any degree of probability to real differences. Latham had already pointed out that in any examination the candidates in the middle are very difficult to distinguish in any meaningful sense, and Edgeworth drew some specific conclusions about the margins within which such distinctions operate. Clearly in any examination a number of those who were successful were as likely as not to be placed differently had they been assessed by another and equally competent examiner. Edgeworth argued that in an honours examination, out of every 1,000 candidates, there were among those who passed at least 120 who obtained marks between 1,800 and 2,000. On this basis the average number of candidates placed owing to chance in the wrong category was about 30, though in one year it might be only 20 and in another rise to 40.[3] Using similar methods to decide how many candidates for the Civil Service would have been safe if their papers had been marked by different examiners, Edgeworth concluded that between one-third and two-thirds would be successful again and that a corresponding proportion would not. In the event of a re-examination in such a case Edgeworth considered that about one-seventh would be displaced. 'Thus, where fifty clerks were appointed, it may be expected – the most probable event is – that seven would be displaced by a re-examination of the same work.'[4]

---

[1] Hartog, *Examinations*, p. 109.
[2] *Journal of Education*, x. p. 470.
[3] Hartog, *Examinations*, p. 114.
[4] *Ibid.* pp. 129–30.

In order to test how far marking might be expected to vary, Edgeworth arranged through the *Journal of Education* for a number of competent persons to mark a piece of Latin prose as if they were marking it for the Indian Civil Service examination. 28 marks were received, varying from 45 to 100. The central value, 'the presumably correct mark', was 78·5. The two highest marks of 100 were each more than double the lowest mark of 45. In such a case it seemed likely that different examiners were using different marking scales. Of course, as has been already explained, the results of an individual paper accentuated such differences, because of the tendency of fortuitous errors to compensate. Thus, on a possible re-examination, fewer changes would take place overall than might at first have been expected.[1]

Only a very superficial account of Edgeworth's work has been given here. In his examples taken from schools, from universities and from the Civil Service, he had for the first time shown statistically the limits both of accuracy and of error within which examinations operate. His results were taken up by Sir Philip Hartog in a book published in 1918, but in his own day he was a lone voice. His ideas are important rather for the twentieth century than for the end of the nineteenth. He begins a debate different in kind from that with which this book has been concerned.

In the twentieth century examinations were to be discussed from the point of view of statistics, of psychology, and later of sociology. In the nineteenth they had been a part of politics, using that word in a very broad sense to cover the whole social structure of the time. Examinations had appeared as one aspect of the theory of open competition which was basic to the Victorian age. They had been promoted in the universities, in the schools and in the public service as tools of greater efficiency and of more even-handed social justice. They had furthered an ideal of individual excellence, from which, it was believed, society must benefit since the whole must advance strictly in relation to the progress of individuals. As the century drew to its close, the balance between individualism and collectivism was changing. Some men, as we have seen, feared that a state-promoted ideal of excellence would prove harmful to individuality. Whatever new balance was to be struck in the new century between individual and collective claims, it would certainly

---

[1] *Ibid.* pp. 121–2; *Journal of Education*, XII, pp. 95–6, 203.

be very different from that which had existed in the 1850s. when the examination structure had come into being.

M. E. Sadler wrote something on this theme in 1898 in a paper on Prussian secondary education:

> The point at issue is how far can England, with her looser organisation and freedom for individual enterprise, get from her secondary schools the kind of intellectual product which will enable her (so far as knowledge comes into the matter at all), to bear up against the presence of the highly-disciplined and well-organized knowledge, which is the outcome of the secondary education of some other countries.[1]

The relationship between the individual and the collective whole is the major theme of English nineteenth-century history. Public examinations had played an important part in a half-century of social, political and educational change, much of which revolved round that relationship. After many vicissitudes, examinations had won their place, not because they were popular, but because they could not be dispensed with. The question of the new century was to be, not whether they should be retained or abandoned, but how their efficiency could be improved. Though Auberon Herbert and F. Y. Edgeworth were writing at the same time, the first was looking back – over the period with which this book has been concerned. The second heralded a new age.

[1] M. E. Sadler, 'Problems in Prussian Secondary Education for Boys, with special reference to similar questions in England', *Education Department, Special Reports on Educational Subjects*, vol. 3, p. 251 (1898).

BIBLIOGRAPHIES

(All books are published in London, unless another place of publication is cited.)

I MANUSCRIPT SOURCES, SCHOOL RECORDS, ANNUAL REPORTS:

Local Examinations Syndicate, Cambridge

Minute Books (from 1862).
Miscellaneous letters.
J. N. Keynes: Commonplace Book.
Jamaica Centre: Minute Book, 1887–1911.
Annual Reports (from 1859).

Delegacy of Local Examinations, Oxford

Minute Books (from 1857).
Annual Reports (from 1858).

Cambridge University Archives

University Papers (1857–).
Guard Books 57 (1, 2, 3) (Local Examinations and Local Lectures).
Guard Books 59 (1, 2) (Oxford and Cambridge Schools Examination Board).

Cambridge University Library

Add. MSS (including the correspondence of J. F. Keynes, 7652.)

Oxford University Archives

Minutes of Hebdomadal Council, 1854–66.
Hebdomadal Council Reports, 1855–64.
Convocation Register, 1854–71.

Bodleian Library, Oxford

Gough Adds. Oxon. (University Notices, University Pamphlets).
Association for Promoting the Higher Education of Women in Oxford: Reports, 1879–1920.,
University of Oxford Local Examinations: Reports on Examinations for Women, 1877–1907.

University of London Library

Minutes of Committees, 1853–66, 1867–80.

Public Record Office

Examiners' Reports on Endowed Schools (Ed. 27).

College of Preceptors

Rough Minute Books, 1854–72, 1872–1904.

Incorporated Association of Headmasters
Reports, 1891–8.

National Society
Minutes of the Committee of Inquiry and Correspondence (1838), and of the Committee of Correspondence (1839–).
Monthly Paper.
Annual Reports.

North London Collegiate School for Ladies
Reports and other Papers.

St Mary's Hall, Brighton
Reports, 1838–97.

Tavistock Grammar School
School Records, 1839–88 (a volume of notes and cuttings).

West Buckland School
Devon County School Register (1863–).

Individual Collections
Acland, Sir T. D., 11th Baronet, Papers (at Killerton, Devon).
Brereton, Prebendary J. L., Letters and Papers.
Fortescue, 3rd Earl – Letters to J. L. Brereton (Cavendish collection, Homerton College, Cambridge).
Macaulay, T. B. – Letters to T. F. Ellis (Trinity College, Cambridge).
Pusey, E. B., Papers and Pamphlets (Pusey House MSS., Oxford).

2 OFFICIAL PUBLICATIONS:
(All references are to *Parliamentary Papers* unless otherwise specified)

Minutes of the Committee of Council on Education, 1847–8, L; 1851, XLIV; 1852–3, LXXIX; 1857–8, XLV.
Papers relating to the Reorganization of the Civil Service, 1854–5, XX.
Reports of Her Majesty's Civil Service Commissioners, 1856–99; 1856, XXII; 1857, III; 1857–8, XXV; 1859, VIII; 1860, XXIV; 1861, XIX; 1862, XXI; 1863, XX; 1864, XXX; 1865, XVI; 1866, XXV; 1867, XXI; 1867–8, XXII; 1868, XVIII; 1870, XIX; 1871, XVII; 1872, XIX; 1874, XVI; 1875, XXII; 1876, XXII; 1877, XXVIII; 1878, XXVII; 1878–9, XXII; 1880, XXI; 1881, XXXI; 1882, XXII; 1883, XXIII; 1884, XXI; 1884–5, XXI; 1886, XX; 1887, XXVII; 1888, XXXIV; 1889, XXVIII; 1890, XXVI; 1890–1, XXVI; 1892, XXVII; 1893–4, XXV; 1894, XXVIII; 1895, XXVI; 1896, XXV; 1897, XXIV; 1898, XXI; 1899, XIX.

Report from the Select Committee on Civil Service Appointments, 1860, IX.

Report of the Commissioners appointed to Inquire into the State of Popular Education in England, vol. I, 1861, XXI, Pt. 1.

Report of the Commissioners appointed by Her Majesty to Inquire into the Education given in Schools in England, not comprised within her Majesty's two recent commissions on popular education and on public schools (Schools Inquiry Commission), 21 vols., 1867–8, XXVIII (vols, I, IV, V, VII, VIII, IX).

First Supplementary and Second Reports of the Commissioners appointed to make Inquiry with regard to Scientific Instruction and the Advancement of Science, 1872, XXV.

First, Second and Third Reports of the Civil Service Inquiry Commission, 1875, XXIII.

Papers relating to the Selection and Training of Candidates for the Indian Civil Service, 1876, LV.

Royal Commission appointed to Inquire into the Civil Establishments of the Different Offices of State at Home and Abroad ... First Report, 1887, XIX; Second Report, 1888, XXVII; Fourth Report, 1890, XXVII.

Royal Commission on Secondary Education (Bryce Commission), 9 vols. 1895, XLIII–XLIX (vols. I, II, III, IV, V, VI).

Education Department, *Special Reports on Educational Subjects*, vol. 3 (1898).

Report of the Committee on the Civil Service 1966–68 (Cmnd 3638, chairman Lord Fulton) (with reprints of both the Northcote–Trevelyan report and the report of Macaulay's committee on the Indian appointments).

3   CONTEMPORARY NEWSPAPERS AND PERIODICALS

Cambridge Chronicle.
Cambridge University Reporter.
Educational Times.
English Journal of Education.
Fortnightly Review.
Jackson's Oxford Journal.
Journal of Education.
Journal of the Royal Statistical Society.
Leeds Mercury.
Manchester Guardian.
Museum and English Journal of Education.
Nineteenth Century.

Transactions and Sessional Proceedings of the National Association for the Promotion of Social Science.

4   GENERAL BIBLIOGRAPHY

Abbott, E. and Campbell, L. *Life and Letters of Benjamin Jowett*, 2 vols., 1897.

Acland, A. H. D. (ed.) *Memoir and Letters of the Rt. Hon. Sir Thomas Dyke Acland* (privately printed), 1902.

Acland, T. D. *The Education of the Farmer reviewed in connection with that of the Middle Classes in general*, 1857.

Some Account of the Origin and Objects of the New Oxford Examinations, 2nd ed., 1858.

Intermediate Schools on a Confessedly Religious Basis, Exeter, 1882.

Adamson, J. W. *'The Illiterate Anglo-Saxon' and Other Essays in Education, Medieval and Modern*, Cambridge, 1946.

Arnold, Matthew *Schools and Universities on the Continent*, 1868.

Higher Schools and Universities in Germany, 1874.

Arnold, Ralph *The Whiston Matter*, 1961.

Arnold, Thomas *Miscellaneous Works*, 1845.

Bamford, T. W. *The Rise of the Public Schools*, 1967.

Barnard, H. *Normal Schools and Other Institutions, Agencies and Means designed for the Professional Education of Teachers*, Hartford, Conn., 1851.

Barry, A. *Educational Prospects in England: A Lecture delivered at King's College, London*, 1874.

Benson, A. C. and Esher, Viscount (eds.) *The Letters of Queen Victoria 1837–1861*, vol. III, 1907.

Birdwood, George C. M. *On Competition and the Indian Civil Service*, 1872.

Blake, Robert *Disraeli*, 1966.

Booth, J. *Examination the Province of the State: or the Outlines of a Practical System for the extension of National Education*, 1847.

Systematic Instruction and Periodical Examination: Two Addresses, 1857.

Bowen, W. E. *Edward Bowen: A Memoir*, 1902.

Brereton, J. L. (1822–1901) *Principles and Plan of a Farm and County School*, Exeter, 1858.

'County Education': A Letter addressed to the Rt. Hon. the Earl of Devon, 1861.

Education as connected with Agriculture, 1864.

County Education: A Contribution of Experiments, Estimates and Suggestions, 1874.

Brereton, J. L. *The Case for Examinations*, Cambridge, 1944.

Browne, G. F. *The Recollections of a Bishop*, 1915.

Bruce, George *Secondary School Examinations: Facts and Commentary*, Oxford (Pergamon Press), 1969.

Burgess, H. J. *Enterprise in Education: The Story of the Work of the Established Church in the Education of the People prior to 1870*, 1958.

Burn, W. L. *The Age of Equipoise*, 1964.

Chandler, G. *An Address delivered at the Opening of the Church of England Metropolitan Commercial School, Rose Street, Soho Square, January 28, 1839*, 1839.

Clough, B. A. *Memoir of Anne J. Clough*, 1897.

Cohen, Emmeline, W. *The Growth of the British Civil Service, 1780–1939*, 1941.

Collins, Philip *Dickens and Education*, 1963.

Crick, B. (ed.) *Essays on Reform, 1967: A Centenary Tribute*, 1967.

Davie, G. E. *The Democratic Intellect: Scotland and her Universities in the Nineteenth Century*, Edinburgh, 1961.

Davies, Emily *The Higher Education of Women*, 1866.

Thoughts on Some Questions relating to Women, 1860–1908, 1910.

Dawes, R. *Hints on an Improved and Self-Paying System of National Education, suggested from the working of a Village School in Hampshire*, 1847.

Suggestive Hints on Improved Secular Instruction, 3rd edn., 1849.

Observations on the working of the Government System of Education and on School Inspection, 2nd edn., 1849.

Remarks on the Reorganization of the Civil Service and its bearing on Educational Progress, 1854.

Mechanics' Institutes and Popular Education: An Address delivered at the Annual Soirée of the Huddersfield Institute, December 13, 1855, 1856.

Demogeot, J. and Montucci, H. *De L'enseignement secondaire en Angleterre et en Ecosse: Rapport addressé à son exc. M. Le ministre de l'instruction publique*, Paris, 1868.

Draper, W. H. *University Extension: A Survey of Fifty Years, 1873–1923*, 1923.

Drescher, S. *Tocqueville and England*, Cambridge, Mass., 1964.

Dunsheath, P. and Miller, M. *Convocation in the University of London: The First Hundred Years*, 1958.

Faber, G. *Jowett: A Portrait with Background*, 1957.

Fitch, J. G. *Proposed Admission of Girls to University Local Examinations*, 1865.

Fortescue, Earl *Public Schools for the Middle Classes*, 1864.

Gilbert, W. S. *Iolanthe, The Savoy Operas*, vol. I, World's Classics edn., 1962.

Gooch, Sir Daniel *Diaries*, 1892.

Green, V. H. H. *Oxford Common Room*, 1957.

Hart, Jenifer 'Sir Charles Trevelyan at the Treasury', *English Historical Review*, vol. LXXV, 1960.

Hartog, P. J. *Examinations and their relation to Culture and Efficiency*, 1918.

Hartog, P. J. and Rhodes, E. C. *The Marks of Examiners*, 1936.

Heeney, Brian *Mission to the Middle Classes: The Woodard Schools, 1848–1891*, 1969.

Herbert, Auberon (ed.) *The Sacrifice of Education to Examination: Letters from 'All Sorts and Conditions of Men'*, 1889.

Hughes, E. 'Sir Charles Trevelyan and Civil Service Reform, 1853–5', *English Historical Review*, vol. LXIV, 1949.

'Civil Service Reform, 1853–5', *Public Administration*, vol. XXXII, 1954.

[Humphreys, E. R.] *England's Educational Crisis: A Letter addressed to the Rt. Hon. Viscount Palmerston*, 1856.

Hussey, R. *A Letter to Thomas Dyke Acland Esq., M.P., on the System of Education to be Established in the Diocesan Schools for the Middle Classes*, 1839.

Kay[-Shuttleworth], J. P. *Recent Measures for the Promotion of Education in England*, 10th edn., 1839.

Kellett, E. E. *As I Remember*, 1936.

Kitson Clark, G. *The Making of Victorian England*, 1962.

Latham, H. *On the Propositions made by the Head Masters of Schools to the University of Cambridge*, Cambridge, 1871.

On the Action of Examinations considered as a means of Selection, 1877.

Lauwerys, J. A. and Scanlon, D. G. (eds.) *The World Year Book of Education, 1969: Examinations*, 1969.

Leclerc, M. *L'Education des classes moyennes et dirigéantes en Angleterre*, Paris, 1894.

Les professions et la Société en Angleterre, Paris, 1894.

Lowe, E. C. *S. Nicolas College and its Schools: A Record of Thirty Years Work*, 1878.

Macalister, E. F. B. *Sir Donald Macalister of Tarbert*, 1935.

Macaulay, T. B. *Speeches, Parliamentary and Miscellaneous*, 2 vols, 1853.

Markby, T. *Practical Essays in Education*, 1868.

Mason Coxe, J. *Middle Class Education: A Letter to the Rt. Hon. the Earl of Devon*, 1865.

[Mathison, G. F.] *How Can the Church Educate the People? The question considered with reference to the Incorporation and Endowment of Colleges for the Middle and Lower Classes of Society*, 1844.

Montgomery, R. J. *Examinations: An Account of their Evolution as Administrative Devices in England*, 1965.

Moore, R. J. 'The Abolition of Patronage in the Indian Civil Service and the Closure of Haileybury College', *Historical Journal*, vol. VII, 1964.

Liberalism and Indian politics, 1872–1922, 1966.

Newman, J. H. *The Idea of a University, Defined and Illustrated*, new edn., 1898.

Norris, J. P. *The Education of the People, our Weak Points and our Strength: Occasional Essays*, Edinburgh, 1869.

O'Malley, L. S. S. *The Indian Civil Service, 1601–1930*, 2nd edn., 1965.

Parkin, G. R. *Life and Letters of Edward Thring*, 2 vols., 1898.

Pattison, Mark *Suggestions on Academical Organisation with especial reference to Oxford*, 1868.

Memoirs, 1885.

Payne, J. *Works*, vol. I, *Lectures on the Science and Art of Education*, 1883.

Peacock, T. L. *Gryll Grange*, Penguin edn., 1947.

Reader, W. J. *Professional Men: The Rise of the Professional Classes in Nineteenth Century England*, 1966.

Richson, C. *The Agencies and Organization required in a National System of Education*, 1856.

Ridding, George *A Letter to the Rev. Henry Latham, M.A., in reply to his Observations*, 1871.

A Letter to Edward Bowen, M.A., in reply to a Pamphlet, 1872.

Ridding, Lady Laura *George Ridding, Schoolmaster and Bishop*, 1908.

Ridgway, James *Oxford Examination of those who are not Members of the University*, Oxford and London, 1858.

Roach, John 'Victorian Universities and the National Intelligentsia', *Victorian Studies*, vol. II, 1959.

Roberts, David *Victorian Origins of the British Welfare State*, New Haven, 1960.

Rogers, Annie M. A. H. *Degrees by Degrees: The Story of the Admission of Oxford Women Students to Membership of the University*, 1938.

Rogers, J. E. Thorold *Education in Oxford, its Methods, its Aims and its Rewards*, 1861.

Roy, Naresh Chandra *The Civil Service in India*, Calcutta, 1958.

Sadler, Sir Michael (and others) *Essays on Examinations*, 1936.

Sandford, E. G. (ed.) *Memoirs of Archbishop Temple*, by Seven Friends, 2 vols, 1906.

Sparrow, John *Mark Pattison and the Idea of a University*, 1967.

Stephen, Barbara *Emily Davies and Girton College*, 1927.

Stewart, W. A. C. and McCann, W. P. *The Educational Innovators, 1750–1880*, 1967.

Stuart, James *Reminiscences*, 1912.

Temple, F. 'National Education', *Oxford Essays*, 1856.
Thomson, J. J. *Recollections and Reflections*, 1936.
Thornton, F. V. *The Education of the Middle Classes in England*, 1862.
Todhunter, Isaac *The Conflict of Studies and other Essays on Subjects connected with Education*, 1873.
Trevelyan, G. O. *Life and Letters of Lord Macaulay*, 2 vols., 1876; popular edn., 1 vol., 1889.
Trollope, Anthony *An Autobiography*, ed. Booth, Bradford A., Berkeley, Los Angeles, 1947.
The Three Clerks, World's Classics edn., 1907.
Tuckwell, W. *Reminiscences of Oxford*, 1900.
Wells, H. G. *The New Machiavelli*, 2nd edn., 1911.
Love and Mr Lewisham, Nelson's Library edn., n.d.
Experiment in Autobiography, 2 vols., 1934.
Wiese, L. *German Letters on English Education: Written during an Educational Tour in 1876*, English trans., 1877.
Wiseman, S. (ed.) *Examinations and English Education*, Manchester, 1961.
Wood, H. T. *A History of the Royal Society of Arts*, 1913.
Woodard, N. *A plea for the Middle Classes*, 1848.
Public Schools for the Middle Classes, 1851.
St Nicolas College: St Saviour's Lower Middle School, 1858.
The Society and Schools of St Mary and St Nicolas College, 1878.
The Scheme of Education of St Nicolas College: in A Letter to the Most Noble the Marquis of Salisbury, 1883.
Wratislaw, A. H. *Middle Class and Non-Gremial Examinations*, Cambridge and London, 1860.

[Cambridge University] *Occasional Papers on University Matters and Middle-Class Education: together with full information on the Local Examinations and Recent University Changes*, 1858–9.
Fifty Years of Progress in Education: A Review of the Work of the College of Preceptors from its Foundation in 1846 to its Jubilee in 1896, 1897.
Report of a Conference on Secondary Education in England convened by the Vice-Chancellor of the University of Oxford, October 10–11, 1893, Oxford and London, 1893.
Report of the Seventy-Third meeting of the British Association for the Advancement of Science, September 1903, 1904.
Trent College School Lists, 1874.
University of London, The Historical Record, 1836–1912, 1912.
University of Oxford, *Delegacy of Local Examinations, 1857–1957* (privately printed brochure).

INDEX

Entries under Cambridge Local Examinations, Cambridge University, Civil Service Examinations, Oxford Local Examinations, *and* Oxford University *are arranged in the order in which the topics occur in the book.*